CW01522040

A Dialogue of the Deaf
Essays on Africa and the United Nations

Further praise for *A Dialogue of the Deaf*

There is no doubt that the contributors in this volume are eminent personalities with intimate knowledge and long experience of the United Nations in particular and international cooperation in general. There is also no doubt that the title of the volume and its contents are a testimony as to how badly Africa has fared in its relations with the United Nations.

Africa's high hopes and expectations have been persistently poorly realized. If this volume, which is a treasure-trove in the literature on Africa and the UN, provokes an agonising reappraisal, it would have served an invaluable service to humanity.

Professor Adebayo Adedeji, CFR
Former Executive Secretary of the UN Economic Commission for Africa
Chair of the South African Peer Review Process

A growing consensus exists that the architecture of global governance is in need of radical overhaul, if we are to advance global equity, effect a fairer distribution of the world's resources and bridge the divide between Africa and the developed world.

Platitudes and well-intended interventions will not be sufficient – well reasoned and researched strategies, pragmatic and incisive analysis and a realistic grasp of current global reality are required. This compilation comprises all of that and more and advances the pursuit of a more just and equitable world.

Jody Kollapen
National Commissioner: Civil & Political Rights
South African Human Rights Commission

African states have a vested interest in the survival and success of the United Nations as the most important repository of multilateralism in the world. This excellent collection of essays makes the most convincing case in support of this global institution and Africa's place in it. A must read.

Dr Chris Landsberg
Director, Centre for Policy Studies, Johannesburg

This unique book written by eminent African scholars and practitioners with intimate knowledge of the UN, represents a timely and valuable appreciation of the importance of Africa's stake in the United Nations and contributes to strengthening understandings of this critical topic. It is essential reading for those interested in Africa's current and future relationship with the world body.

Scholastica Kimaryo
UNDP Resident Representative & Coordinator of the UN System in South Africa

A Dialogue of the Deaf
Essays on Africa and the United Nations

Edited by Adekeye Adebajo and Helen Scanlon

For Dr Dominique Jacquin-Berdal
Friend, scholar, activist and daughter of Africa

In memoriam, 1966–2006

First published in 2006 by
Fanele – an imprint of Jacana Media (Pty) Ltd

Jacana Media (Pty) Ltd
10 Orange Street
Sunnyside
Auckland Park 2092
South Africa
(+27 11) 628-3200
www.jacana.co.za

© The Centre for Conflict Resolution, 2006

All rights reserved.

ISBN   1-77009-263-3
        978-1-77009-263-1

Cover design by Jacana Media
Set in Bembo 11/13pt
Printed by Interpak Books
See a complete list of Jacana titles at www.jacana.co.za

Contents

Contributors... vii

Foreword... xiii
Archbishop Njongonkulu Ndungane

Acknowledgements...xvii

List of Acronyms xix

Introduction 1
Adekeye Adebajo and Helen Scanlon

SECTION 1: AFRICA'S STAKE IN UN REFORM

Chapter 1 Chronicle of a Death Foretold:
The Rise and Fall of UN Reform...................................... 19
Adekeye Adebajo

Chapter 2 Crafting the UN High-level Panel Report:
An Insider's Perspective... 45
Mary Chinery-Hesse

Chapter 3 African Divisions, Western Dominance........................ 57
James Jonah

Chapter 4 The UN, NEPAD and the Commission for Africa........ 75
Ibrahim Gambari

SECTION 2: SOVEREIGNTY AS RESPONSIBILITY

Chapter 5 Africa's Responsibility to Protect 89
Musifiky Mwanasali

Chapter 6 The International Challenge of State Failure
and Internal Displacement 111
Francis Deng

Chapter 7 The UN Human Rights Council:
From Rights to Responsibility?..131
Helen Scanlon

Chapter 8 A Tale of Two Tragedies: Rwanda and Darfur.............147
Henry Anyidoho

SECTION 3: AFRICA'S DEVELOPMENT AND HUMAN
            SECURITY CHALLENGES

Chapter 9 Nyerere's Challenge:
Deconstructing the Washington Consensus..167
Margaret Legum

Chapter 10 Aligning HIV/AIDS and Security:
The UN and Africa 183
Angela Ndinga-Muvumba

Chapter 11 Tackling Security Threats:
International Organised Crime 207
Peter Gastrow

SECTION 4: AFRICAN ACTORS AND RESPONSES

Chapter 12 South Africa, the UN, and Human Rights.................227
Kader Asmal

Chapter 13 Towards a Symbiotic Partnership:
The UN Peacebuilding Commission and the Evolving
AU/NEPAD Post-conflict Reconstruction Framework......................243
Tim Murithi

Chapter 14 Terrorism and Counter-terrorism:
Dialogue or Confrontation? 261
Mwesiga Baregu

Conclusion 275
Helen Scanlon

Selected Reading...283

Index..291

Contributors

Adekeye Adebajo is Executive Director of the Centre for Conflict Resolution, Cape Town, South Africa. He served as Director of the Africa Programme of the New York-based International Peace Academy between 2001 and 2003. During the same period, Dr Adebajo was an Adjunct Professor at Columbia University's School of International and Public Affairs. He previously served on UN missions in South Africa, Western Sahara and Iraq. Dr Adebajo is the author of *Building Peace in West Africa: Liberia, Sierra Leone and Guinea-Bissau*; *Liberia's Civil War: Nigeria, ECOMOG, and Regional Security in West Africa*; and co-editor of *Managing Armed Conflicts in the Twenty-First Century* and *West Africa's Security Challenges: Building Peace in a Troubled Region*. He was a member of the international advisory group to the UN High-level Panel on *Threats, Challenges and Change*.

Henry Anyidoho is currently the leader of the United Nations Assistance Cell for the African Union mission on Darfur. Born at Tanyigbe in the Volta Region of Ghana, General Anyidoho was commissioned into the Ghanaian army's Signal Corps in 1965. A graduate of the US Marine Staff College in Virginia, he served in various capacities in Ghana's armed forces, including as Commanding Officer of the Ghana Military Academy and Commander of the Northern Command of the Army. General Anyidoho was the Deputy Force Commander and Chief of Staff of the United Nations Assistance Mission for Rwanda (UNAMIR) in 1994. After forty-one years of military service, he headed the UN Observers for Cameroon–Nigeria Mixed Commission. He is decorated with the Distinguished Service Order for Gallantry and is the author of a book on his tenure in Rwanda: *Guns Over Kigali*.

Kader Asmal has been a member of South Africa's parliament since 1994, serving as Minister of Water Affairs and Forestry until 1999 and then as Minister of Education from 1999 to 2004. Prior to his return to South Africa from exile in 1990, he was a law professor at Trinity College, Dublin, Ireland for 27 years, specialising in human rights, labour and international law. Professor Asmal was a founder member of the British anti-apartheid movement as well as the Irish anti-apartheid movement. He was vice-president of the World Commission on the Oceans (1995–1998) and chairperson of the World Commission on Dams (1997–2001). In 2005 he was made an officer of the Order of the *Légion d'Honneur*, the highest decoration for gallantry in France. He has written and co-edited many books including: *Human Rights, Reparations and Reconciliation*; *Legacy of Freedom: The ANC's Human Rights Tradition*; and *South Africa's Nobel Laureates: Peace, Literature and Science*.

Mwesiga Baregu is Professor of Political Science and International Relations at the University of Dar-es-Salaam, Tanzania. Until 2003, he headed the Peace and Security Research Programme at the Southern African Political Economy Series Trust (SAPES) in Harare, Zimbabwe. He is a member of the Executive Council of the International Peace Research Association and the Africa Peace Research and Education Association. Professor Baregu is editor of *Preventive Diplomacy and Peacebuilding in Southern Africa*; *The Conflict Matrix and Research Agenda*; and co-editor of *From Cape to Congo: Southern Africa's Evolving Security Challenges*.

Mary Chinery-Hesse is the Chief Adviser to the President of Ghana. She was a member of the UN High-level Panel on Threats, Challenges and Change. Dr Chinery-Hesse was previously Deputy Director-General of the UN's International Labour Organisation and was Resident Representative of the United Nations Development Programme in Sierra Leone, Tanzania, the Seychelles and Uganda. Before joining the United Nations, she was Principal Secretary, Ministry of Finance and Economic Planning and Secretary of the National Economic Planning Council in Ghana. She also served as Chairperson of the Commonwealth Expert Group of Eminent Persons on Structural Adjustment and Women, which prepared the book *Engendering Adjustment*.

Francis Deng served as the United Nations Secretary-General's Special Representative on Internally Displaced Persons between 1992 and 2004. He is a Professor at the University of Johns Hopkins' School of Advanced International Studies in Washington DC, having been a senior fellow in Foreign Policy Studies at the Brookings Institution, also in Washington DC. Professor Deng was formerly Sudan's Minister of State for Foreign Affairs, has served as the Sudanese Ambassador to the United States, Scandinavia and Canada, and was a human rights officer at the UN Secretariat's Division of Human Rights in New York. In 2006, Professor Deng was awarded the Rome Prize for Peace and Humanitarian Action, sponsored by the city of Rome, Italy, for his work on internal displacement. He is the author of numerous books including *Masses in Flight: The Global Crisis of Internal Displacement; Protecting the Dispossessed: A Challenge for the International Community*; and *Conflict of Identities in the Sudan*.

Ibrahim Gambari is Under-Secretary-General for Political Affairs at the United Nations Secretariat in New York. Professor Gambari served as Special Representative of the Secretary-General and Head of the United Nations Mission to Angola, from September 2002 to February 2003. Before joining the UN Secretariat, Professor Gambari was Foreign Minister of Nigeria and the longest-serving Permanent Representative of Nigeria to the UN between 1990 and 1999. He was the last chairman of the UN Special Committee Against Apartheid. Professor Gambari has authored several books in the field of international relations including: *Political and Comparative Dimensions of Regional Integration: the Case of ECOWAS; Party Politics and Foreign Policy: Nigeria under the First Republic*; and *Theory and Reality in Foreign Policy Making: Nigeria after the Second Republic*.

Peter Gastrow has been the Cape Town Director of the Institute for Security Studies, South Africa, since 1998. He studied economics and law before establishing his own legal practice as an advocate of the Supreme Court of South Africa. Mr Gastrow thereafter served as a Member of Parliament and a member of the National Peace Committee. After South Africa's 1994 election, he became the special adviser to South Africa's Minister for Safety and Security, assisting with the transformation of

South Africa's Police Service. He is author of *Bargaining for Peace: South Africa and the National Peace Accord*; *Organised Crime in the SADC Region: Police Perceptions*; and editor of *Penetrating State and Business: Organised Crime in Southern Africa*.

James Jonah worked in the United Nations Secretariat from 1963 until 1994 in various capacities. At the time of his retirement from the UN he was Under-Secretary-General for Political Affairs, where his areas of focus included Africa, the Middle East and Global Election Monitoring. Dr Jonah is a Senior Fellow at the Ralph Bunche Institute for International Studies in New York. He served Sierra Leone as Minister of Finance, Development and Economic Planning, and as Permanent Representative of Sierra Leone to the United Nations. In 2001, Dr Jonah won a Carnegie Scholar Grant to prepare his memoirs. He has published extensively on Africa and the UN and holds a PhD in Political Science from the Massachusetts Institute of Technology.

Margaret Legum is an independent economist based in Cape Town, South Africa. She is an experienced consultant and trainer with a background in counselling, education, management and journalism. She holds an MA in Economics from Cambridge University in England, and helped to found the South African New Economics Network: an independent network for the creation of a just and sustainable economic system. Ms Legum had previously formed the Centre for Anti-Racism and Anti-Sexism Trust (CARAS) on her return from exile in the early 1990s. She is a regular contributor to the South African print media. Her most recent book *It Doesn't Have to be Like This* was published in 2002.

Tim Murithi is a Senior Researcher at the Centre for Conflict Resolution, University of Cape Town. From 1999 to 2005, Dr Murithi worked as a Programme Officer for the Programme in Peacemaking and Preventive Diplomacy at the United Nations Institute for Training and Research (UNITAR) in Geneva, Switzerland. He has worked as a Consultant on Conflict Resolution for the Organisation of African Unity, the United Nations Development Programme in Sierra Leone, the UN-affiliated University for Peace, the United Kingdom's Department for International Development and the Canadian Ministry of Foreign

Affairs. Author of numerous publications, his most recent book is entitled *The African Union: Pan-Africanism, Peacebuilding and Development*.

Musifiky Mwanasali is a Political Affairs Officer at the UN Secretariat in New York. He previously served as Regional Adviser for the Office of the UN High Commissioner for Human Rights in Central Africa, and as a political analyst in the Conflict Management Centre at the Organisation of African Unity in Addis Ababa, Ethiopia. Dr Mwanasali has also held teaching and research posts in academia and in think-tanks – including the New York-based International Peace Academy – in both Africa and the US. He has published extensively on African security issues.

Angela Ndinga-Muvumba is a Senior Researcher at the Centre for Conflict Resolution in Cape Town, and head of its HIV/AIDS and Security project. Before joining the CCR, Ms Ndinga-Muvumba served as a Political Officer in the Bureau of the Chairperson of the Africa Union Commission in Addis Ababa, Ethiopia. She worked with the International Peace Academy's Africa Programme between 2001 and 2004. Ms Ndinga-Muvumba has served as a consultant for the UN's HIV/AIDS and Governance Commission. She holds a Master's degree in International Affairs from Columbia University's School of International and Public Affairs in New York, and has published several scholarly articles and book chapters.

Helen Scanlon is a Senior Researcher at the Centre for Conflict Resolution in Cape Town, focusing on the UN, human rights and gender issues. She has worked at the University of Cape Town since 2002 in both a teaching and research capacity. Between 2002 and 2004, Dr Scanlon was a research fellow in UCT's Department of Historical Studies and has taught on a number of undergraduate and graduate courses within the University's Humanities Faculty. Dr Scanlon was also based at UCT's African Gender Institute, where she contributed to both teaching and research. She has published a number of scholarly articles and is author of *Representation and Reality: Portraits of Women's Lives in the Western Cape*.

Foreword

The Most Reverend Njongonkulu Ndungane
Archbishop of Cape Town

THIS VOLUME, WRITTEN by eminent African scholars and practitioners on the United Nations (UN), is a particularly timely and welcome addition to the literature. If we are to have a UN that is truly representative of all its members, then the African perspective must be more adequately enunciated and understood than has previously been the case.

A few years ago, a journalist asked me: "Archbishop, what sort of world would you like to see?" The answer came to me immediately: "A world with a human face: where every individual has all that is necessary to meet their basic needs and to live with dignity".

After the last century's two World Wars, humanity began increasingly to understand that we are all one single global family. We came to believe that people of every culture, every faith and no faith, can live and work together for the common good. We must not lose sight of this vision that underlies the UN system, founded in 1945. The Universal Declaration on Human Rights of 1948 clearly states:

> Everyone has the right to a standard of living adequate for the health and well-being of himself and of his family, including food, clothing, housing and medical care and necessary social services, and the right to security in the event of unemployment, sickness, disability, widowhood, old age or other lack of livelihood in circumstances beyond his control.
>
> *General Assembly Resolution 217 A (III), December 1948*

This commitment should be the cornerstone of all we do, in all our policymaking – nationally and internationally – in public and private sectors. As part of customary international law, it should certainly be an unquestionable priority of every global and regional body, regardless of whether human rights is its stated focus.

The reform of the UN system remains a live issue and concerns a lot more than who sits on the Security Council! As the late South African Communist Party activist, Joe Slovo, once said, "The real question is not whether a system works, but for whom it works."

For far too long, the UN system has benefited the wealthy at the expense of the poor, and the powerful at the expense of the weak. The challenge to the whole UN system in the twenty-first century is to put people first – and especially those who most need protection, assistance, support, or perhaps even a voice. As this rich volume clearly shows, discussions on UN peacekeeping and conflict resolution are futile if they are not part of wider policies to tackle the undermining contexts in which instability can thrive – with poverty being the greatest challenge.

Interdependence remains a human reality. It is also a political, economic, environmental and security reality. True security is found not in military strength, but in ensuring that every person has access to the essentials of a fully human life. Pursuing this goal is the type of security spending the world needs most.

Half of the world's population of six billion people live on less than two dollars a day; indeed, over 300 million people in sub-Saharan Africa live on less than *one* dollar a day. Extreme poverty is increasing, and so is global hunger. Add to this the devastation caused by the HIV and AIDS pandemic which, along with tuberculosis and malaria, affects our continent disproportionately, as one chapter in this book illustrates.

I am optimistic that through the United Nations and linked initiatives such as the Millennium Development Goals, which aims to halve global poverty by 2015, we have an unprecedented opportunity to create a world with a human face. As Nobel Prize winner, Jonas Salk, has noted, "We are the first generation in human history where large numbers of ordinary people are taking responsibility for the future of an entire species".

In this world of which I dream, success is measured by quality of life for all, not in quantities of dollars for some. As we try to build "A More

Secure World" – in the words of the UN High-level Panel on *Threats, Challenges and Change* – we need the political will to tackle poverty and all the other threats to our safety and stability in Africa. The only safe world is one of peace through justice, where everyone is guaranteed – in practice, and not just on paper – these basic human necessities, these basic human rights, of life. Only when every individual is assured of these fundamentals, can we all become fully human in the true spirit of *Ubuntu*. Then we can be what we are meant to be. This is why this book is such a valuable contribution to African efforts to engage the UN to achieve these noble goals.

Acknowledgements

THIS BOOK WOULD not have been possible without the assistance and cooperation of many people. First and foremost, we would like to thank the authors for their contribution to the two policy seminars organised by the Centre for Conflict Resolution (CCR) at the University of Cape Town, South Africa, on the United Nations reform process in May 2004 and April 2005. Both meetings formed the basis of this volume.

We would like to thank our partners, the Friedrich Ebert Stiftung in Mozambique, and the United Nations Foundation and the Rockefeller Foundation, both in New York, for co-implementing and funding this project. CCR would also like to thank the other funders of its Africa Programme: the governments of Denmark, Netherlands, Sweden, Norway and Finland as well as the United Kingdom's Department for International Development (DFID) and the Rockefeller Brothers Fund (RBF) in New York. We appreciate the authors' tireless revisions of their initial chapters and their patience during the process of bringing this project to fruition. We would further like to thank the other participants at these seminars – too numerous to list – who provided insight into the role of the UN in Africa which helped to inform this collection. In addition, we would like to thank Caroline Smith and Russell Clarke at Jacana Media for their input, support and efficiency.

We would also like to acknowledge our colleagues at the Centre for Conflict Resolution whose assistance and support ensured the successful completion of this volume: Neeran Naidoo and his colleagues in the Communications cluster assisted extensively with the design of the book as well as in selecting and sourcing photographs; Tim Murithi made useful comments on the entire manuscript; while Yaliwe Clarke gave useful input on several chapters. Selma Walters provided invaluable administrative support, while Cavan Davids, Ismail Noordien and their colleagues facilitated budget and payment issues.

We hope that this book will contribute significantly to an understanding among specialists and the general public of the UN and Africa's stake in issues of peace, security and socio-economic development. This volume, written by eminent African scholars and practitioners, is the first book of its kind to offer pan-African perspectives on the UN's past, current and future challenges. The timing is particularly propitious, following the increased attention on the global body in the aftermath of the UN reform process in September 2005 and continuing efforts to meet the UN Millennium Development Goals' aim of halving poverty by 2015. We hope that this volume will contribute to fostering a greater understanding of peace, security and socio-economic issues in the 50-year "dialogue of the deaf" between the rich north and the global south.

Adekeye Adebajo and Helen Scanlon
Cape Town, 2006

List of Acronyms

ADB	African Development Bank
AENF	Alliance of Eritrean National Forces
AMIS	AU Mission in Sudan
AMU	Arab Maghreb Union
ANC	African National Congress
APRM	Africa Peer Review Mechanism
ASF	African Standby Force
AU	African Union
AWA	AIDS Watch Africa
BBTG	Broad-Based Transitional Government
CAR	Central African Republic
CCR	Centre for Conflict Resolution
CHA	Consortium of Humanitarian Agencies
CIA	Central Intelligence Agency
CJTF-HOA	Combined Joint Task Force – Horn of Africa
COO	Chief Operating Officer
CSSDCA	Conference on Security, Stability, Development and Cooperation in Africa
DITF	AU Darfur Integrated Task Force
DPKO	Department of Peacekeeping Operations
DRC	Democratic Republic of Congo

EACTI	East African Counter-terrorism Initiative
ECCAS	Economic Community of Central African States
ECOMOG	ECOWAS Cease-fire Monitoring Group
ECOSOC	Economic and Social Council
ECOWAS	Economic Community of West African States
EU	European Union
FATF	Financial Action Task Force Against Money Laundering
FBI	Federal Bureau of Investigation
G-8	Group of Eight Industrialised Countries
G-20+	Group of 20+
G-77	Group of 77
GDP	Gross Domestic Product
GFATM	Global Fund to Fight AIDS, Tuberculosis and Malaria
GNP	Gross National Product
HCFA	Humanitarian Ceasefire Agreement
HIPC	Heavily Indebted Poor Countries
HSGIC	Heads of State and Government Implementation Committee
IASC	Inter-Agency Standing Committee
ICC	International Criminal Court
ICISS	International Commission on Intervention and State Sovereignty
ICRC	International Committee of the Red Cross
IDA	International Development Association
IDPs	Internally Displaced Persons
IGAD	Intergovernmental Authority on Development
ILO	International Labour Organisation
IMF	International Monetary Fund
IOM	International Organisation for Migration
IPA	International Peace Academy

JEM	Justice and Equality Movement
LPA	Lagos Plan of Action
MDGs	Millennium Development Goals
MSF	*Médecins Sans Frontières*
NEPAD	New Partnership for Africa's Development
NGOs	Non-governmental organisations
OAS	Organisation of American States
OAU	Organisation of African Unity
ODA	Official Development Assistance
OECD	Organisation for Economic Cooperation and Development
OHCHR	UN Office of the High Commissioner for Human Rights
OPEC	Organisation of Petroleum Exporting Countries
OSCE	Organisation for Security and Cooperation in Europe
PAP	Pan African Parliament
PEPFAR	President's Emergency Plan for AIDS Relief
PSC	AU Peace and Security Council
RECs	Regional Economic Communities
RPF	Rwandese Patriotic Front
RTLM	*Radio-Television Libre de Mille Collines*
SADC	Southern African Development Community
SANDF	South African National Defence Force
SAPs	Structural Adjustment Programme / Policies
SLA/M	Sudan Liberation Army / Movement
SPLA	Sudan People's Liberation Army
SPLM	Sudanese People's Liberation Movement
SSR	Security Sector Reform

TASO	AIDS Support Organisation
UNAIDS	Joint UN Programme on HIV/AIDS
UNAMIR	UN Assistance Mission for Rwanda
UNCTAD	UN Conference on Trade and Development
UNDP	UN Development Programme
UNHCR	UN High Commissioner for Refugees
UNICEF	UN Children's Fund
UNIDO	UN Industrial Development Organisation
UNMIS	UN Mission in Sudan
UNODC	UN Office on Drugs and Crime
WHO	World Health Organisation
WMDs	Weapons of Mass Destruction
WTO	World Trade Organisation

Introduction

Adekeye Adebajo and Helen Scanlon

IN 1990 KENYAN scholar, Ali Mazrui, described the relationship between America and the Third World as a "dialogue of the deaf". He noted that while Americans are gifted communicators, they are poor listeners. Mazrui argued that humanity was becoming Americanised because of the United States' (US) ability to communicate effectively (for example through Hollywood and the export of its culture abroad), but that America's external relations were not being humanised since Americans remain bad listeners.[1] This view aptly highlights the difficulties that the George W Bush administration faced in seeking to win the support of the global community of states at the United Nations for its unilateral and controversial invasion of Iraq in 2003. Not only was Washington unable to secure a clear, legal mandate for the intervention – facing strong opposition from even western allies such as France and Germany – this incident underlined the importance of maintaining support for actions through listening to others and pursuing enlightened policies. In the case of Iraq, the US, as the most powerful state in the history of contemporary world politics, discovered that it had power without legitimacy, while the UN rediscovered that it had legitimacy without power. The UN and US thus need each other in order to advance global peace. If the powerful need the UN, the case for a strong UN is even more critical for the weak; a category in which the overwhelming majority of African states belong. The reform of international political and financial institutions like the World Bank, the International Monetary Fund (IMF) and the World Trade Organisation (WTO) is

1

therefore critical for the continent's development and security needs. Africa stands to gain or lose the most from any future UN reform.

Africa and the West have engaged in a "dialogue of the deaf" at the UN and other international forums since the continent's "lost decade"[2] of the 1980s. The dialogue runs as follows: Africans call for an annulment of what they see as an unpayable external debt of $290 billion and note that they have paid back $550 billion out of an initial debt of $540 billion between 1970 and 2002; the West continues to roll over the debt and offers periodic "debt relief" for an ailing African patient. Africans call for the West to meet aid targets of 0.7 per cent of Gross National Product (GNP) set as far back as 1970; the West responds by continuing to maintain average annual aid levels of about 0.3 per cent and to make persistent unmet promises to reach the target of 0.7 per cent. Finally, Africans call on the rich world to live up to its free trade principles by eliminating agricultural subsidies that prevent the continent from growing out of poverty; the West continues to maintain subsidies of over $311 billion that by 2001 had surpassed the entire economic strength of sub-Saharan Africa.

The report *A More Secure World: Our Shared Responsibility,*[3] was submitted to UN Secretary-General, Kofi Annan, by his appointed High-level Panel on *Threats, Challenges and Change* in December 2004. The Panel had been mandated in 2003 to examine the main global threats and challenges to peace and security and to make recommendations to the UN Secretary-General for a collective response to these threats. The crafting of the UN High-level Panel report involved 43 worldwide meetings and informal consultations with civil society actors, including one of six Panel meetings taking place in Addis Ababa, Ethiopia, in April 2004. Three African members served on the Panel: Salim Ahmed Salim, former Secretary-General of the Organisation of African Unity (OAU); Amre Moussa, Secretary-General of the Arab League; and Mary Chinery-Hesse, former deputy Director-General of the UN's International Labour Organisation (ILO).

The findings of the UN's High-level Panel report dominated debate on peace, security and development issues in 2005. Civil society actors played an important part in convening meetings to increase public awareness and to elicit support for the findings of the report. In order to avoid a hierarchy of security issues, the report dealt with both "hard" (terrorism, and nuclear and biological weapons) and "soft" (socio-economic problems, HIV/AIDS and international organised crime) security threats, as well as two additional "baskets" of threats: interstate and intrastate conflicts.

At a meeting in Swaziland in February 2005, the African Union's (AU) committee of fifteen foreign ministers met in Mbabane, Swaziland, to craft a common African response to the UN High-level Panel report. Their report became known as the "Ezulwini Consensus". The comprehensive document – the only common response by any region to the High-level Panel report – called for two permanent seats with veto power for Africa on a reformed fifteen-member UN Security Council to add to its existing three rotating seats, as well as two additional rotating seats on a reformed Council of twenty-six. The report also called for a strengthening of the UN General Assembly to make it more democratic, and advocated that the UN's Economic and Social Council (ECOSOC) be empowered to play a major role in implementing the Millennium Development Goals (MDGs) aim of halving poverty by 2015, so as to link security more closely to development. The AU foreign ministers called for strengthened peacekeeping in Africa, including the increased financing of African regional organisations by the UN. They supported the idea of establishing a UN Peacebuilding Commission; rejected the proposal for a Human Rights Council with universal membership (which they felt would hamper the body's effectiveness and duplicate the work of the UN's third committee); and backed the idea of a "responsibility to protect" doctrine and a common definition of terrorism. Ezulwini also advocated increased access to, and support for, HIV/AIDS treatment, care, research and healthcare systems. The ministers further questioned the sustainability of Africa's debt burden of $290 billion and greater transparency in negotiations at the World Trade Organisation.[4]

Since October 2003, the Cape Town-based Centre for Conflict Resolution (CCR) – which has conceived and edited this book – has been implementing a vision to transform the Centre from being a principally South African body into a uniquely pan-African organisation. This vision is grounded in the Centre's new Africa Programme. One of the key areas of policy research is on the United

Nations' role in Africa. This has involved the organisation of two important policy seminars on the UN held in May 2004 (one of the 43 regional meetings organised for the High-level Panel) and April 2005, which involved senior officials in the Secretariat of the UN High-level Panel in New York.[5] These seminars brought together African policy-makers, civil society actors and academics and provided a forum for articulating African interests and responses to the UN reform process. The first seminar in May 2004 set out to consider the United Nations, Africa's regional organisations and future security threats for the continent. The objective of the meeting was to generate policy proposals to strengthen relationships between the UN and African organisations for the continent's future security. The second seminar set out to consider African perspectives on the High-level Panel report of December 2004 and UN Secretary-General, Kofi Annan's March 2005 *In Larger Freedom: Towards Development, Security and Human Rights For All* report.[6] This meeting also sought to examine both reports' recommendations, to devise strategies for disseminating African perspectives and recommendations to the UN community, and to consider how best to raise awareness about the reports on the continent prior to the sixtieth anniversary UN summit in September 2005.

The recommendations of the reports have since been widely disseminated in Addis Ababa, Berlin, New York, London, Maputo, Maseru, Mauritius, Windhoek, Cape Town and Pretoria. Short summaries of some of the papers presented at the meeting were published as a special supplement in South Africa's *Mail & Guardian* on the eve of the General Assembly summit on UN reform in September 2005.[7] This volume of essays, which have been thoroughly updated, thus represents a further effort to disseminate this work. The book is the first published volume that provides African perspectives on the key issues related to the UN in the areas of peace; security; aid; trade; development; human rights; organised crime; HIV/AIDS; and terrorism. Three eminent South African scholars are joined by eleven non-South African scholars and practitioners from the Democratic Republic of the Congo (DRC), Ghana, Kenya, Nigeria, Sierra Leone, Sudan, Tanzania, Uganda and Britain. This introduction will highlight the key issues in the UN reform process in 2005, explaining the significance of these issues for Africa. The book is arranged around four broad themes: Africa's stake in UN reform; its "responsibility to protect" victims of human rights abuses; key economic development and human security challenges such as HIV/AIDS and international organised crime; and the response of key African actors to the challenges of human rights, peacebuilding and terrorism. The unifying theme of the book is the need for a dialogue over the efficacy of the UN and the continent's security and development challenges in the post–Cold War era.

Key Issues in the UN Reform Process

The need for strengthening the role of the UN in aiding Africa's peacekeeping and promoting economic development on the continent is clear: nearly half of the fifty UN peacekeeping missions in the post–Cold War era have been in Africa; the continent currently hosts the largest and most numerous UN peacekeeping missions in the world; Africa has produced the last two UN Secretaries-General – Egypt's Boutros Boutros-Ghali (1992–1996), and Ghana's Kofi Annan (1997–2006); much of the UN's socio-economic and humanitarian efforts are located in Africa, and the world body has established sub-regional offices in West Africa, the Great Lakes and Central Africa as well as peacebuilding offices in Liberia, Guinea-Bissau and the Central African Republic (CAR). Today, half of the UN's seventeen peacekeeping missions are in Africa, and nearly 90 per cent of its personnel are deployed on the continent. But despite the importance of the UN to the continent, there is still a paucity of knowledge about the organisation and how to access it to serve the continent's needs among many African practitioners and policymakers. This was reflected, for example, in a regional meeting in Johannesburg, South Africa, in March 2001 with diverse African actors who discussed the UN's Brahimi report on peacekeeping of August 2000.[8]

This book reflects strong and diverse African perspectives – from both scholars and practitioners – on the relevance and the role of the United Nations in conflict management and development issues on the continent in the post–Cold War era. The recent discussions and disagreements about the reform of the United Nations on its sixtieth anniversary in September 2005 culminated in a disappointingly watered-down reform package. There were commitments to establish a Peacebuilding Commission and a Human Rights Council as well as pledges over the "responsibility to protect" civilians from human rights abuses. However, notable failures in the reform package for Africa were UN Security Council reform; concrete commitments to debt cancellation, fair trade and increased aid; and systematic and substantial support for African peacekeeping efforts.

Concerns thus remain regarding the need to re-evaluate the multilateral dimensions of the United Nations and the efficacy of the institution as it currently exists. Addressing the organisation's current relevance has stirred considerable debate over its present and future role. Prompted by these developments, this book provides an analysis of the distinct and multi-faceted relationship that the UN has had with Africa in the post-Cold War era. This unique collection draws together essays from a variety of African policy-makers, academics and civil society activists including: Ibrahim Gambari, UN Undersecretary-General for Political Affairs and the most senior African at the UN after its Secretary-General, Kofi Annan; Mary Chinery-Hesse, one of the three African members of the United Nations High-level Panel set up by Kofi Annan in 2003; James Jonah and Francis Deng, former UN Undersecretaries-General for Political Affairs and Internally Displaced Persons respectively; and General Henry Anyidoho, former UN deputy force commander in Rwanda during the 1994 genocide. Kader Asmal, South Africa's former education minister and former chair of the country's parliamentary defence portfolio, has also contributed a chapter on South Africa and human rights within the UN context.

When the UN was created in 1945, its central mandate was to prevent the horrors of the Second World War being repeated. Accordingly, its structures were primarily devoted to preventing wars between states at a time when most of the world's nations were still largely under colonial rule. The past sixty years have witnessed enormous changes in the world's political geography. However, while the world has transformed with the end of the Cold War, the UN's power structures have remained virtually unchanged. The UN Security Council's permanent membership continues to reflect the victorious powers of the Second World War: the US, Britain, France, Russia and China. African countries, in collaboration with the Group of 77 (G-77) developing countries at the UN, mounted sustained attacks on apartheid South Africa and championed decolonisation efforts consistently from the

1960s. The UN has mushroomed from an initial 51 members in 1945 to 192 members in 2006, and now incorporates former colonies which have since transformed into nation states. Among these are 53 African countries that constitute over a quarter of the UN's membership.

Stark global political divisions after the controversial US-led invasion of Iraq in 2003 underscored the urgent need for reviewing the structure of the UN. The fact that the invasion occurred without UN Security Council authorisation precipitated a crisis in the international system and led to questions over the efficacy of current international norms and institutions for maintaining peace and security. These events prompted the UN Secretary-General, Kofi Annan, to announce plans to elicit suggestions for reform through a High-level Panel on *Threats, Challenges and Change*. At the time Annan noted: "We have come to a fork in the road. This may be a moment no less decisive than 1945 itself, when the United Nations was founded".[9]

Recommendations in the High-level Panel report of December 2004 included strategies aimed at bolstering multilateralism and counteracting the numerous new security threats of the twenty-first century. The report's innovation from previous analyses of global security threats was its insistence that there was a clear link between development issues and security, and a focus on human security as well as traditional military security. The Panel recognised that the scourge of poverty and disease provides a potentially grave threat in the twenty-first century. The report therefore focused on both "soft" security threats which developing countries prioritise, and "hard" security threats which richer countries are mainly concerned with. Kofi Annan's 2005 report responding to the High-level Panel, *In Larger Freedom*, went further and explicitly linked poverty to security and human rights. The UN's Millennium Development Goals also aim to halve global poverty, infant mortality and illiteracy by 2015.

The identification of security and development as global security threats has clear implications for Africa and provides the bedrock of this collection of fourteen rich essays. The debates on UN reform have provided an opportunity for reflection on Africa's priorities in relation to the international community. This book is a collection of experiences, historical insights and foresights into the needs and desires of the African continent as it charts a course for the twenty-first century. The essays show both an appreciation of African political and socio-economic realities and also provide concrete recommendations over how to address the continent's concerns through a multilateral approach. Since the tragedy of the Rwandan genocide in 1994, more extensive conflict management mechanisms have been developed on the continent and there are plans by the AU to establish an African Standby Force (ASF) by 2010. There is a clear and increasing desire among Africa's leaders and civil society actors to create a *Pax Africana* on the continent: a peace established and consolidated largely through the efforts of Africans.[10] Africa's security mechanisms, however, remain fledgling and under-resourced. Although the desire to meet Africa's needs has not yet been fulfilled, this book reflects concerns and strategies for the future relationship between the UN and Africa.

Contents of the Book

The focus of the first section of the book is the UN and Africa's stake in the largely disappointing reform process in 2005. Suggestions for reforming the United Nations have included creating a Security Council that reflects the 21st century, a strengthened Human Rights Council, and a Peacebuilding Commission for post-conflict reconstruction. Improved collaboration between the UN and Africa's regional organisations such as the African Union, the Southern African Development Community (SADC), the Economic Community of West African States (ECOWAS), the Intergovernmental Authority on Development (IGAD), the Economic Community of Central African States (ECCAS) and the Arab Maghreb Union (AMU) has also been suggested.

An introductory essay by Adekeye Adebajo, a Nigerian scholar, provides a context for understanding the UN reform process. The author assesses the main outcomes for Africa of the UN summit in September 2005, provides the context for understanding the thirteen other essays in the book, and recommends strategies for Africa to be able to influence the UN in defence of its own interests. As one of three African members of the sixteen-member High-level Panel, Ghana's Mary Chinery-Hesse provides an insider's perspective of the process leading to the crafting of the 2004 report on UN reform. Chinery-Hesse details the challenges that the three African members on the Panel faced in shifting the understanding of global security threats beyond those focused on terrorism and "hard" security issues to a realisation that development was also an international security concern. She argues that it is important that Africa not lose the little ground gained through the Panel's report in terms of broadening the understanding of security to encompass human security issues.

In the following chapter, James Jonah details the recent debate on UN reform with a particular focus on the Security Council, and provides an assessment of why the issues raised remain important for Africa. The Sierra Leonean scholar–diplomat critiques the recommendations for UN reform as too favourable to powerful Western interests and explores the need for the Millennium Development Goals to be realised in Africa. While recommendations exist for the creation of new institutions and reforms to address "hard" threats such as terrorism, he notes that no obligations exist for powerful governments to fulfil their commitments to combating "soft" threats such as poverty and infectious diseases. Jonah further argues that overcoming Africa's development concerns are vital to addressing security issues on the continent. To enable these, he calls for the democratisation of the UN Security Council and strengthening of the UN General Assembly, offering tangible recommendations for future strategies.

As Nigeria's UN Under-Secretary-General for Political Affairs, Ibrahim Gambari's chapter provides a clear overview of the debates and issues of this book, with a particular focus on the New Partnership for Africa's Development (NEPAD) of 2001 and British premier, Tony Blair's Commission for Africa report of 2005. Gambari outlines the background and perceived need for UN reform as well as the evolving relationship of the continent with the UN since its foundation. As both scholar and diplomat, he notes how control of decision-making within the UN has become increasingly skewed towards western powers and, as a result, argues that there is a need to promote and encourage a unified continental approach to promoting African interests. Concerted action on the part of Africa and its international partners to help overcome obstacles to the continent's development are of prime importance. This will pave the way for an Africa that depends more on its competence and productive capacity than the world's compassion to survive and succeed. A strong and prosperous Africa is in the world's interest. This requires a clear identification and articulation of Africa's concerns, needs and priorities, which are the subject of the rest of the book.

The second section of the book specifically addresses key issues of concern to Africa in the area of the "responsibility to protect". The UN High-level Panel report of 2004 adopted the ideas of the Canadian-sponsored International Commission on Intervention and State Sovereignty (ICISS) which argued that, if governments are unwilling or unable to protect their citizens from serious harm, then the international community has a duty to protect them, ignoring the principle of non-intervention for a higher goal. This section addresses those organs and issues that are linked to governments' responsibilities to their citizens. The evolving "responsibility to protect" doctrine in Africa, the plight of internally displaced persons, the transformation of the Human Rights Commission into a more effective Human Rights Council, and the twin tragedies of Rwanda and Darfur are the specific subjects of this section.

Congolese scholar and UN official, Musifiky Mwanasali, starts the section by exploring the creation in July 2004 of the African Union's fifteen-member Peace and Security Council (PSC), the decision-making organ established for the prevention, management and resolution of conflicts. He then provides a rich analysis of Africa's emerging "responsibility to protect" doctrine which has challenged traditional notions of sovereignty. Mwanasali argues that the AU's new concept of "non-indifference" – in stark contrast to the Organisation of African Unity's obsession with non-interference in the internal affairs of member states – demonstrates the AU's determination to be more proactive in preventing and resolving African conflicts. The chapter provides a sober analysis of the legacy of the OAU as well as an optimistic assessment of the potential that lies in the AU.

Sudanese scholar and former UN Under-Secretary-General for Internally Displaced Persons between 1992 and 2004, Francis Deng, investigates the important challenge posed by "failed states" like Somalia and Liberia. He sees internal displacement as not only constituting a humanitarian and human rights crisis, but also an international political and security issue. The crucial problems of national sovereignty and the "responsibility to protect" doctrine are both explored, and a thorough historical analysis of these concerns is provided. Through the case study of Sudan, Deng assesses the internal displacement challenges of the international community and the need to develop ways of preventing the arbitrary displacement of populations, responding to the protection and assistance needs of those already displaced, and finding durable solutions to these crises. He argues that there is also a challenge for states to create conditions of peace and security which would prevent or discourage further conflict, human rights violations and resulting displacement.

Through an analysis of the creation of the UN Human Rights Council in March 2006 to replace the discredited Human Rights Commission, British scholar Helen Scanlon questions its significance for the African continent. She explores the establishment of the Human Rights Council within the context of the growth of human rights concerns by the United Nations since its creation and the relevance of these developments for Africa. This chapter investigates some of the failures of the Human Rights Commission within its historical context; its growing politicisation as well as what its recent metamorphosis can potentially present for Africa. Although the Council represents one of the few significant outcomes of Annan's 2005 drive for UN reform, the ability of the Human Rights Council to be insulated from the politicisation that occurred with its predecessor remains uncertain. Nonetheless, the significance of the protection of human rights for Africa's long-term security and development has been gaining widespread recognition and thus the mandate and powers of the Human Rights Council is a priority to actors on the continent.

Through a rich comparison with Sudan's Darfur region, General Henry Anyidoho, UN deputy force commander in Rwanda, provides a unique contribution of personal involvement in the UN during the Rwandan genocide in 1994. His powerful, and sometimes disturbing account of events in Rwanda provides a sobering analysis of the UN's failure to prevent the atrocities that unfolded. Anyidoho details the lack of political will by the west, the critical role of Non-Governmental Organisations (NGOs), and the clear need for post-conflict reconstruction. The Ghanaian general further provides pertinent recommendations for peacekeeping and peacemaking in other parts of Africa such as Darfur, based on his own personal experience in both cases, to ensure that such tragedies do not reoccur.

Section Three addresses some of the economic development and human security challenges that affect the African continent in the twenty-first century. The recognition of both "hard" and "soft" threats as international security issues is of obvious interest to Africa. Collective security necessitates addressing the security concerns of the entire global community by promoting development through aid, trade and debt annulment, as well as addressing human security issues such as HIV/AIDS and international organised crime. Focusing on the causal factors of Africa's current inequitable relationship with the West, South African economist, Margaret Legum, incisively probes some of the circumstances around Africa's $290 billion debt crisis. She explores some common misconceptions about Africa's economic plight and in turn paves the way for understanding the need for UN reform through a more holistic analysis of the historical background of the current crisis. Responses which call on the West to recognise the importance of poverty as a "security" threat are potentially strengthened by detailing the root causes of that poverty and deconstructing the "Washington Consensus". Legum also calls for unity in confronting western trade barriers, and discusses the politics of foreign aid to Africa.

Ugandan scholar Angela Ndinga-Muvumba argues that, since large segments of Africa's population and national armies are afflicted by, and will succumb to, HIV/AIDS, the disease has major implications for national and human security on the continent. After assessing the disappointing results of the UN reform process in this area, Ndinga-Muvumba calls on African institutions and civil society actors to play a leading role in efforts to combat the disease and demands that the international community assist African governments in strengthening health infrastructure. Transnational crime as a factor in the erosion of human security and in undermining the ability of some states to maintain law and order is the subject of South African analyst Peter Gastrow's essay. He argues that currently, in many African countries, transnational organised crime poses a more immediate and serious threat to human security than does terrorism. Gastrow further notes that this is an area that can be addressed provided that the necessary political will and international support are forthcoming. Emphasis should be placed on increased coordination in providing technical and development assistance to strengthen criminal justice systems in Africa, and not only through the establishment of yet another fund. Suggestions on how to tackle the problem includes proper adoption and implementation of the concept of "collective security", implementing the UN Convention against transnational organised crime, and encouraging international support to strengthen the rule of law in Africa.

The fourth and final section of the book shifts the debate away from a focus on overall UN reform to deal with the response of African actors to human rights, peacebuilding and international terrorism. The essay by South African scholar–politician, Kader Asmal, discusses human rights issues within the context of South Africa's liberation struggle, calling for Africans to remain committed to the universalisation of these rights. The largest consensus in UN circles for reform is perceived to be the establishment of a Peacebuilding Commission within the UN Secretariat – the subject of Kenyan scholar, Tim Murithi's analysis. The Commission seeks to improve UN post-conflict planning, focusing particularly on establishing institutions, ensuring financing, and improving coordination of UN bodies and other key regional and global actors. This Commission will interact with both the UN Security Council and its Economic and Social Council, and involve the participation of international financial institutions. Murithi also focuses attention on the evolving AU/NEPAD post-conflict reconstruction framework and calls for a symbiotic relationship between this body and the new UN Peacebuilding Commission.

In the final essay of the book, Mwesiga Baregu, a Tanzanian scholar, traces the links between international terrorism, increasing global socio-economic disparities and globalisation. He notes that while terrorism is currently seen as a principle threat in the West, in Africa poverty, disease and inter- and intra-state conflicts are more important threats to the region. Baregu expresses concern that America's "war on terrorism" has created polarisation in Africa to rival that engendered by the Cold War. The establishment of a US military base in Djibouti in 2002 and the hasty passage by African governments of counter-terrorism legislation have led to criticism that Africa has again become a pawn in world politics. Baregu notes that terrorism is a global phenomenon arising from global processes and therefore requires global cooperation to counter it effectively. He suggests a focus on the root causes that breed terrorism, and not just applying military tools to tackle the symptoms of terrorism.

Overall, the depth of this edited collection lies in the unique contributions of rich essays by a pan-African team of scholars and practitioners. The premise throughout these analyses remains that Africa can and should be a partner rather than a problem for the international community. Debates on the reform of the UN have opened a unique window of opportunity to strategise on how Africa can best build effective multinational and multilateral institutions and support effective multilateral action. The acceptance of the relationship between non-traditional security issues such as poverty and health, and collective international security are crucial, and African concerns must be raised articulately to impact on future UN policy and the reform of the world body. This book clearly demonstrates that critical to any revitalisation of the United Nations and reaffirmation of its mandate, Africa must be an intrinsic partner to the work at hand. Only then can the "dialogue of the deaf" between Africa and the West become a fruitful exchange.

Notes

[1] Mazrui, A: *Cultural Forces in World Politics* (London: James Currey, 1990), p.116.

[2] This phrase was coined by Adebayo Adedeji, who served as Executive Secretary of the UN Economic Commission for Africa (ECA) from 1975 to 1991.

[3] *A More Secure World: Our Shared Responsibility,* Report of the United Nations Secretary-General's High-level Panel on *Threats, Challenges and Change* (United Nations Department of Public Information: DPI/2367, December 2004).

[4] See African Union, Draft Recommendations at the Ministerial Committee of Fifteen on the Report of the High-level Panel on the Reform of the UN System. 20–22 February 2005. Mbabane, Swaziland. CTTE/15/Min/ReformUN/Draft/Recomm. (I).

[5] See "The New Partnership for Africa's Security: The United Nations, Regional Organisations, and Future Security Threats in Africa", *CCR Seminar Report*, October 2004; and "A More Secure Continent: African Perspectives on the UN High-level Panel Report, A More Secure World: Our Shared Responsibility", *CCR Seminar Report*, May 2005. Available at www.ccrweb.ccr.uct.ac.za

[6] *In Larger Freedom: Towards Development, Security and Human Rights For All*, Report of the UN Secretary-General; follow-up to the outcome of the Millennium Summit. 21 March 2005, A/59/2005.

[7] CCR: "Special Supplement on UN Reform" in *Mail & Guardian*, 9–15 September 2005.

[8] International Peace Academy and the Centre on International Cooperation: "Refashioning the Dialogue: Regional Perspectives on the Brahimi Report on UN Peace Operations", *Regional Meetings* (Johannesburg, Buenos Aires, Singapore and London, February–March 2001), pp.6-11.

[9] Secretary-General Address to the General Assembly: New York, 23 September 2003. See http://www.un.org/webcast/ga/58/statements/sg2eng030923 (accessed 24 April 2006).

[10] See Mazrui, A: *Towards a Pax Africana* (Chicago: University of Chicago Press, 1967).

Section One

©Louise Gubb/Trace Images

Africa's Stake in UN Reform

Chronicle of a Death Foretold:
The Rise and Fall of UN Reform[1]

Adekeye Adebajo

UNITED NATIONS REFORM is dead. Over 150 heads of state met in New York in September 2005 to recite obsequies for yet another ill-fated effort to reform the UN. The lifeless corpse of UN reform was dead on arrival by the time world leaders flew into the "Big Apple". The event left UN Secretary-General Kofi Annan's legacy – already badly tarnished by Iraq's oil-for-food scandal – in tatters. The 101 recommendations of Annan's High-level Panel on UN reform were cynically derided by critics as the "101 Dalmatians" (after the animated Disney cartoon). Spectacular failures in the UN reform process included:

- The inability to reform the anachronistic fifteen-member UN Security Council on which America, Russia, China, France and Britain still sit as veto-wielding permanent members, when seventy per cent of the issues discussed on this undemocratic body relate to Africa;

- No substantive and concrete measures being taken to improve the UN's peacekeeping capacity in Africa despite the organisation deploying half of its peacekeeping missions in the world and nearly ninety per cent of its peacekeepers to the continent; and

- Continued disappointment on aid, trade and debt issues amidst the frugality and empty promises of the rich world in the face of the depressing reality that most African countries will miss the

UN Millennium Development Goals (MDGs) target of halving poverty by 2015.

This chapter will assess Africa's stake in the UN reform process in the seven key areas of peacekeeping; UN Security Council reform; humanitarian intervention and peacebuilding; the New Partnership for Africa's Development (NEPAD) and democratic governance; sustainable development, trade and aid; HIV/AIDS as a security threat; and international terrorism. We will also assess why these interests were predictably and largely unfulfilled in the UN reform process that culminated in the disappointing General Assembly session in New York between September and December 2005.

The UN High-level Panel and the Millennium Declaration

The December 2004 report, *A More Secure World: Our Shared Responsibility*,[2] submitted to the UN Secretary-General, Kofi Annan, by the High-level Panel on *Threats, Challenges and Change* generated considerable debate, particularly among the "chattering classes" in New York. In the aftermath of the illegitimate and illegal US-led military invasion of Iraq which had been launched without the authorisation of the UN Security Council, Annan set up a High-level Panel to study global security threats[3] in November 2003. The Panel was mandated to examine the main global threats and challenges to peace and security and to make recommendations to the UN Secretary-General by December 2004 for a collective response to these threats. (See Chinery-Hesse in this volume).

It is important to note that the five-year review of the UN Millennium Declaration of September 2000 provided a focus for UN reform and was the basis of Kofi Annan's March 2005 report to the UN General Assembly, *In Larger Freedom*.[4] American economist Jeffrey Sachs' Millennium Development Project had also submitted a report *Investing in Development: A Practical Plan to Achieve the Millennium Development Goals* two months earlier.[5] The UN Secretary-General's March 2005 report sought not only to assess progress towards the Millennium Development Goals, but also to respond to the report of the UN High-level Panel and recommend actions to be taken at the UN General Assembly session in September 2005 in the areas of development, collective security, human rights, and strengthening UN institutions.[6] The Millennium Declaration of 2000 had sought to generate international consensus on meeting Africa's special needs in four key areas on which this chapter will focus: building peacekeeping capacity in cooperation with Africa's regional organisations; strengthening democratic governance; promoting sustainable development by providing development assistance, enhancing private capital flows, and building capacity for trade; and developing partnerships to combat HIV/AIDS. In this chapter, we will also focus on three other important issues in the UN reform process: reforming the fifteen-member UN Security Council; humanitarian intervention and peacebuilding; and international terrorism.

If Africa is to meet the Millennium Development Goals' aim of halving poverty by 2015, the continent will require an average annual economic growth rate of 7 per cent, double the current rate of about 3.5 per cent. During the 1990s – another "lost decade" like the 1980s – the continent's growth rate was a feeble 2.1 per cent. Thirty-two of the world's 49 Least Developed Countries (LDCs) are in Africa, making it essential that the continent's special needs are urgently addressed by institutions like the UN.

Blue Helmets, Burning Brushfires: UN Peacekeeping in Africa

The need for strengthening the UN's role in keeping Africa's peace and promoting economic development on the continent is clear: nearly half of the fifty UN peacekeeping missions in the post-Cold War era have been in Africa; the continent currently hosts the most numerous and largest UN peacekeeping missions in the world; Africa has produced the last two UN Secretaries-General – Egyptian, Boutros Boutros-Ghali, and Ghanaian, Kofi Annan; much of the UN's socio-economic and humanitarian efforts are located in Africa; and the world body has established sub-regional offices in West Africa, the Great Lakes and Central Africa, as well as peacebuilding offices in Liberia, Guinea-Bissau and the Central African Republic (CAR). Today, half of the UN's 17 peacekeeping missions are in Africa, and nearly 90 per cent of its personnel are deployed on the continent. But despite the importance of the UN to the continent, there is still a paucity of knowledge about the organisation and how to access it to serve the continent's needs among many African practitioners and policymakers. This was reflected, for example, at a regional meeting in Johannesburg, South Africa, in March 2001 with diverse African actors who discussed the UN's Brahimi report on peacekeeping of August 2000.[7]

The Brahimi report sought to strengthen the UN's peacekeeping capacity and introduced innovations such as pre-approving spending of funds for peacekeeping missions; improving the rapid deployment of civilian personnel to UN missions, as well as communication between headquarters and the field; and increasing the size of the UN's Department of Peacekeeping Operations (DPKO) from 400 to 600.[8] This report, named after its chair, Algeria's Lakhdar Brahimi, was, however, disappointingly short on details on how to improve relations between the UN and Africa's sub-regional organisations: the continent's main peacekeeping preoccupation. The report's constant warnings that the UN should not undertake certain missions where it could not guarantee success, was seen by many in Africa as prejudiced code for avoiding African conflicts after UN debacles in Somalia (1993) and Rwanda (1994). A report named after one of Africa's most illustrious public servants had thus ironically ignored the continent's most urgent peacekeeping needs.

Unlike the Brahimi report of August 2000, the High-level Panel report of December 2004 seemed at first to give priority to relations between the UN and Africa's regional organisations. This approach was lauded by a prominent African on the Panel, Salim Ahmed Salim, former Secretary-General of the Organisation of African Unity (OAU). Salim sat in Addis Ababa, Ethiopia, for 12 years between 1989 and 2001 experiencing the frustrations of seeking the assistance of the UN Security Council in many African conflicts such as Burundi, Liberia, and Sierra Leone. Sir David Hannay, another Panel member and former British permanent representative to the UN, was another strong supporter of strengthening ties between the UN and Africa's regional organisations, having worked closely with Ibrahim Gambari, Nigeria's former permanent representative to the UN and later UN Under-Secretary-General for Political Affairs, on these issues between 1993 and 1995. The UN High-level Panel held one of its meetings in Addis Ababa in April 2004 and met with senior African Union (AU) officials and African civil society actors to gain their own perspectives on relations with the UN. At the time, it was felt that this was a clear sign of the Panel's desire to focus on the UN's ties with African actors and institutions. But in the end, the Panel's report devoted about 5 paragraphs out of 302 to Africa's most important peacekeeping challenge. Like the Brahimi report before it, another high-level group had failed to grasp the UN/regional cooperation nettle, despite assurances from high-level members during their meetings that this was a key area of high priority.

Kofi Annan's report to the General Assembly of March 2005, *In Larger Freedom,* calls on donors to devise a 10-year capacity-building plan with the African Union, which is developing an African stand-by force based on five sub-regional brigades built around the Southern African Development Community (SADC), the Economic Community of West African States (ECOWAS), the Economic Community of Central African States (ECCAS), the Intergovernmental Authority on Development (IGAD) and the Arab Maghreb Union (AMU). This should be ready by 2010. Both Annan's report and the UN High-level Panel report of December 2004 advocated UN financial support for Africa's regional organisations. This is particularly welcome in light of the AU's peacekeeping efforts in Sudan's Darfur region that forced it to decide, in March 2006, to hand the mission over to the UN. Africa must, however, remain vigilant to ensure that this ten-year capacity-building plan is implemented, given the penchant of the Group of Eight (G-8) industrialised countries to make similar unfulfilled promises since 2002.

In the first four-and-a-half decades of the UN's existence, there was only one UN peacekeeping operation in Africa – the controversial Congo intervention between 1960 and 1964. The UN only returned to Africa as a peacekeeper some 25 years later in 1989 when it administered apartheid South Africa's military withdrawal from Namibia and supervised that country's first democratic election. Over the next decade, 17 peacekeeping operations were undertaken by the UN in Africa. There were the relative successes in Namibia and Mozambique, but also spectacular failures in Somalia and Rwanda.[9]

The cooperation between the UN and the Nigerian-led ECOWAS in Liberia and Sierra Leone yielded some positive results. However, this relationship was also characterised by serious challenges such as tensions between the ECOWAS Cease-fire Monitoring Group (ECOMOG) and the UN over strategy, division of labour, the sharing of scarce resources, as well as conditions of service and remuneration. In addition, there was often poor communication and a lack of trust between both organisations. There still remains a pressing need to establish a proper division of labour between the UN and Africa's fledgling security organisations which need to be greatly strengthened. Rwanda's Arusha agreement of 1993, the Democratic Republic of the Congo's (DRC) Lusaka accord of 1999, and the Algiers accords of 2000 that ended the Ethiopia/Eritrea conflict, all clearly revealed the military weakness of the OAU/AU whose members lacked the resources to implement agreements they had negotiated without UN peacekeepers. In Sierra Leone and Liberia, the UN took over peacekeeping duties from ECOMOG in 2000 and 2003 respectively. The UN also took over the AU mission in Burundi and the ECOWAS mission in Côte d'Ivoire in 2004. The UN Security Council has not done enough to strengthen the capacity of African regional organisations and to collaborate effectively with them in the field. The willingness of western peacekeepers, who have both the equipment and resources, to continue contributing to UN missions in Africa remains important. (See Anyidoho and Mwanasali in this volume). In 2004, 40 per cent of peacekeepers deployed in Africa and 31 per cent of troops deployed outside the continent were contributed by African armies. It is therefore also critical that an apartheid system of peacekeeping not be created within the UN.

The Ethiopia/Eritrea case provides an example of the potential for cooperation between the UN and Africa's regional organisations. The UN and the OAU eventually cooperated in the deployment of peacekeepers to the Horn of Africa in 2001 after the OAU, under its Algerian chair, Abdelaziz Bouteflika, had mediated an accord that the UN was asked to implement. After difficult experiences with ECOMOG in Liberia and Sierra Leone between 1993 and 2000, there is still great unease within the UN Security Council and Secretariat in New York about working alongside regional peacekeepers. There was, for example, much hostility directed against the continuing presence of Nigerian peacekeepers in Sierra Leone in 1999 within the UN Secretariat.[10] The UN's peacekeeping efforts in Ethiopia/Eritrea and the critical support of western governments for the UN operations in Mozambique, Sierra Leone, Liberia, Sudan, Côte d'Ivoire and Congo, however demonstrate the importance of external actors to peacekeeping missions in Africa.

UN Security Council Reform: Fifteen Men on a Powder Keg[11]

The reform of the UN Security Council – the most discussed proposal on the UN reform agenda – is now dead. Amidst the horse-trading between African foreign ministers and the G-4 (Group of Four: Japan, Germany, Brazil and India), Chinese intransigence, American and Russian ambivalence and the anti-permanent membership "spoilers" of Pakistan, Italy, Canada and Mexico in the Uniting for Consensus group, it was hard to discern a clear direction in a surreal process of smoke and mirrors. Some background is important in understanding this strange debate.

Every effort at reforming the Security Council – the UN's most powerful decision-making body – has in the last 40 years failed. The effort in 2005 was therefore no exception. The UN's Open-ended Working Group on Council Reform, established in December 1993, has long been dismissed in New York as "the Never-ending Working Group".[12] The five permanent members of this anachronistic Council – America, Britain, China, France and Russia – still reflect the victorious alliance of the Second World War in 1945. With a reconstituted Council, Africa would have had an enhanced presence at the top table of global diplomacy to help ensure that, with consistently strong representation, its security concerns are taken more seriously. This is particularly important since about 70 per cent of the Council's deliberations focus on Africa and nearly 90 per cent of UN peacekeepers are deployed on the continent. The UN Security Council must thus still be democratised to include more consistently strong African representation. The continent should also build a peacekeeping coalition at the UN with Asia and other regions that have contributed to UN peacekeeping efforts in Africa to ensure that the world body does not ignore future genocides in places like Rwanda.

At a meeting in Swaziland in February 2005, AU members called for two permanent seats with veto power for Africa to add to its existing three rotating seats, as well as two additional rotating seats on a reformed Security Council of 26. This became known as the Ezulwini Consensus.[13] The UN High-level Panel suggested an increase in Council membership from 15 to 24 members, the creation of six new permanent members without veto power, and 13 rotating two-year non-permanent seats in addition to the five veto-wielding permanent members. Under this proposal, Africa would have obtained two permanent seats and an additional rotating seat to add to the three it already holds. This, option A, was the most popular, while option B called for 8 four-year renewable seats and 11 two-year rotating seats in addition to the five permanent members.

After a meeting in London in August 2005 between African and G-4 foreign ministers, it appeared that the Africans would have to drop their veto demand in exchange for the G-4 agreeing to lobby for 26 instead of its preferred 25 seats. An acrimonious meeting of AU leaders in Addis Ababa in August 2005 exposed the continent's deep divisions on this issue, as countries like Egypt, Libya, Algeria and Zimbabwe reportedly opposed the pragmatic approach of Nigeria and South Africa to drop the unrealistic insistence on a veto. This lack of African consensus contributed significantly to the failure to achieve Security Council reform at the September 2005 summit. The African bloc of 54 states – about a quarter of the 192-strong General Assembly membership – was unable to play the bridging role required to reach the 128 votes needed to obtain a two-thirds majority for expanding the Security Council.

Disputes also emerged as to which country would fill the two permanent African seats. Egypt, Nigeria and South Africa all declared their candidacies. Kenya, Libya and Senegal also expressed interest. It is important, in case the issue of UN Security Council reform re-emerges in future, to assess the strengths and weaknesses of Africa's three leading candidates in this Byzantine contest: Nigeria, South Africa and Egypt. Cynics dismissed Nigeria as too "anarchic", Egypt as too "Arab" and South Africa as too "albinocratic". In its favour, Nigeria – Africa's most populous state with a population of about 130 million and the sixth largest oil-producer in the Organisation of Petroleum Exporting Countries (OPEC) – has an impressive peacekeeping record dating back to the UN's protracted Congo crisis in the 1960s, up until the more recent Liberia and Sierra Leone peacekeeping missions in the 1990s. Nigeria organised a UN anti-apartheid conference in 1977 and chaired its anti-apartheid committee for much of its existence. It has produced impressive UN technocrats like Ibrahim Gambari (UN Under-Secretary-General for Political Affairs) and Adebayo Adedeji (former Executive Secretary of the UN Economic Commission for Africa [ECA]). Nigeria is, however, in the throes of a difficult transition from 15 years of military misrule, and continues to suffer from the excesses of a profligate political class and communal strife that have resulted in over 10 000 deaths since 1999. Problems by disaffected armed militias clamouring for a greater share in Nigeria's oil wealth shut down a third of its oil production in 2005. It is therefore unclear whether Nigeria will be a force for stability or instability in Africa.

South Africa has several advantages: the constitutional democracy of Africa's richest country – albeit with massive inequalities – is widely admired; it has produced four Nobel peace laureates in Albert Luthuli, Desmond Tutu, Nelson Mandela and F. W. De Klerk; and Thabo Mbeki has won much praise for his peacemaking efforts in Congo, Côte d'Ivoire and Burundi. South Africa, a respected member of the global South, also has wide-ranging trade interests in Asia, Europe and the Americas, an evolving partnership with Brazil and India, and the country organised two high-profile UN summits on race and sustainable development. On the negative side, South Africa's military, academic and economic institutions are still seen as white-dominated, and memories of the country's destructive destabilisation of the region in the 1980s still linger amidst concerns over whether many South Africans have truly embraced an African identity.

Finally, Egypt has a proud history of international peacekeeping and produced a UN Secretary-General, Boutros Boutros-Ghali, who served between 1992 and 1996. But Egypt has been accused of having its body in Africa and its heart and head in the Middle East. The apparent Arab League support for Cairo at a meeting in Algiers, Algeria, in 2005 reinforced this perception. Egypt's legendary leader, Gamel Abdel Nasser, had also annoyed black Africans in the early 1950s by talking patronisingly of "diffusing the light of civilization into the furthest parts of the virgin jungle".[14] The country's current leader, Hosni Mubarak, has until recently been seen as detached from African affairs, rarely attending AU and NEPAD meetings. Questions continue to be raised about Egypt's democratic and human rights record, with the 77-year old Mubarak adding to his 24-year rule in flawed elections in 2005.

Sovereignty as Responsibility: Humanitarian Intervention and Peacebuilding

The UN High-level Panel report of December 2004 adopted the ideas of the Canadian-sponsored International Commission on Intervention and State Sovereignty (ICISS) on the "responsibility to protect", which argued that if governments are unwilling or unable to protect their citizens from serious harm, then the international community has a duty to protect them, ignoring the principle of non-intervention for a higher goal. Five criteria are laid out to legitimise such interventions:

1. The seriousness of the threat must justify the use of force;
2. The purpose of the military action must be to avert the specific threat;
3. All non-military options must have been exhausted;
4. The use of military force must be proportionate to the threat; and
5. The chances of military action to meet the threat must be high.[15]

In his landmark *An Agenda for Peace*, published in 1992, UN Secretary-General Boutros Boutros-Ghali argued forcefully for humanitarian intervention and advocated the use of regional security arrangements to lighten the UN's heavy peacekeeping burden. UN Secretary-General, Kofi Annan, has also been a vociferous proponent of humanitarian intervention. As Annan noted, "States are now widely understood to be instruments at the service of their peoples, and not vice-versa... Nothing in the UN Charter precludes recognition that there are rights beyond borders".[16] Annan's promotion of humanitarian intervention and his support of Francis Deng's (his Sudanese former Special Representative for Internally Displaced Persons between 1992 and 2004) idea of "sovereignty as responsibility"[17] has met with strong opposition from many leaders, particularly in developing countries. They fear that such interventions might be used to threaten their own sovereignty by powerful states. This is ironic considering that the AU's Constitutive Act of 2000 has one of the most interventionist systems in the world in cases of genocide, egregious human rights violations, unconstitutional changes of government, and situations that have the potential to lead to regional instability. (See Mwanasali and Deng in this volume).

Related to the idea of humanitarian intervention is the concept of peacebuilding, which if effectively undertaken, can help avoid such interventions through early prevention of conflicts. Peacebuilding is often associated with the "second generation" of UN missions in the post-Cold War era in places like Angola, Mozambique, Namibia and Somalia, where efforts were made to adopt a holistic approach to peace. Not only are diplomatic and military tools employed in building peace, but today's peacebuilders also focus on political, social, and economic aspects of societies emerging from civil war in an effort to address the root causes of conflict. Peacebuilding thus aims to promote not just political peace, but also social peace and the redressing of economic inequalities that could lead to further conflict.[18] Both the UN High-level Panel and the UN Secretary-General's 2005 report *In Larger Freedom* backed the establishment of a Peacebuilding Commission as well as a Peacebuilding Support Office within the UN Secretariat, and the UN General Assembly agreed to the Commission in September 2005. (See Murithi in this volume).

The Peacebuilding Commission aims to improve UN post-conflict planning, focusing particularly on establishing institutions, ensuring financing in the period between the end of hostilities and the convening of donor conferences, and improving coordination of UN bodies and other key regional and global actors. This Commission would interact both with the UN Security Council and the UN Economic and Social Council (ECOSOC), and would involve the participation of international financial institutions. The Peacebuilding Commission is to be composed of 31 members from the Security Council, ECOSOC, and the highest financial and troop-contributors to the UN. A multi-year standing fund is to be established with voluntary contributions. Due to pressure from developing countries, the Commission will focus largely on post-conflict reconstruction and not on conflict prevention. Many Africans are, however, sceptical – based on UN experiences in Rwanda, Sierra Leone, Liberia, and the Central African Republic – and feel that this Commission may represent a new alchemy that will not make much difference in mobilising the resources required for post-conflict reconstruction efforts in Africa.

Not Yet Uhuru: NEPAD, the APRM and Democratic Governance

Many of Africa's leaders have recognised that the continent cannot achieve economic development and security without promoting democratic governance: one of the four key areas of the UN Millennium Declaration of 2000's plan for meeting Africa's special needs. In October 2001, African leaders from South Africa, Nigeria, Senegal and Algeria spearheaded the New Partnership for Africa's Development, which seeks greater western aid, investment and debt relief in exchange for a self-monitored voluntary peer-review system of "good governance".[19] NEPAD has six sectoral priorities: education, health, regional infrastructure, agriculture, market access and the environment. The NEPAD Democracy and Governance programme calls on African leaders to commit themselves to political and economic "good governance", free and fair elections, and accountable and transparent management of their economies. Countries are also to submit themselves to an African Peer Review Mechanism (APRM). 25 African countries have so far signed up for review, with APRM missions having visited Ghana, Rwanda, Mauritius, Kenya, Uganda, Nigeria and South Africa. Work is also continuing with Algeria, Egypt, Mali, Mozambique and Senegal.

Under the APRM process, each country prepares a national programme of action after undertaking a self-evaluation which involves government officials, civil society and the private sector. The APRM Panel of Eminent Persons[20] then submits a country review report to help governments identify institutional, policy and capacity weaknesses, before recommending remedies to these shortcomings. The peer review mechanism is intended to encourage countries to adopt sound policies, priorities and standards for political, economic, development and sub-regional and continental integration through shared experiences. The three key features of the APRM are: first, the reviews must be competent, credible and free of political manipulation; second, Africans must "own" the process; and third, the review is non-confrontational. The process itself has five stages:

1. The Panel of Eminent Persons studies the political, economic and corporate governance as well as the development environment of countries under review based on background documents produced by the APRM Secretariat in South Africa, as well as material from national, sub-regional and international organisations.

2. Political parties, parliamentarians, the private sector and civil society are consulted.

The suggestion by the UN Conference on Trade and Development (UNCTAD) in September 2004 that the international community cancel Africa's debilitating debt of $290 billion must be strongly supported. It is significant to note, as a recent UNCTAD report does, that between 1970 and 2002 Africa borrowed $540 billion and paid back about $550 billion in principal and interest. [25] The West must open its markets to freer and fairer trade with Africa. Development assistance must also be urgently increased to 0.7 per cent of the national incomes of rich countries; a target set as far back as 1970. Donors need to coordinate their efforts better, and richer countries from Asia must join the group of current largely western donors to contribute more to global development efforts.

American economist Jeffrey Sachs' sensible call for the World Bank's International Development Association (IDA) to increase its annual programme from $8 billion to $25 billion, half of which should go to African countries, also deserves support. The IDA should, as Sachs argues, provide grants rather than loans. [26] Only few African countries have so far seen an effective alleviation of their debt burden under the World Bank's Heavily Indebted Poor Countries (HIPC) initiative. Even the countries that have reached HIPC's completion point cannot sustain their debt levels since growth and export levels have been overestimated and oil imports rose astronomically in the 2004–2006 period. Monstrous, corrupt autocrats such as Zaire's Mobutu Sese Seko, Somalia's Siad Barre and Liberia's Samuel Doe, many of whom were fed with western grants and loans during the Cold War era, largely accumulated Africa's debts. Even with raging conflicts, grinding poverty and an AIDS pandemic that threatens to wipe out large populations on the continent, these governments cannot continue to be forced to use a quarter or more of their export earnings on servicing debts that everyone knows can never be repaid. Scarce resources that should go towards health and education must not continue to be used to service unpayable debts. (See Legum in this volume).

Africa's share of global trade declined from about 6 per cent in the early 1980s to only 2 per cent today. [27] The global trading system, as represented by the inequities of the World Trade Organisation (WTO) and the two Bretton Woods institutions – the World Bank and the International Monetary Fund (IMF) – must be urgently reformed in ways that give greater voice to Africa. African and other southern representation in the highest decision-making organs of these organisations must be urgently increased. Unfair trade practices by rich countries also make it harder for Africa to grow its economies out of poverty. Most industrialised countries impose high tariffs on agricultural and manufactured goods, the areas of comparative advantage for African states. This has led to grotesque distortions between North and South; while rich European Union (EU) countries provided subsidies of $913 per cow to their farmers in 2000, they contributed only $8 of aid to each African citizen. While the US provided its farmers with cotton subsidies of $10.7 million per day in 2000, it provided only $3.1 million of aid per day to the whole of sub-Saharan Africa. Rich countries agricultural subsidies of $311 billion exceeded the total national income of sub-Saharan Africa of $301 billion in 2001.[28]

In recognition of the pernicious effects of these agricultural subsidies, the WTO's Doha Trade Round agreed to their elimination in 2001, though significantly no timetable was set for this process. These subsidies must be eliminated urgently with a clear plan of the quantity of reductions per year. Even as subsidies and tariffs cripple Africa's economic prospects, the rich world has become less generous with development assistance. Between 1990 and 2001, official development assistance fell from 0.33 per cent to 0.22 per cent of the gross national income of donors. If the Millennium Development Goals' aim of halving poverty by 2015 is to be achieved in Africa and the rest of the developing world, a minimum of $100 billion a year will have to be found by the industrialised world. This figure would still represent only 0.43 per cent of the national income of Organisation for Economic Cooperation and Development (OECD) countries. Countries like Brazil, India, China, South Africa and Nigeria are increasingly organising efforts with other members of the Group of 20+ (G-20+) in the Doha trade round to present a more powerful bloc that can more effectively defend southern interests from the protectionist excesses of the profligate north.[29]

"Making Poverty History": Geldof, the G-8 and Africa

In concluding this section, we focus on the G-8 meeting in London in July 2005 and its significance in meeting the UN Millennium Declaration of 2000. The Live8 campaign by Bob Geldof, the narcissistic, fading Irish rock star, "to make poverty history" was naively admirable but also somewhat disturbing to watch. Here was a dynamic individual who was helping to perpetuate the stereotype of the "dark continent" as a helpless place of poverty and disease which the white musical minstrels of a new age would help to overcome. Geldof's stubborn refusal to include African singers on the lily-white stage was breathtakingly insensitive. The blacks wheeled out as props on stage were famine victims and schoolchildren in a drama in which whites remained the main actors in another African "tragedy". It was therefore a relief to see Nelson Mandela addressing the Johannesburg concert in June 2005. A BBC (British Broadcasting Corporation) documentary titled "Geldof in Africa" showed the pop star waltzing around Ethiopia in a hat and scruffy clothes, mouthing generalisations about "Africa" and "modernity" encroaching on the continent. Geldof waxed philosophical about his approach to "making poverty history" in December 2005: "There are those who will stand outside the tent peeing in, there are those who will be inside the tent peeing out – and then there are the others who will stand inside the tent peeing on the ground where they stand… By peeing so wantonly, so copiously, you can stink the place up so much that they want you out – at a reasonable price."[30] The fact that two Irish rock stars – Geldof and Bono, of the band U2 – are at the forefront of these campaigns is a clear sign of the poverty of genuine leadership on these issues.

Regarding the 2005 G–8 meeting itself, there had been euphoric talk about a "Marshall Plan" for Africa and an Alice-in-Wonderland-like expectation that this club of eight rich men would somehow be swayed by the tuneful ballads of white musical messiahs into "saving" Africa from itself. Britain's energy – with its Commission for Africa (See Gambari in this volume) – was admirable. But, in the end, what has sometimes been described as Tony Blair's "muscular born-again Christianity" failed to find sufficient converts to the faith. The "holy trinity" of trade, debt and aid dominated the discussions on Africa. The Gleneagles accord promised to begin to lift western export subsidies that harm African agricultural products, to double aid to Africa to $50 billion by 2010 and to write off $55 billion of debt involving 14 African countries. There were also promises to support African peacekeeping and the battle against AIDS, as well as infrastructure projects. But as often occurs in these cases, the devil was in the detail: there was no timetable for eliminating farm subsidies; only about a third of the promised aid was new money; and, based on recent experience, future fiscally-conscious western governments are unlikely to honour these pledges. The debt write-off for Africa represents only a drop in a large debt ocean of $290 billion.

Only the Scandinavians and the Dutch have managed consistently, over the last three decades, to contribute 0.7 per cent of their gross national income to foreign aid. Despite France's frequent attempts to portray itself as a champion of African interests, not only has its aid fallen far short of its rhetoric, but London is correct in criticising Paris' insistence on maintaining profligate annual EU agricultural subsidies of about $50 billion which remain one of the biggest obstacles to Africa's capacity to develop. While the US spends $450 billion annually on its military hardware, it devotes a meagre $15 billion to its development "software", underlining Washington's lopsided priorities. So, what is to be done? The food mountains of the rich must be demolished and the dumping of agricultural products on the poor halted. Fortress Europe must tear down its ramparts, while Uncle Sam must stop feeding his gluttonous, corpulent farmers more subsidies lest they choke on this poison. These must be done not just out of some altruistic feeling of charity, but to take advantage of the potential of trade with an African market of 850 million consumers. Otherwise, all the efforts of musicians, politicians and activists will turn out simply to have been much ado about nothing.

Deadly Peacekeeping: HIV/AIDS as a Security Threat

The scourge of the HIV/AIDS pandemic has had a particularly devastating effect on Africa as recognised by the UN reform process which called for greater resources in combating the disease and strengthening Africa's health systems. (See Ndinga-Muvumba in this volume). HIV/AIDS has become the leading cause of death among adults on the continent. There are an estimated 25.8 million Africans affected by the disease, representing 60 per cent of the global figure, and 22 million Africans have died of the disease. During the 1990s, the spread of HIV/AIDS also had a devastating effect on families and communities. The loss of productive capacity among families affected by HIV/AIDS had a major impact on food production and nutritional well-being. To make matters worse, HIV/AIDS transmission rates and the progression of the disease tend to be higher in under-nourished populations, trapping them in a vicious cycle of hunger and disease.[31]

The disease constitutes a serious constraint to the growth and stability of many African economies and societies, and could reverse their hard-won development gains over the last four decades.

Since large segments of Africa's population and national armies are afflicted by and will succumb to HIV, the disease has major implications for national security on the continent. Africans need to become part of debates on AIDS that have tended to be dominated by western scholars and policymakers. While much research has focused on the socio-economic impact of AIDS, the security and governance dimensions of the disease have been under-researched. African institutions and actors must therefore play a leading role in such efforts, grassroots organisations must continue to be supported and African governments must be assisted to strengthen domestic health infrastructure and promote anti-AIDS campaigns. Such support can be channelled through bodies like the Joint UN Programme on HIV/AIDS (UNAIDS), the World Health Organisation (WHO), the Global AIDS Fund and local NGOs in Africa.

The security dimension of AIDS has three elements: the implications for national security of having large parts of the most productive members of society – those between the ages of 15 and 45 – succumb to the disease; the high prevalence rates of the disease in national armies; and the spread of AIDS by international peacekeepers and their infection by local populations. According to some estimates, 40 to 60 per cent of the national armies of Angola and the DRC, a third of Botswana's army, and 23 per cent of South Africa's defence force are HIV positive. [32] This situation could lead to armies not being able to deploy whole contingents to peacekeeping missions. It could also result in a lack of the cohesion necessary to maintain force structures, adversely affect combat readiness, and lead to massive increases in military spending. Such concerns led to South Africa's army declaring HIV to be one of its most strategic concerns in 1999. The discovery by Uganda's leader, Yoweri Museveni, of high prevalence rates among his soldiers in 1986 led to one of the most determined responses to the disease. A guerrilla movement that had just seized power at the time recognised the long-term implications for its continued grip on office of the decimation of its army by this invisible enemy.

Peacekeepers have spread HIV both in areas in which they are deployed and once they return to their home countries. They are also vulnerable to infection by local populations. This has led to the supreme irony of those charged with security becoming agents of insecurity. At the urging of the Security Council in 2000, the UN now distributes condoms and booklets on HIV to all its peacekeepers in the field, and encourages countries to promote voluntary testing. In establishing the UN mission in the Congo in 2000, the Security Council wrote unprecedented clauses into its resolution on the prevention of HIV/AIDS, once again reinforcing the growing recognition of the link between HIV and security. The UN Security Council (in 2000) and General Assembly (in 2001) held unprecedented sessions on HIV/AIDS as a security threat.

African leaders gathered in Abuja, Nigeria, in April 2001 to focus on the AIDS issue, and resolved in the resultant Abuja Declaration to devote 15 per cent of their economic output to the health sector. A five-year review of this meeting was held in Abuja in May 2006. The meeting found that this target is currently not being met, except by Botswana. More positively, South Africa has started to provide anti-retroviral drugs to HIV sufferers. Such efforts must be accelerated. Foreign donors have also increased their contributions to the fight against AIDS, providing $4.7 billion in 2003 (compared to $200 million in 1996). The UN has estimated, however, that $15 billion a year will be needed to combat the disease by 2007. Donors must ensure that this target is met in order to be able to counter one of the continent's greatest security threats. Weak health infrastructure in Africa must also be strengthened, as both the UN High-level Panel and Kofi Annan's 2005 *In Larger Freedom* report argued, since they could still constrain the fight against AIDS despite the declining costs of drugs to treat the disease which have plummeted by more than 95 per cent since 1998. There are also other life-threatening diseases like tuberculosis and malaria on which African governments must expend their scarce resources, providing another important rationale for supporting Africa's anti-AIDS battle more generously. Some progress is finally being reported in the fight against AIDS. Africans must, however, remain at the forefront of this titanic battle for the continent's future, while outsiders have an important role to play in helping the continent reclaim its future.

Weapons of the Weak? International Terrorism

The final issue to be addressed in the UN reform process is international terrorism, which was one of the areas in which consensus failed to emerge in September 2005. The profound concerns in Africa about US President

George W Bush's "war on terrorism" is that new justifications will be found to back autocratic allies who support America in its declared hunt for terrorists, rather than supporting democratic allies and principles. (See Baregu in this volume). The establishment in 2002 of a US military base and a Joint Task Force Horn of Africa Command in Djibouti, comprising 900 soldiers, with the goal of tracking terrorists in the region, may yet come to mirror the American support of autocratic governments in Kenya, Somalia and Sudan during the Cold War. The support of these regimes was justified at the time by the need to protect strategic sea-lanes used for transporting oil from the Middle East. Having established security relations with Djibouti, the United States has strengthened security ties with Eritrea. Washington also maintains strong ties with Ethiopia with the aim of benefiting from the intelligence network of the pre-eminent military power on the Horn of Africa.

American fears of Africa becoming a sanctuary for terrorists were further heightened by terrorist attacks on an Israeli airliner and Israeli tourists in a hotel in Mombasa in November 2002. Reports have noted that American Central Intelligence Agency (CIA) agents are collaborating with Somali warlords in pursuit of terrorist suspects inside Somalia.[33] Some African regimes appear to be taking advantage of these fears to crack down on domestic dissent. In a striking replay of the American government's response to the attacks of September 11, Morocco rushed anti-terrorism legislation through its rubber-stamp parliament, allowing capital punishment against terror suspects. This followed the deadly suicide attacks in Casablanca in May 2003. Other countries like Tanzania are also drawing up anti-terrorism legislation that civil libertarians have criticised as giving governments too much power to clamp down on genuine dissent. These concerns were further confirmed by the autocratic Liberian leader Charles Taylor's decision, before his ousting in 2003, to castigate his domestic opponents as "terrorists" and his holding of dissidents as "unlawful combatants". Eritrea has accused its exiled Alliance of Eritrean National Forces (AENF) opponents of having links to al-Qaida, while Ethiopia has branded its opponents in Oromo areas as being involved in "international terrorism".

Concluding Thoughts: Hard Times, Great Expectations

In concluding this essay, it is pertinent to note that Charles Dickens' classic *A Christmas Carol* captures well the tragic fate of UN reform during the General Assembly session between September and December 2005. In this tale, Ebenezer Scrooge, a grumpy miser, is visited by three ghosts which point him to his past, present and possible future; a frightening experience that forces Scrooge to change his nasty ways. The three main potential successes of a largely disappointing UN reform process are akin to these three ghosts. The Ghost of Christmas Past represents the international community's "responsibility to protect" victims of massacres and genocide like the one in Rwanda in 1994; the Ghost of Christmas Present is symbolised by continuing efforts to establish an effective Human Rights Council that has the "teeth" to keep in check and discipline offenders; the Ghost of Christmas Future is represented in the establishment of a Peacebuilding Commission to mobilise resources for post-conflict reconstruction efforts.

As earlier noted, the idea behind the "responsibility to protect" is that the international community has a duty to protect populations from serious harm if governments are unwilling or unable to do so. Governments thus cede the right to non-intervention in their internal affairs if such protection is not provided. Many governments in Africa and the global south criticised this notion as an opportunity for more powerful countries to undertake "regime change" and other self-interested interventions in weaker countries under the cloak of protecting civilians – as America is widely accused as having done in Iraq.

The efforts to create a Human Rights Council have been driven largely by the concerns of the US and other western countries that the UN's Human Rights Commission was ineffectual and allowed countries like Cuba, Libya and Sudan to sit on the Commission, thus weakening its credibility. Washington and its allies favoured a body elected by two-thirds of the UN's members rather than by regional blocs. America's critics have retorted that flagrant human rights abuses in Iraq's Abu Ghraib prison, Afghanistan and Guantánamo Bay expose the hypocrisy of the "hyperpower" and ask in vain: "Who will police the self-appointed global policeman?". African governments – in the Ezulwini Consensus on UN reform in February 2005 – also questioned the need for a human rights body with universal membership. They called instead for an organ that would report to the UN's Economic and Social Council. A 47-member Council eventually emerged by April 2006 in which members would be nominated by regional blocs and approved by a two-thirds majority in the UN General Assembly. (See Scanlon in this volume). Finally, the idea of a Peacebuilding Commission that was agreed in September 2005 won the most support in UN circles. As noted earlier, the Peacebuilding Commission will involve key UN members with political, financial and peacekeeping clout, and along with regional development banks, the World Bank and the IMF, seek to mobilise the resources to ensure that countries like Sierra Leone, Liberia, Angola and the DRC remain stable after fighters have laid down their arms.

But despite progress on these three issues, the recent experiences of UN members in delivering on their promises do not offer much hope for success. These "reforms" could result in a "responsibility to protect" doctrine that is flouted with impunity in Darfur and the eastern Congo; a Human Rights Council that fails to sanction human rights violators; and a Peacebuilding Commission that is unable to mobilise the necessary resources to ensure that countries remain peaceful. The rich world will most likely continue its stinginess. This, even as it makes empty promises while refusing to make genuine cuts in trade-distorting agricultural subsidies (as evidenced in WTO talks in Hong Kong in December 2005) that prevent farmers in poor countries from selling more of their products abroad. Like the fabled Oliver Twist, Africa will most likely have to continue holding out its begging bowl to ask for more from the rich world. But like Ebenezer Scrooge, the rich world must stare the ghosts of Christmas in the face and change its miserly ways. Otherwise, in the Dickensian world of African politics, great expectations will continue to be dashed by the harsh reality of hard times. The fate of UN reform truly has been a chronicle of a death foretold.

Notes

[1] This chapter is based on an unpublished paper prepared for the Southern African Regional Poverty Network (SARPN), and presented at a seminar on "Human Security, Conflict and Poverty in SADC" in Mauritius on 31 August 2005. The chapter is also partly based on Adebajo, A and Landsberg, C: "The Millennium Declaration Goals: Meeting Africa's Special Needs" an unpublished paper prepared for Columbia University and presented in New York on 30 September 2004.

[2] *A More Secure World: Our Shared Responsibility*, Report of the United Nations Secretary-General's High-level Panel on Threats, Challenges and Change. Published by the United Nations Department of Public Information DPI/2367, December 2004.

[3] Members include Robert Badinter, Joao Soares, Gro Harlem Brundtland, Mary Chinery-Hesse, Gareth Evans, David Hannay, Enrique Iglesias, Amr Moussa, Satish Nambiar, Sadako Ogata, Yevgeny Primakov, Qian Qichen, Nafis Sadik, Salim Ahmed Salim, and Brent Scowcroft. See UN Press Release, SG/A/857.

[4] *In Larger Freedom: Towards Development, Security and Human Rights For All*, Report of the UN Secretary-General, Follow-up to the outcome of the Millennium Summit. 21 March 2005, A/59/2005.

[5] See Sachs, J: "The Millennium Project: From Words to Action", in Heinbecker, P & Goff, P (eds.): *Irrelevant or Indispensable? The United Nations in the 21ˢᵗ Century* (Ontario, Canada: Wilfrid Laurier University Press, 2005), pp.19-23.

[6] *In Larger Freedom.*

[7] International Peace Academy/Center on International Cooperation, *Refashioning the Dialogue: Regional Perspectives on the Brahimi Report on UN Peace Operations*, Regional Meetings, February-March 2001, Johannesburg, Buenos Aires, Singapore and London, pp.6-11. http://www.cic.nyu.edu/projects/projects.html (accessed 7 July 2006).

[8] See *Report of the Panel on United Nations Peace Operations*: (Brahimi Report), 21 August 2000, S/2000/809.

[9] For African perspectives on UN peacekeeping, see Adebajo, A: "From Congo to Congo: United Nations Peacekeeping in Africa after the Cold War," in Taylor, I & Williams, P (eds.): *Africa in International Politics: External Involvement on the Continent* (London: Routledge, 2004); Gambari, I: "The United Nations" in Baregu, M & Landsberg, C (eds.): *From Cape to Congo: Southern Africa's Evolving Security Challenges*, (Boulder and London: Lynne Rienner, 2003); Jonah, J: "The United Nations," in Adebajo, A & Rashid, I (eds.): *West Africa's Security Challenges: Building Peace in A Troubled Region* (Boulder and London: Lynne Rienner, 2004); and Zacarias, A: *The United Nations and International Peacekeeping* (London: I B Tauris and Co., 1996).

[10] Jonah, "The United Nations", p.331.

[11] This title is borrowed from Boyd, A: *Fifteen Men on a Powder Keg: A History of the UN Security Council* (London: Methuen, 1971).

[12] See Mahbubani, K: "The Permanent and Elected Council Members" in Malone, D M (ed.): *The UN Security Council: From the Cold War to the 21st Century* (Boulder and London: Lynne Rienner, 2004), pp.253–66.

[13] See African Union, Draft Recommendations at the Ministerial Committee of Fifteen on the Report of the High-level Panel on the Reform of the UN System. 20–22 February 2005. Mbabane, Swaziland. CTTE/15/Min/ReformUN/Draft/Recomm. (I).

[14] Quoted in Mazrui, A: "Africa and Egypt's Four Circles" in *On Heroes and Uhuru-Worship* (London: Longman, 1967), p.111.

[15] See Evans, G: "When is it Right To Fight?" in *Survival*, vol.46 no.3, Autumn 2004, p.75.

[16] Annan, K: "Two Concepts of Sovereignty" in *The Economist*, 18-24 September 1999, p.49.

[17] See Deng, F *et al.: Sovereignty as Responsibility: Conflict Management in Africa* (Washington, DC: The Brookings Institution, 1996).

[18] See Boutros-Ghali, B: *An Agenda For Peace*, (New York: United Nations, 1992); Franck, T: "A Holistic Approach to Building Peace" in Otunnu, O & Doyle, M (eds.): *Peacemaking and Peacekeeping for the New Century* (Lanham, New York, Boulder and Oxford: Rowman & Littlefield Publishers Inc., 1998); and The World Bank: *Post-Conflict Reconstruction: The Role of the World Bank* (Washington D.C.: The World Bank, 1998.).

[19] See for example Adedeji, A: "From Lagos to NEPAD" in *New Agenda*, Issue 8, Fourth quarter 2002, pp. 32–47; International Peace Academy: "NEPAD: African Initiative, New Partnership?" in a report of a policy seminar in New York, July 2002; and Landsberg, C: "From African Renaissance to NEPAD... and back to the Renaissance" in *Journal of African Elections*, vol.1 no.2, September 2002, pp.87–98.

[20] The members of the APRM Eminent Persons Panel are: Professor Adebayo Adedeji from Nigeria; Ambassador Bethuel Kiplagat of Kenya; Dr. Graça Machel from Mozambique; Dr. Dorothy Njeuma from Cameroon; Ms. Marie-Angelique Savané from Senegal; and Dr. Chris Stals from South Africa.

[21] This paragraph is based on Adedeji, A: "NEPAD's Africa Peer Review Mechanism: Progress and Prospects." Keynote address at the Centre For Conflict Resolution policy seminar on *Building an African Union for the 21st Century: Relations with the RECS, NEPAD and Civil Society*, Cape Town, South Africa, 20–22 August 2005.

[22] See the insightful article by Landsberg, C: "SA should take heed of the harsh criticisms against NEPAD" in *City Press*, 12 March 2006, p.28.

[23] See Bond, P (ed.): *Fanon's Warning: A Civil Society Reader on the New Partnership for Africa's Development*, Second Edition, (Trenton and Asmara: Africa World Press, 2005).

[24] This term is borrowed from Patrick Bond.

[25] United Nations Conference on Trade and Development, *Economic Development in Africa. Debt Sustainability : Oasis or Mirage?* (New York and Geneva: United Nations, 2004), p. 9.

[26] Sachs, J: "Doing the Sums on Africa" in *The Economist*, 20 May 2004.

[27] Thaker, P: "Africa: Hope or Hype?" in *The Economist,* "The World in 2006", p.82.

[28] United Nations Development Programme: *Human Development Report* (Oxford: Oxford University Press, 2003), pp.155–56.

[29] See, for example, Hugueney, C: "The G-20: Passing Phenomenon or Here to Stay?" in *Friedrich Ebert Stiftung Briefing Paper*, March 2004.

[30] See "Geldof's Year" in *The Guardian* (London), Section G2, 28 December 2005, p.2.

[31] UNDP and UNICEF: *The Millennium Development Goals in Africa*, p. 9.

[32] See Elbe, S: *Strategic Implications of HIV/AIDS*, Adelphi Paper 357 (Oxford: Oxford University Press, 2003).

[33] Sciolino, E: "At a Traumatic Moment, Morocco's King is Mute," in *The New York Times*, 27 May 2003, p.A3.

2

Crafting the UN High-level Panel Report: An Insider's Perspective

Mary Chinery-Hesse

THE MAIN OBJECTIVE of the High-level Panel on *Threats, Challenges and Change* was to make proposals to ensure that the United Nations (UN)[1] would be up to the task of facing the challenges of the twenty-first century, that the UN would be perceived to be representative and democratic and that the world body would be strengthened and its decision-making given sufficient "teeth" to effectively promote peace and stability in the face of today's threats. In addition to this, every part of the globe should feel confident that it is well served by the organisation, that collective action would be the preferred option over unilateralism, and that global security would be perceived as a shared responsibility of all.

The African members of the sixteen-member High-level Panel – Tanzanian Salim Ahmed Salim, the former Secretary-General of the Organisation of African Unity (OAU), Egyptian Amre Moussa, Secretary-General of the Arab League and myself, a Ghanaian national and former deputy Director-General of the UN's International Labour Organisation (ILO) – believed that Africa's voice had been muted within the UN. After the Panel, could it be justly claimed that Africa's interests have been fully catered for in the High-level Panel report of December 2004? I believe the jury is still out in this regard.

The composition of the Panel – referred to by a cynical section of the international press as "the geriatrics" due to the fact that there were several septuagenarians on the Panel – was well-conceived by the UN Secretary-

General, Kofi Annan. Its membership was drawn from individuals who have actually been at the helm of affairs as leaders in their countries – the politically savvy, but also those with an intimate knowledge of the international system, as well as development practitioners and military leaders.[2] Of course, in the High-level Panel process, north–south divisions between rich and poor countries were also present. The intention of the UN Secretary-General was to ensure, to the greatest extent possible, that a balance would be struck between the needs and interests of the various countries and regions of the world. This was a recognition that, in a world of inter-connected threats and challenges, the broadest interests are best served by global cooperation, based on accommodating diverse points of view, and, as much as possible, finding common ground to facilitate consensus-building.

The crafting of the report involved 43 worldwide meetings and informal consultations with civil society actors. Several governments took the initiative and committed resources to the organisation of seminars, symposia and workshops to which Panel members were invited to participate and to hear diverse views. In addition, civil society organisations and other non-governmental organisations (NGOs) in regions other than Africa organised similar gatherings. Our fear was that the special concerns of Africa, as perceived by Africans themselves, would be completely lost in the barrage of opinions with which the Panel was inundated.

The High-level Panel process was aided by the insistence of the three African members that an exception to an earlier decision that Panel meetings be held only in those countries that host the headquarters of UN organisations should be made, and for a regular meeting to convene in Addis Ababa, Ethiopia: the seat of the African Union (AU).

We addressed a joint letter to the AU, which invited the heads of Africa's sub-regional organisations such as the Southern African Development Community (SADC), the Economic Community of West African States (ECOWAS), the Intergovernmental Authority on Development (IGAD), the Economic Community of Central African States (ECASS) and the Arab Maghreb Union (AMU), to tell their own story of their experiences and evolving conflict resolution mechanisms.

The Addis Ababa meeting, which took place in April 2004, had another purpose. Again, on the insistence of the Africans on the Panel, a forum was held on the sidelines of the meeting to solicit the views of African civil society on UN reform. The refreshing ideas that emanated from the gathering informed many of the conclusions in the report. A major problem, however, was how to ensure that African public opinion would be adequately reflected in the Panel's report. The Panel Secretariat in New York established an internet website to solicit public opinion on the remit of its work. Due to lack of sufficient access to cyberspace, African input in this process was minimal.

The three Africans on the Panel were approached, as were other members, by governments from other regions that deemed it important to convince the Panel of their particular stance on critical issues. The ambassadors of these governments also consulted us frequently when we were in our own countries.

African leadership, by contrast, largely ignored the exercise and did not make any effort to proffer their views to us. We did our best, under the circumstances, and took the initiative to garner ideas whenever opportunities arose. In that sense, we suffered a certain degree of frustration. The African media was also largely uninterested in the Panel's work. The High-level Panel was not considered to be newsworthy. There was very little we could do since there were prohibitions on Panel members' direct interaction with the press in order to obviate leaks from our deliberations – not that this was foolproof.

Were African voices heard in terms of the final outcome of the High-level Panel report? The first major challenge was to test the resolve of Panel members from developing countries on two counts. First, should deliberations be driven by the initial motivation for the establishment of the Panel, namely the 9/11 terrorist bombings of the World Trade Centre in New York and its aftermath? This would entail a key focus on how to confront terrorism through the use of force and international diplomacy and thus risk nuclear Armageddon. Alternatively, the Panel could take a more wide-ranging approach to global security which would also involve attempting to address the root causes of terrorism. (See Baregu in this volume).

The second challenge was to convince the entire Panel to agree that threats should not be classified into "hard" and "soft" categories. A threat is a threat is a threat, and from this understanding, there was no room for an approach which would create a hierarchy of threats.

Those on the Panel who felt that adopting this approach would mean that we would be diverted from our core objectives, argued that there were other initiatives launched by the United Nations dealing with the development-biased "soft" threats, which in their view necessitated long-term solutions outside the current UN reform process. Indeed, major UN and other international conferences, such as the 2002 International Conference on Financing for Development in Monterrey, Mexico, and the UN Summit on Sustainable Development in South Africa in 2002, had been devoted to these themes.

With the UN and global security having reached what Kofi Annan described as a "fork in the road", should the Panel stray into such territory rather than focus on more immediate "hard" threats? As one Panel member noted, an apt analogy would be to compare the current global situation to that of a patient suffering from many undesirable maladies. Should one treat a chronic condition like diabetes or hypertension – which may ultimately kill the patient – with the same urgency and attention that one would give to a stroke or heart attack which would lead to immediate death? These views on the need to address only "hard" security threats were strongly expressed, despite a clear commitment in the terms of reference of the Panel that advocated the need for a broad engagement with peace and security issues.

The responsibility of the Panel, as set out in Kofi Annan's speech to the UN General Assembly of 2003 was quite clear.[3] First, the Panel was to examine current global challenges to peace and security. Second, it was to consider the contribution that multilateral action could make in addressing these challenges. Third, the Panel was to review the functioning and relevance of the major organs of the UN. Finally, we were to recommend ways of strengthening the UN through the reform of its principal institutions.

The dominant focus of the High-level Panel was intended to be on global threats to peace and security. However, we were also tasked with examining other international challenges in so far as these affect wider threats. Without consideration of the root causes, would one not be treating the symptoms of the disease rather than providing an enduring cure for the patient?

An examination of the Panel's report revealed which opinions dominated prioritising security threats. The Panel finally came to the conclusion that "one man's perception of threat could be another man's 'so what'?" We acknowledged the fact that perceptions of what constitutes threat differs markedly across the globe, depending on one's geographical location and station in life.

The report accepted that the current challenges facing the African continent were primarily human security concerns related to the urgent tasks of development: extreme poverty and the associated limitations on life expectancy, disparity of income both between and within societies, pandemics such as HIV/AIDS and environmental degradation were all threats that could not be ignored or given sufficient priority. (See Legum and Ndinga-Muvumba in this volume). These factors threaten many African people as directly as weapons of mass destruction, making development centered on the eradication of poverty an indispensable basis of collective security on the continent. The Panel also made recommendations over strengthening global public health capabilities and disease monitoring (particularly HIV/AIDS) and response initiatives, among others. The undisputed conclusion was that mutual understanding and ties of solidarity were indispensable in realising collective security on these issues.

It is obvious, but worthy of repetition, that global threats to peace in the past were often driven by Cold War rivalries that were generally tackled through state-centred responses. In this context sovereign states could, at least in theory, be committed and held accountable through international treaties. The global geo-political realities characterised by the increased involvement of non-state actors in conflicts in the post-Cold War era were, however, a factor that the Panel could not ignore. It was obvious that current threats include not only those posed by the proliferation of nuclear and other types of weapons of mass destruction – including chemical and biological weapons – but also the possibility of the possession of these weapons by international terrorist groups.

The Panel discussed whether traditional notions of deterrence could apply in these circumstances, since non-state actors can acquire the same level of destructive power once held only by sovereign states. There is no doubt that current scientific and technological developments can only lead to the further fashioning of more lethal weapons whose proliferation could potentially be facilitated through the use of the internet.

What would be the significance of such a development for Africa? We

49

must recall that the continent has been on the receiving end of terrorist acts in recent times, as evidenced by the bombings of US embassies in Dar-es-Salaam, Tanzania and Nairobi, Kenya in August 1998. In Nairobi, 213 people were killed in the explosion and an estimated 4 000 injured; in Dar-es-Salaam, the attack killed at least 12 people and wounded 85 people. Most of the casualties were Africans. These events, and the countless travel warnings issued as a result of suspected terrorist attacks, have clear implications for activities such as tourism, which constitute an important source of income for many African countries.

In addition, the Panel recognised that poverty potentially provides a breeding ground for civil conflict and the recruitment of terrorists. Indeed, this was one of the major arguments for positing the poverty paradigm as an essential instrument in tackling global peace and security issues.

The growing problem of drug trafficking was also seen as an issue which could assist in focusing attention on development issues (See Gastrow in this volume). It is well known that illegal narcotics have become an important financial instrument of international terrorism. An Africa that is poor and disadvantaged can easily become not only a production and transit point for the narcotics trade, but also an attractive destination for other global criminal networks. Again, poverty can be an important factor in making conditions more favourable in this regard.

It was obvious to the Panel that the existence of failed states, in which governance capacity is eroded and governments are unable to prevent humanitarian catastrophes, genocide, mass human loss and refugee exodus, creates barriers to global peace and security. (See Deng in this volume). Africa currently suffers a disproportionate number of intra and interstate conflicts to which the international community has had to commit resources. The three African members of the Panel thus insisted that sufficient attention be devoted to this critical issue.

The causes and remedies of Africa's conflicts received much consideration on the Panel agenda, as did the issue of conventional and light weapons and landmines. These topics also received particularly thorough investigation at the Panel meeting that convened in Addis Ababa in April 2004. In my view, the major breakthrough for Africa in this process was the Panel's recognition of the role of regional institutions within the context of global peace and security. At the Addis Ababa meeting, the

Panel was extremely impressed with, and many members were unaware of, the arrangements that were currently in place for conflict resolution in Africa, fashioned under the umbrella of the AU.

It was clear that there was a need for a division of labour between the UN Security Council and the AU's 15-member Peace and Security Council (PSC) in terms of peacekeeping, and that proper and timely financial arrangements need to be put in place to support the efforts of the AU and African regional institutions. In this regard, the Panel's recommendation of supporting a ten-year capacity-building programme for peacekeeping through the AU was a significant step, which Kofi Annan also supported in his March 2005 report that responded to, and built upon, the Panel's report.[4]

Panel members noted the laudable steps that African institutions had taken towards promoting self-reliance in peace and security issues, many of which have not been widely publicised and acknowledged by the international community. African diplomats must thus take urgent steps to improve perceptions which sustain the stigma of dependency and helplessness with which Africa is commonly associated. Furthermore, homegrown solutions to peace and security issues on the continent are critical. However, there remains a risk that less relevant models will be imposed on Africa unless the continent communicates better the proven success of its own tested peace and security mechanisms and structures.

Regarding the reasons for the establishment of the Panel, the issue of a collective security system as opposed to unilateral action in defiance of the UN Charter engaged much of the Panel's attention. The Panel's report covers the rationale for its recommendations regarding this aspect quite adequately. It is however noteworthy that, during debates on pre-emptive strikes that preceded the attack on Iraq in 2003, African leaders did not have a consistent stance on what line of action would be in the best interest of the continent. African governments took positions individually in what was deemed to be their national interests. There would have been nothing wrong with this approach if this had been a result of consultations at the continental level, but this was not apparent to Panel members.

What we do know is that countries, on occasion, rushed legislation through their national parliaments on one terrorism-related issue or another, ahead of other pressing domestic legislation. This and other complaints were aired at the Addis Ababa civil society forum with the Panel in April 2004. One recurrent point made was that "rogue regimes" might be able to avoid sanctions from the international community over bad governance and human rights issues by proclaiming their willingness to join an anti-terrorism coalition.

The other issue which absorbed the attention of the High-level Panel was that of the "responsibility to protect"; the principle of sovereignty enshrined in the United Nations Charter which recognises the responsibility of states to protect their own citizens. (See Mwanasali in this volume). Should traditional notions of sovereignty ever be set aside so that responsibility shifts to the international community? What could justify legitimate interference in the internal affairs of a sovereign state by the international community? At what stage can a decision be made that a national authority is unwilling or unable to protect its own citizens? Most importantly, who makes the decisions, considering the power structure of a world in which double standards in decision-making appear to be the norm rather than the exception? Could such a development not pose an inherent risk that weaker members of the United Nations might be victimised because they do not toe a preferred line or buy into a particular ideology promoted by a powerful state and its allies?

The discussions in Addis Ababa in April 2004 clarified the situation for us, and we found ourselves ready to join the consensus that such collective action would be justified in cases of genocide, ethnic cleansing and crimes against humanity. The Panel attempted to define many of these concepts, including terrorism, either overtly or covertly. Nonetheless, several definitional difficulties still need to be ironed out to ensure a common understanding of concepts.

The role of the AU and other sub-regional institutions in this issue, and the consultation machinery in such circumstances, will need to be carefully negotiated. The conclusion of the High-level Panel was that diplomatic, humanitarian and other non-aggressive initiatives – including sanctions – should first be exhausted, and the use of force through a decision by the UN Security Council must be an absolute last resort after all attempts at peacemaking have failed. In this regard, the Panel recommended that the mediation capacity of the UN, as well as its capacity to undertake peace-support operations – and when warranted, peace-enforcement – be strengthened.

Other issues that the Panel deliberated on at length related to the issue of rapid response and the need for the United Nations to have improved rapid deployment options. In recognition of the current situation in which the global supply of peacekeepers is shamefully inadequate, the Panel urged that countries be more willing to provide and support military deployments. Obviously, richer members of the United Nations would need to make greater efforts to have contingents ready for peace operations, and equally importantly, they must provide the necessary financial and logistical support for rapid mobilisation of troops.

Noting the importance of the human rights component in conflict prevention and peacebuilding, the High-level Panel focused on this issue, eventually making recommendations that clearly do not have the full support of many African governments. These governments are extremely cautious about the Panel's recommendation to place the protection of human rights under the auspices of the UN Security Council due to the current power structure of that body. (See Scanlon in this volume).

The Panel also considered the current weak institutional infrastructure of the UN for assisting countries emerging from conflict. If not properly managed, this could lead to the resumption of conflicts in places like Liberia, Sierra Leone and Angola. As the High-level Panel report noted, in half of the cases of conflicts in the post-Cold War era, wars restart due to inadequate post-conflict peacebuilding.[5] The Panel's solution was to recommend the establishment of a Peacebuilding Commission with an early warning capacity to identify countries at risk of violent conflict. This Commission would also be tasked with undertaking measures aimed at prevention as well as galvanising and sustaining the interest of the international community in post-conflict peacebuilding for long-term recovery. (See Murithi in this volume).

Regarding the reform of the UN and its organs and more broadly, institutional strengthening, it is ironic that for the majority of countries – especially the richer ones – this has been the principal item of interest. Indeed, even in a narrower sense, the main focus of some powerful members has been on the reform of the UN Security Council. The High-level Panel faced great difficulties during the consultation stage of its work to convince governments to pay equal attention to other aspects of its remit.

Specific recommendations were made, apart from the expansion of the Security Council, for the creation of the position of a second deputy

Secretary-General responsible for peace and security issues, who would prepare early warning reports and strategy options in support of the UN Secretary-General. This recommendation was not accepted by Kofi Annan in his March 2005 report. Other recommendations, of course, related to the reform of the UN General Assembly and its Economic and Social Council (ECOSOC), to strengthen its role as a development forum.

Concluding Thoughts

The UN Secretary-General, Kofi Annan, issued his synthesising report in March 2005. This report was important, since it not only drew on the High-level Panel report, but also on the recommendations of the Jeffrey Sachs report on the Millennium Development Goals, as well as the Cardoso report on civil society.[6] Both of these reports deal, in greater depth, with social, economic and development issues, and provide the international community with an opportunity to consider whether the nexus between peace and development has been appropriately captured in the Panel's report.

Can one genuinely claim that the High-level Panel did a great job? I can claim that we did our best, all things considered. Personally, I would have wished that issues of gender, social justice, and all the ramifications of the pain of stigmatisation, marginalisation and exclusion were better factored into our deliberations. Perhaps this is too much wishful thinking as the world turns.

As a development practitioner, I was quite surprised at the way in which issues to which I attach great importance were so easily pushed to the back-burner. It was personally frustrating that the UN General Assembly and its economic arm, ECOSOC, were not given the same high profile as the UN Security Council. I hope that Africa will not be caught up in this tide but can steer international discourse to balance these issues in future debates.

The important issue in the aftermath of the publication of all these reports and the failure so far to implement many of these recommendations, is how Africa can ensure that it does not lose the little ground that it has gained from these processes. Through the Panel, the concept of peace and security was broadened to include human security concerns, and to establish firmly that development and security are inextricably linked.

The power dynamics in the "brave new world" outside the Panel requires a completely different set of negotiating skills to ensure that these factors remain on the agenda.

How can Africa keep the issue of poverty on the "front-burner" during future UN negotiations? It is important that African voices are raised during the formulation of reports such as ours, rather than at the end of the process, only to be confronted with a *fait accompli*, and at that futile stage attempting to introduce changes in the margins while on the defensive. Africa clearly has pressing bread-and-butter issues that absorb most of the time of its leaders. There is, however, no justification for largely ignoring an exercise the outcome of which is expected to make significant changes to the international political and socio-economic architecture, and to introduce a new model for global governance that will affect the lives of Africa's 800 million people.

Notes

[1] *A More Secure World: Our Shared Responsibility,* Report of the United Nations Secretary-General's High-level Panel on Threats, Challenges and Change. Published by the United Nations Department of Public Information DPI/2367, December 2004.

[2] Members of the High-level Panel included: Anand Panyarachun, Chair (Thailand); Robert Badinter (France); João Baena Soares (Brazil); Gro Harlem Brundtland (Norway); Mary Chinery-Hesse (Ghana); Gareth Evans (Australia); David Hannay (United Kingdom); Enrique Iglesias (Uruguay); Amre Moussa (Egypt); Satish Nambiar (India); Sadako Ogata (Japan); Yevgeny Primakov (Russian Federation); Qian Qichen (China); Nafis Sadik (Pakistan); Salim Ahmed Salim (United Republic of Tanzania); and Brent Scowcroft (United States).

[3] See http://www.un.org/webcast/ga/58/statements/sg2eng030923 (accessed 12 January 2006).

[4] *In Larger Freedom: Towards Development, Security and Human Rights For All,* Report of the UN Secretary-General; follow-up to the outcome of the Millennium Summit. 21 March 2005, A/59/2005.

[5] *A More Secure World: Our Shared Responsibility,* Report of the United Nations Secretary-General's High-level Panel on Threats, Challenges and Change. Published by the United Nations Department of Public Information DPI/2367, December 2004, p.70.

[6] See Sachs, J: *The Millennium Development Project: Practical Action Plan to Combat Poverty,* available at www.unmilleniumproject.org/reports/fullreport.htm; and Panel of Eminent Persons on United Nations–Civil Society Relations: *We the Peoples: Civil Society, the United Nations and Global Governance: Report of the Panel of Eminent Persons on United Nations–Civil Society Relations* at http://www.un-ngls.org/Final%20report%20-%20HLP.doc (accessed 12 March 2006).

3

African Divisions, Western Dominance

James Jonah

ANY THOROUGH EXAMINATION of the United Nations (UN) High-level Panel report on *Threats, Challenges and Change* should consider that reform in the United Nations system has been an ongoing debate since the organisation's creation in 1945.[1] The UN Secretary-General, Kofi Annan, has himself reminded us that reform is a process and not an event. Indeed, since the establishment of the UN, the organisation has experienced a whole array of reform proposals. While some have been successfully adopted and implemented, the majority have remained on the drawing board gathering dust.

The predicament is that individual or groups of member states have often embarked only on reform measures that they benefited from and ignored those that they disliked. For example, some western powers such as the United States have only grudgingly accepted reforms promoted by developing countries like the establishment of the United Nations Conference on Trade and Development (UNCTAD) and the United Nations Industrial Development Organisation (UNIDO).

Explanations by two major organisation theorists, James March and Johan Olson, may offer insights into why governments behave the way they do over the reform of international organisations.[2] In their 1989 study of attempts to make comprehensive governmental reorganisation in the US during the twentieth century, March and Olson concluded that lofty rhetoric, political deal-making and periodic cultural rituals often created the illusion of progress where none existed. It has been said that all large organisations need to go through the ritual of repeating the rhetoric of reform in every new administration with few results, and the United Nations is no exception.[3]

So why then the great drama about the 2004 report of the High-level Panel? It would appear that the urgency of this set of reform proposals is linked to the controversy over the US intervention in Iraq in March 2003, carried out without explicit UN Security Council authorisation. Although this rationale is generally accepted, many member states did not agree with Kofi Annan that the United Nations had "come to a fork in the road". Accordingly, they did not believe that it was imperative for decisions to be taken on the recommendations made by the High-level Panel at the UN General Assembly's historic 60th session which started in September 2005. For example, a coalition of over 100 member states, together with China, insisted that more time was required to reach a consensus on the recommendations of the Panel.

The African Posture

How did African states react to these developments? While the Non-Aligned group in the UN was explicit in its criticism of some of the key recommendations of the High-level Panel, the African Group was increasingly perceived to be ambivalent at best. The Latin American and Asian members of the Non-Aligned group hinted that African governments should not have allowed "sentiments" for "one of their own"– Kofi Annan – to rule them and urged the Africans to examine the recommendations of the Panel objectively and dispassionately. The mistake that African states seem to have made is to allow the debate over UN reform to be controlled by western states, pundits and academics. Any quick perusal of the mainstream international media would reveal that the western conception of acceptable UN reform gained the most ground in the run up to the September 2005 summit. One can not blame these analysts for articulating their point of view. Africa, however, needed to be more energetic in presenting its own case for reform since these proposals may adversely affect the vital interests of African states.

During the summit itself, African states adopted a far more robust position. They joined all the members of the Group of 77 (G-77) developing countries[4] and China in formulating their common position to the summit Outcome Document of September 2005.[5] The major gripe of the G-77 and China is that the UN Secretary-General's proposals – which were the basis of the outcome document – were unbalanced and reflected the views of the western member states.[6]

The UN High-level Panel report, *A More Secure World: Our Shared Responsibility* and the companion report of the Secretary-General, *In Larger Freedom: Towards Development, Security and Human Rights for All,* offer much food for thought.[7] There is much in these two reports that Africa should readily embrace. Equally, there are sections of these reports that Africa must be wary of. Africa should welcome the fact that the reports raised the profile of development issues in their recommendations. They placed the Millennium Development Goals (MDGs) of 2000 at the centre of national and international poverty reduction strategies. Significantly, conditionality for permanent membership of the Security Council by any new industrialised state is the fulfilment of the 0.7 per cent Gross National Product (GNP) target for Official Development Assistance (ODA) set as far back as 1970. (See Legum in this volume).

Reforming the Economic and Social Council

Africa should be disappointed that in evaluating the UN Economic and Social Council (ECOSOC), the High-level Panel conceded much to the position of some of the western powers. Ignoring the great debate sponsored by the G–77 on the need for global negotiations, the report asserted that it would not be realistic for ECOSOC to become the world's central decision-making body on matters of trade and finance, nor for it to direct the programmes of the UN's specialised agencies or the international financial institutions.[8] The section on ECOSOC in the summit's outcome document contained no specific reform proposals and blandly stated that, in order for ECOSOC to perform its functions, its organisation of work, agenda, and current method of work should be changed.

The High-level Panel did warn that no recommendation should ignore underlying power realities lest they be doomed to failure or irrelevance. However, the Panel also noted that recommendations that merely reflect distributions of power and make no effort to strengthen international principles are unlikely to gain the widespread adherence necessary to alter international behaviour. Furthermore, the UN Secretary-General and High-level Panel repeatedly underlined that sovereign states are the basic and indispensable building blocks of the international system, and that the United Nations remains the only global organisation that tackles development, security and human rights issues holistically.

It is no secret that western industrialised powers favour the Bretton Woods institutions – the World Bank and the International Monetary Fund (IMF) – for essential decisions on economic and financial matters, and tend to sideline ECOSOC. The weighted voting in the Bretton Woods institutions has allowed the preponderance of influence to lie with the rich world to the detriment of developing countries. It was therefore timely that Trevor Manuel, South Africa's Minister of Finance and Chairman of the Development Committee of Ministers that oversees the World Bank, drew attention to this imbalance in April 2005. According to the *Financial Times* of London, Manuel advised that the Bank's shareholders should examine voting shares at the Fund and the Bank and act to address this imbalance within the next year.[9] Japan's Finance Minister, Sadakazu Tanigaki, also called for a review of Asia's representation in the IMF in order to avert the questioning of the Fund's relevance.

Proposal for a Peacebuilding Commission

With regard to post-conflict peacebuilding, having assessed the UN's peacekeeping operations, the High-level Panel drew attention to the existence of an institutional gap. Members noted that the UN system lacked an organisation that could effectively address the problems of assisting countries in their transition from war to peace. The Panel therefore recommended that the UN Security Council, in collaboration with ECOSOC, establish a Peacebuilding Commission and a Peacebuilding support office within the UN Secretariat. African states, however, have to be convinced that adequate and predictable resources will be available to finance such post-conflict recovery programmes and ensure that the continent is not left out of benefitting from any standing fund for peacebuilding. In light of the neglect of post-conflict cases such as Liberia, Sierra Leone, Guinea-Bissau and the Central African Republic (CAR), financing is crucial. As is well known, many peacebuilding operations, particularly in Africa, have been hampered primarily due to funding problems posed by disarmament, demobilisation and reintegration (DDR) programmes. (See Murithi in this volume).

Humanitarian Intervention – to what Purpose?

It is difficult to fathom the High-level Panel's recommendations over certain issues vital to Africa's interests. A close study of the Panel's report suggests that its members prioritised recommendations palatable to western states. In adopting this posture, the report jeopardised the interests of small and medium-sized states. One wonders whether the UN Secretary-General's assertion that the Panel addressed, in a comprehensive manner, "the security concerns of all states – rich and poor, weak and strong" is correct.[10] Even when the Panel acknowledged the indispensable nature of sovereign states, it identified the critical importance of consultation with civil society actors. However, the strongest and most vibrant civil society groups represented by robust non-governmental organisations are mostly based in the West.

The High-level Panel's discussion and recommendations with respect to humanitarian intervention was disappointing for Africa. Surely, members of the Panel must have been familiar with the remarks and observations of the Non-Aligned states when the 2000 Brahimi report on UN peace operations was first published.[11] The report, produced under the leadership of Algerian diplomat Lakhder Brahimi, was commissioned by the UN Secretary-General in 2000 to undertake a thorough review of the United Nations' peace and security activities in the wake of the UN's debacles in Somalia (1993) and Rwanda (1994). The report made a number of recommendations aimed at tackling shortcomings in the UN's existing activities such as the call for a realistic mandate for peacekeeping operations.

The Brahimi report was warmly received by western states but African states, along with the other members of the Non-Aligned group, were very cautious towards some of its recommendations. Southern governments were particularly critical of what they perceived as support for intervention by the United Nations in the internal affairs of member states. Despite these reservations, the High-level Panel appears to have given short shrift to the stated concerns of developing countries. The Panel itself remarked that what often passes for "collective security" today is simply a system providing protection to the rich and powerful. Similarly, it was noted that the international community's selective responses to threats has further fuelled the divisions between rich and poor states. Yet, it was deemed vital that situations in which threats are primarily internal and matters arise over the "responsibility to protect" a state's own citizens are tackled fairly. This is fair enough, but the panel enters potentially dangerous territory when it states that "the principle of non-intervention in internal affairs cannot be used to protect genocidal acts or other atrocities, such as large-scale violations of international humanitarian law or ethnic cleansing which can properly be considered a threat to international security and as such provoke action by the Security Council".[12] The disturbing aspect of this thinking is that the Panel noted: "We endorse the emerging norm that there is a collective international responsibility to protect, exercisable by the Security Council".[13]

The Panel went to great lengths to define the conditions under which the UN Security Council can act in cases of humanitarian intervention. The most significant condition is that the Council should act only after the most careful consideration and when it is abundantly clear that failure to protect might result in genocide. Although these caveats are necessary and appropriate, they do not offer adequate safeguards for small and medium-sized states in an international community of powerful, predatory military states. History – and recent history at that – is replete with examples of powerful states using various pretexts to encroach on the autonomy and security of weak states. Once the principle of non-intervention has been eroded, weak states are at the mercy of strong states. What is now required is a thorough and balanced approach to the problem. While there is an international responsibility to ensure that genocide and other gross violations of human rights are not tolerated, the solution to such situations should be sought through joint initiatives. We should remember that we do not live in an equitable and just international community. Accordingly, an absolute consensus must emerge as to how best create acceptable rules and norms to govern the international use of force and intervention in sovereign states. (See Mwanasali in this volume).

Enlargement Of The UN Security Council

Anyone familiar with previous attempts at enlarging the membership of the UN Security Council may be puzzled by the High-level Panel's recommendation over this sensitive issue. (See Adebajo in this volume). What was apparent during the substantive discussions on the issue between 1996 and 1998 and thereafter was that there existed a wide diversity of views among member states on this issue. African states had joined other Non-Aligned members in supporting an enlargement of both permanent and non-permanent seats. While the global south supported the inclusion of Germany and Japan as new permanent members, they also called for permanent membership for representatives from Africa, Asia and Latin America. At the Organisation of African Unity (OAU) summit in Harare, Zimbabwe in 1997, African states called for two permanent seats for the continent on an expanded Council. They also rejected any attempt to institutionalise two categories of permanent members – the original five permanent members exercising the right of veto and new permanent members having no right of veto.

Within this context it was puzzling that Model A, proposed by the High-level Panel, endorsed the view of the current western permanent members (France, Britain and the United States) that new permanent members be denied the right of veto. The Panel, perhaps reflecting a deeper division among member states, failed to reach consensus on this sensitive issue. Panel members themselves apparently held divergent views on the problem of enlargement.

Africa was right to have rejected two categories of permanent membership since the UN Charter is supportive of its stance. There is no reference in the Charter to the "right of veto" and what is now referred to as the "right of veto" is intrinsically tied to permanent membership. Article 27 of the Charter merely calls for the "concurring votes" of the permanent members when the Council makes substantive decisions. Therefore, it would be anomalous to have new permanent members without the right of veto.

It is understandable that the High-level Panel members would not wish to increase the number of permanent members with the right of veto. While the veto can perform a useful role in the deliberations of the Security Council and is thus a worthwhile mechanism, it is the potential misuse of the veto that has created difficulties in the Council. It would have been preferable for the Panel to have worked out strategies to limit the abuse of the veto rather than create two new categories of permanent membership: the preferred route of Washington and London.

When the UN Charter was crafted in 1945, it was hoped that the permanent members would use the right of veto judiciously and sparingly and only in exceptional circumstances. However, in the era of the Cold

War, when the Soviet Union found itself in a minority on the Security Council, Moscow frequently used the veto as a form of protection. This was clearly an abuse of the right of veto, which was in essence reserved for situations when the use of force was contemplated under Chapter VII of the Charter.

At other times, western powers abused the right of veto. In 1956, both Britain and France used the veto to block action against them by the Council following their joint intervention, in collaboration with Israel, in the Suez Canal. In subsequent years, the US used the veto to protect Israel against adverse action by the UN Security Council with respect to Israel's policy on Jerusalem and the settlements in the West Bank. Most regrettably for African states, Washington and London either used or threatened the use of the veto to oppose comprehensive economic sanctions against apartheid South Africa.

In view of these considerations, Model B could have gained wider support among UN member states. Under Model B, there would be no new permanent seats. However, eight rotating new seats would be established to serve a renewable four-year term and one non-renewable seat would be added to serve for a two-year term. These non-permanent seats would be divided among the major regional areas. Under Plan B, Africa would have a total of six seats – two four-year renewable, and four two-year non-renewable.

I suggested earlier that a coalition of member states from small and medium-sized states, together with China, were not happy with Model A for a variety of reasons. Perhaps, should there be a future agreement to limit the use of the veto only to matters related to the use of force, African states should be ready to give serious consideration to Model A. This would offer two permanent seats to Africa. Of course, even though Nigeria, South Africa, Kenya, Egypt and Senegal all expressed interest in permanent membership, Africa never reached consensus on their representatives. In the end, the reform of the Security Council failed to make it into the final document in September 2005.

A month before the September 2005 Summit in New York, African leaders met in Addis Ababa, Ethiopia, to determine whether they could amend Africa's position as embodied in the Sirte Declaration of September 1999 and the Ezulwini Consensus of February 2005 on the right of veto in order to accommodate the wishes of Germany, Japan, Brazil and India (the G–4, or Group of Four). While reaffirming their common position, the Addis Ababa summit of August 2005 formed a Committee of Ten, headed by president Ahmed Kabbah of Sierra Leone, with a mandate to explain Africa's position to other members of the UN. The Committee of Ten consulted the UN's five permanent members before issuing its report in October 2005. The report reaffirmed Africa's demand for two permanent seats with the full rights of veto. President Kabbah's report further urged all African states to campaign for the strengthening of the power and authority of the UN General Assembly. This confirmation of the African position virtually killed the initiative launched by Germany, Japan, Brazil and India.

Reforming the General Assembly and the Commission on Human Rights

The High-level Panel made critical comments about the performance of the UN General Assembly and the UN Commission on Human Rights. It is obvious that, for African countries, membership of the General Assembly represents an affirmation of their equal sovereign status with other states. Nevertheless, the voting procedures in the General Assembly have not been fully accepted by powerful western powers. If possible, these states would institute a system of weighted voting in which countries derive votes based on their financial contributions to the organisation, as exists in the Bretton Woods institutions. In any event, the Panel lamented the General Assembly's unwieldy and often static agenda. Few would disagree that better conceptualisation and shortening of the General Assembly's agenda is necessary. However, African states should vigorously oppose all efforts to diminish the importance and authority of the General Assembly.

Furthermore, some western powers' criticism of the Commission on Human Rights is related to its composition. (See Scanlon in this volume). Indeed, African states have been criticised – particularly by the US – for nominating certain "unworthy" states such as Sudan, Libya and Zimbabwe as members of the Commission. This has apparently contributed to the Commission's perceived loss of credibility. Despite this perception, would the Panel's proposal to expand the membership of the Commission to include all members of the United Nations, or the UN Secretary-General's replacement of the Commission with a smaller standing Human Rights Council based on certain membership criteria, have had the expected result of a more credible human rights body?

The history of the United Nations suggests an uncertain outcome. Perhaps members of the Panel did not adequately take into consideration the history of the UN during its first decade. At that time, both east and west insisted that only "peace-loving" states could become members of the UN. A provision which was initially meant to exclude so-called "enemy states" like Germany and Japan from UN membership thus created an impasse when a number of applicants were rejected because both east and west disagreed on which states were truly "peace-loving". Recognising this fault, a global agreement was reached during which 16 new member states were admitted to the organisation in 1955. This marked the end of the criterion of "peace-loving" as a qualification for membership to the UN. It is possible that any effort to clinically define which state is suitable for membership in the proposed Human Rights Council may meet a similar fate.

Regional Organisations

Unfortunately, the High-level Panel's treatment of regional organisations missed an excellent opportunity to formulate reliable guidelines aimed at regularising the relationship between the Security Council and regional bodies in the area of peace and security. While the rhetoric had validity, the actual recommendations were too tentative. Here again, the impression was given that the Panel was too cognisant of the reluctance of the US – as the largest contributor to the peacekeeping budget (of about 22 per cent) – to endorse the principle that financing of regional peacekeeping operations should be borne by the United Nations. We now find ourselves in the rather unusual situation in which the UN Security Council claims the right either to control or supervise regional peacekeeping operations, but has refrained from providing the necessary logistical support and financing for these initiatives, as was the case in Liberia and Sierra Leone in the 1990s.[14]

The High-level Panel could have made it clear that Chapter VIII of the UN Charter envisaged close cooperation between the Security Council and regional organisations, particularly in the area of peace and security. The days when antagonistic relations between the Security Council and regional bodies such as the Organisation of American States

(OAS) prevailed are over. Now relationships are cordial, and the Security Council has on many occasions complimented the efforts of regional peacekeeping operations such as the Economic Community of West African States Ceasefire Monitoring Group (ECOMOG) in West Africa. At the Secretariat level in New York, there is meaningful cooperation between the UN's Department of Peacekeeping Operations (DPKO) and the recently formed Commission of the African Union (AU) in Addis Ababa, Ethiopia, particularly in the cases of Burundi and Sudan's Darfur region. The Panel could have built on these experiences and made authoritative recommendations for the UN Security Council to work out arrangements through which it could delegate some peacekeeping responsibilities to regional organisations.

There is sufficient evidence to suggest that the Security Council is now over-burdened by demands for peacekeeping operations around the world. Judging from certain recent mistakes in UN peacekeeping missions in Africa, particularly in Rwanda, Somalia and Angola in the 1990s, it may be to the mutual benefit of all if the Council is able to call on credible and experienced regional peacekeeping mechanisms to act on its behalf. This would of course mean that the burden of financing such missions would be taken on by the UN. The proposal for the United Nations to train regional peacekeepers is appropriate. However, this is an inadequate solution. The provision of logistical support and financing are indispensable.

Regional peacekeeping arrangements such as ECOMOG in Liberia and Sierra Leone have proved themselves. In many instances, they have performed better than UN peacekeeping operations under similar conditions or in the same theatre of deployment, despite their lack of adequate logistical support and financing. African states should therefore press harder to ensure that any future agreed reform measures in the peace and security context include UN financial support for peacekeeping operations undertaken by regional organisations.

Reforming the UN Secretariat

It is surprising that, in recent years, UN member states have relaxed their efforts in monitoring carefully the workings of the Secretariat in New York. In the 1970s and 1980s, there were more introspective reviews of the staffing of the UN Secretariat. For example, in the 1970s, it was argued that the Secretary-General was too preoccupied with political and security matters and had little time for economic and social issues. To meet these concerns, a senior post, just below the rank of the Secretary-General, was established. The new post of Director-General for Development and International Economic Cooperation was tasked with coordinating all the UN's economic activities. The post and the resulting staffing changes did not make much impact and it was abolished in 1992 by then UN Secretary-General, Boutros Boutros-Ghali. Similarly, in 1986 the UN Secretary-General, Javier Perez de Cuellar, set out to restructure the staffing of the UN Secretariat and created an early warning office – the Office for Research and the Collection of Information (ORCI). This office was also abolished in 1992 during the reform initiative undertaken by Boutros-Ghali.

Many resolutions have called for the streamlining and rationalisation of posts within the UN Secretariat. Recently, member states have taken a more *laissez-faire* approach. Why? In the past, it was generally the western powers that expressed concerns about the proper functioning of the UN Secretariat. Under present circumstances, nationals of these same western powers are in a commanding position in the UN Secretariat and have virtually replaced many of the nationals of developing countries in key policy-making positions. Africa, in particular, has suffered heavily. Although the UN Secretary-General is from Africa, nationals of the western powers largely control the top departments of the Secretariat. As a result, being programme managers, rich countries have gained enormous power and influence in recruitment, promotion and career development at the UN.

Although there is currently a growth in the number of UN professional staff, we no longer hear the previous complaints about the need to curb recruitment. Western nationals now occupy many of these new posts. The High-level Panel also took a rather moderate approach to the reform of the Secretariat, which, in fact, is one of the principal organs of the organisation. Instead of tackling head-on the regrettable erosion of the international civil service, the Panel merely made reference to articles 100 and 101 of the UN Charter. Under these provisions, the international character of the Secretariat was underlined. Furthermore, the articles provided the foundation for the international civil service which is characterised by the independence and integrity of UN staff.

The Panel made no critical linkages between the palpable low morale among staff members and the gradual abandonment of some of the key principles of the international civil service. However, its members did propose that the UN Secretary-General be given a free hand in the professional staffing of the Secretariat. Nevertheless, "benign neglect" of secretariat matters by member states has lowered the effective profile of Africans in senior positions within the Secretariat.

Africa must demonstrate greater concern, and must remain alert in discussions of the proposed "buy-out" of UN staff contracts. Make no mistake: when you hear talk about "dead wood" or "staffing with the right people to undertake the tasks at hand", watch out! Such people may invariably have African staff members in mind. There remains a pernicious but unarticulated assumption in United Nations circles that African staff members are, at best, marginally competent. The reality that this perception is woefully erroneous and without foundation is beside the point. What matters is that these assumptions, even though baseless, nonetheless tend to influence policy and action at the UN. Therefore, African governments must be active when reform measures within the Secretariat are being discussed. Significantly, Kofi Annan, in his *In Larger Freedom* report of March 2005, differed from the High-level Panel when he rejected one of the Panel's key reforms of the Secretariat: the appointment of a second deputy Secretary-General to deal with peace and security. The Secretary-General clearly prefers a strengthened cabinet system.

Concluding Thoughts

The reform process in the United Nations has had a beneficial impact on the African Group at the UN. With the end of the Cold War and the increase in member states due to the break-up of the eastern European bloc, the African Group had failed to adjust to its reduced strength in a General Assembly of 192 member states (an increase from 150). The African Group misjudged the implications of having two Africans as head of the UN Secretariat since 1992. Since the commencement of the term of office of Kofi Annan in 1997, the influence and prestige of the African Group has gradually diminished. Keen observers of the politics of the United Nations have always known that the African Group should change tactics and collaborate more with like-minded delegations in the Non-Aligned movement, the companion G-77, and China. That does not mean that the African Group should not formulate a common African position on a number of critical issues. This, however, requires recognition that Africa can achieve better results when it works within a larger group. Otherwise western states, which have shown considerable skills in dividing their adversaries, will always prevail.

Although the development came rather late in the reform process, the African Group started regularly aligning its position with the G-77 and China on key reform proposals, particularly those relating to secretariat and management reforms. At the time of writing in 2006, the G-77 and China had an effective and articulate leadership, represented by the delegation of South Africa and its permanent representative, Dumisani Khumalo. What is crystal clear to the G-77 and China is that the balance of forces within the UN Secretariat has shifted perilously in favour of the US and western states. Not only do they now occupy many key positions in the UN Secretariat, they may as well have written most of the policy and reform proposals emanating from the office of the Secretary-General.

The major problem is that there has been a discernible decrease in the status and credibility of the international civil service.[15] A good many of the occupants of key positions in the Secretariat either care little about their obligations as international civil servants or lack any intrinsic appreciation for the requirement of the service. Owing to this deficiency, these officials appear to have adopted the inclination to use their best efforts to be in the "good books" of what they consider the world's sole superpower: the United States. The UN is an international organisation that must be fully aware of the interests of the other 191 members of the organisation. Failure to do this could lead, as has recently happened with the Iraq oil-for-food scandal, to officials in the Secretariat perceiving the UN Secretariat as a commercial corporation. It is this misperception that is at the heart of the divergence of views and positions between the office of the Secretary-General and the G-77 and China. When there is lack of trust in the impartiality of the UN Secretariat, it is almost impossible to expect the majority of member states to delegate significant mandates to the UN Secretary-General. As one African representative put it recently, it is unfair for the Secretary-General to submit reports to the General Assembly which only consider the views of some member states since this then obligates the African Group to try to uphold their own interests against a Secretary-General from their own region.

Spin-doctors and some sectors of the media have painted the G-77 and China as opposed to any reforms of the United Nations. The African group has joined the G-77 in insisting that they are in favour of reform but not reform which diminishes the power and authority of the General Assembly in which the south has a majority. There are areas in which the G-77 – including African states – has shown great flexibility, such as in the efforts to establish a Peacebuilding Commission. African states have now agreed to accept the establishment of a voluntary multi-year standing Peacebuilding Fund for post-conflict peacebuilding, although they would have preferred a more stable financing of the commission. In addition, they have signed on to the request of the UN Secretary-General to set up a peacebuilding support office in the Secretariat to be financed with existing resources. (See Murithi in this volume).

Attention should be drawn to the fact that a controversy has arisen between the G-77 and China on the one hand and the office of the Secretary-General on the other. The dispute is over what was approved by the September 2005 summit in New York. The Secretariat and the western powers have been maintaining that the outcome document approved key reform measures. The G-77 and China have pointed out that, according to the agreed document, the Secretary-General should submit proposals for the consideration and approval of member states. They have therefore begrudged the fact that, in the UN Secretary-General's budget proposal in 2006, he presented estimates for reform measures as if they had already been approved by member states.

This misunderstanding is at the heart of the threat that was made by the Permanent Representative of the US, John Bolton, regarding the approval of the regular biennial budget of 2006–2007. Washington threatened to agree only a three-month budget if key reform measures had not been approved by the end of December 2005. The key measures for the US were the Human Rights Council, the ethics office in the Secretariat and management reforms. But Kofi Annan had already informed the General Assembly that his proposals on some reform measures would only be submitted in the resumed session of 2006. That is why the majority of member states – not only the G-77 and China – opposed the American position on the budget. But since theoretically every member state has a veto on the budget, the issue was highly problematic.

One final important point should be mentioned. The major difficulty surrounding current debates about management and secretariat reform at the UN is linked to the Secretary-General's intention to introduce the concept of a Chief Operating Officer (COO) into the organisation. This misguided proposal is based on the model of a commercial corporation without fully taking into account the provision of Article 97 of the UN Charter, which makes the Secretary-General "the Chief Administrative Officer of the Organisation". The overwhelming majority of member states and the UN staff association are opposed to a "commercial" model, believing that it would be a mistake for UN reform. It should be observed that a US bipartisan Task Force on the United Nations issued a report in June 2005 and *inter alia* recommended that the UN Secretariat needed to have a single, very senior official in charge of daily operations – the role of Chief Operating Officer – which Paul Volker, former head of the US Federal Reserve and chair of the 2005 investigation into the UN oil-for-food scandal, has also strongly endorsed. Despite the "lofty rhetoric, political deal-making and periodic cultural rituals", progress on UN reform remains stilted. Whether this round of UN reform proves to be an event or a process still remains to be seen.

Notes

[1] *A More Secure World: Our Shared Responsibility,* Report of the United Nations Secretary-General's High-level Panel on Threats, Challenges and Change. Published by the United Nations Department of Public Information DPI/2367, (December, 2004).

[2] March, J & Olsen J: *Rediscovering Institutions: the Organisational Basis of Politics* (New York: Free Press; Toronto: Maxwell Macmillan, 1989).

[3] For a comparison of UN reforms and re-organisation in the public sector in general see Kanninen, T: *Leadership and Reform: The Secretary General and the Financial Crisis of the Late 1980s* (The Hague: Kluwer Law International, 1995).

[4] The Group of 77 is a loose coalition of developing countries at the UN, which was set up to promote their economic interests and to improve the developing world's negotiating capacity. From its initial 77 members, the organisation has since grown to 133 members.

[5] (A/601/2.1) 20 September 2005.

[6] (A/601/2.1) 20 September 2005.

[7] *A More Secure World: Our Shared Responsibility,* Report of the United Nations Secretary-General's High-level Panel on Threats, Challenges and Change. Published by the United Nations Department of Public Information DPI/2367, (December, 2004); and *In Larger Freedom: Towards Development, Security and Human Rights For All,* Report of the UN Secretary-General, Follow-up to the outcome of the Millennium Summit. (March 2005), A/59/2005.

[8] *A More Secure World: Our Shared Responsibility.*

[9] *Financial Times,* London, 18 April 2005.

[10] *A More Secure World: Our Shared Responsibility.*

[11] See Report of the Panel on UN Peace Operations (Brahimi Report) 21 August 2000, S/2000/809. Available at http://www.un.org/peace/reports/peace_operations/ (accessed 21 March 2006).

[12] *A More Secure World: Our Shared Responsibility.*

[13] *A More Secure World: Our Shared Responsibility.*

[14] Jonah, J: "The United Nations" in Adebajo, A & Rashid, I (eds.): *West Africa's Security Challenges: Building Peace in a Troubled Region* (Boulder and London: Lynne Rienner Publishers, 2004) pp. 319–47.

[15] See Jonah, J: "An Independent International Civil Service" in Ask, S & Mark-Jungkvist, A (eds.): *The Adventure of Peace: Dag Hammarskold and the Future of the UN* (New York: Palgrave Macmillan, 2005), pp. 165–77.

4

The UN, NEPAD and the Commission for Africa

Ibrahim Gambari

THE YEAR 2005 WAS one of "good hope" for Africa. The main source of this potential "good hope" and expectations for the continent, was not so much the convergence of important reports and summit meetings during the year (such as the reports by UN Secretary-General Kofi Annan's High-level Panel on *Threats, Challenges and Change*;[1] Jeffrey Sachs' report on the Millennium Declaration;[2] the UN Secretary-General's *In Larger Freedom*;[3] the United Kingdom (UK)-led Commission on Africa; and the summits of the Group of Eight Industrialised Countries (G-8), the European Union and the sixtieth summit of the UN General Assembly), but the growing commitment by African leaders themselves to addressing the continent's peace and security, development and democratisation challenges. The determination of African leaders to make a difference in meeting these challenges is demonstrated by the progress made in the new institutions which they have established, notably the African Union (AU) and the New Partnership for Africa's Development (NEPAD).

In this regard, through NEPAD's African Peer Review Mechanism (APRM), by mid-2005, 23 African governments had volunteered to subject their countries to the scrutiny of an independent Eminent Panel that assesses compliance with agreed political, economic and corporate governance standards. Countries that receive high marks in the independent reviews – indicating their compliance with democratic principles, corporate standards of accountability and transparency, the protection of human rights, and the existence of an independent judicial system – are to be recognised for good practices. Those that fail to reach the standards set by the review will be assisted to raise their levels of democratic governance. (See Adebajo in this volume).

African leaders are also expanding their diplomatic as well as peacekeeping efforts to enhance peace and security across the continent. The highly publicised and truly devastating conflicts in Sudan's Darfur region tends to mask a more positive trend on the African continent. In 1998, 14 countries in Africa were experiencing armed conflict or civil strife and another 11 were undergoing severe political crises and turbulence. This gloomy picture has shifted dramatically and positively in six years. By 2004, only six African countries were embroiled in armed conflict and few others were facing deep political crisis.

Recognising that prevention is much less costly than rebuilding societies devastated by war, disease and poverty, the AU is now developing a peacekeeping and intervention force (See Mwanasali in this volume). African peacekeeping troops have already been used in Burundi and Darfur in 2004; in January 2005 the AU, in collaboration with the Intergovernmental Authority on Development (IGAD), approved a plan to send peacekeepers to Somalia to facilitate the return of the new government.

On the economic front, many African governments are increasing their budget allocations to human development-oriented priorities in line with the United Nations Millennium Development Goals (MDGs) of 2000. By 2003, five African countries – Angola, Burkina Faso, Chad, Equatorial Guinea and Mozambique – had already achieved the levels of economic growth needed to reach the Millennium Development Goal of halving poverty by 2015. Nevertheless, the MDG budgetary goals for health (15 per cent of national spending), agriculture (10 per cent) and clean water and sanitation (5 per cent) are exacting for countries in which debt repayments often account for more than 25 per cent of their annual budgets. Most African countries are therefore unlikely to meet the Millennium Development Goals. (See Legum in the volume).

This chapter proposes to fulfil two tasks: first, to offer the reflections of a UN "insider" – from my vantage point as Under-Secretary-General for Political Affairs on the report of the High-level Panel on *Threats, Challenges and Change* which informed the Secretary-General's own report *In Larger Freedom*; and second, to assess the work of the British-led Commission on Africa as it relates to NEPAD.

The Report of the High-level Panel on Threats, Challenges and Change

In his January 2005 address to the AU summit in Abuja, Nigeria, UN Secretary-General Kofi Annan noted that the implementation of the UN High-level Panel's recommendations would save more lives in Africa than in any other continent. He pointed out that the report acknowledged that "poverty and infectious diseases such as AIDS, which affect so many millions every year in Africa are among the gravest threats to international peace and security". Annan further observed that "any effort to build an effective collective security system must place prevention and the fight against poverty at its heart, [hence] it calls for more concerted action to achieve the Millennium Development Goals".[4]

Some positive recommendations from the high-level panel report

CONCEPTUAL

The nexus between peace and development

The UN High-level Panel's insistence on the connection between contemporary threats to security is particularly important. Addressing terrorism, civil war and extreme poverty cannot be done in isolation. According to the High-level Panel, "hard" and "soft" security issues should be tackled with equal seriousness. (See Chinery-Hesse in this volume). When the Panel considered the question of what constitutes a security threat, it was confronted with diverse perceptions over this issue among world leaders. The government and people of the Central African Republic (CAR), for instance, are not as likely as those of the United States to consider weapons of mass destruction to be a perceptible threat to their security. Poverty and its associated limitations on health and life possibilities are greater concerns for the CAR government and citizens than for America's government and people. Poverty can, for example, lower life expectancy as dramatically as war.

Development is an "indispensable foundation" of collective security. The eradication of poverty and disease is an essential part of efforts to achieve a safer world in the twenty-first century. Those industrialised powers worried about terrorism should be equally concerned about narrowing the global disparity between rich and poor. While poverty is not a direct cause of terrorism in any simple way, factors such as limited economic opportunities and a lack of strong governance institutions can create conditions that can be more easily exploited by those seeking to recruit new members to terrorist causes. (See Baregu in this volume).

Conflict prevention

The High-level Panel report contains many proposals to prevent intra and interstate conflicts and other global threats, with development identified as the first line of response. Development, according to the report:

> [S]erves multiple functions. It helps combat the poverty, disease and environmental degradation that kill millions and threaten human security. It is vital in helping states prevent or reverse the erosion of state capacity, a key to meeting almost every class of threat. And it is part of a long-term strategy for preventing civil war, and for addressing the environments in which both terrorism and organized crime flourish.[5]

Panel members criticised the "shockingly late and shamefully ill-resourced" global response to HIV/AIDS, and called on the international community to rebuild global public health capacity, disease monitoring and response as defences against both naturally occurring epidemics and terrorists using biological weapons. (See Ndinga-Muvumba in this volume).

Peacebuilding

The High-level Panel report also addresses issues that arise during and after violent conflict, including the capacities necessary for peace enforcement, peacekeeping, peacebuilding and the protection of civilians. The report suggested that the global supply of available peacekeepers was insufficient, and tasks UN member states to be prepared to provide and support military deployments. Rich countries, in particular, should have contingents ready for peace operations, and provide the financial and logistical resources to mobilise these when and where they are needed.

PROPOSALS FOR INSTITUTIONAL CHANGE

The peacebuilding commission

The High-level Panel also recommended the creation of a new United Nations body, a Peacebuilding Commission – which would identify countries at risk of violent conflict, organise prevention efforts and "marshal and sustain the efforts of the international community in post-conflict peacebuilding".[6] This would involve efforts by the UN Security Council, the UN's Economic and Social Council (ECOSOC), and donors and national authorities to fill a crucial gap by providing the necessary attention to countries emerging from conflict. (See Murithi in this volume).

Reform of the UN

Panel members also found that the UN "has been much more effective in addressing the major threats to peace and security than it is given credit for, but that nonetheless major changes are needed" in order to be "effective, efficient and equitable in providing collective security for all" in the twenty-first century.[7] Among the most significant structural changes recommended by the High-level Panel was the expansion of the UN Security Council – its most powerful body – from 15 to 24 members. In this respect, the Panel suggested two options: one involved the addition of new permanent members to the Council with no veto powers, the other was based on the introduction of rotating four-year, renewable seats to be regionally distributed, also without veto power. (See Adebajo as well as Jonah in this volume).

In addition, the report recommended changes to the UN General Assembly, ECOSOC and the Commission on Human Rights, and in the UN's relations with regional organisations. The Panel also proposed strengthening the UN Secretary-General's critical role in peace and security. To be more effective, it proposed that Kofi Annan should be given substantially more latitude to manage the UN Secretariat, and in turn, should be held accountable over the exercise of greater authority.

Process of cooperation

The High-level Panel report further noted that the collaboration between the UN and regional organisations, such as the AU, is critical for the maintenance of global security and prescribed a number of principles to govern a more structured partnership between them. For example, the recommendation on the use of assessed contributions to support peacekeeping operations undertaken on behalf of the UN Security Council may be particularly useful to the AU to assist its peacekeeping operations in Africa.

SOME AREAS THAT NEED MORE ATTENTION

One failure of the High-level Panel's report was that it did not provide a comprehensive development and humanitarian strategy for Africa. For example, the report did not identify sources for the much-needed humanitarian assistance for conflict-ravaged countries, nor did it specify mechanisms to help developing countries alleviate extreme poverty and curb the spread of infectious diseases. The explanation for not doing so is that the Panel was tasked to examine economic and social issues only as they relate to peace and security. American economist, Jeffrey Sachs' report of January 2005 on the Millennium Declaration of 2000 filled part of this gap by devising strategies to meet the MDGs.[8] According to Kofi Annan, during his address at the 2005 AU summit in Abuja, most of the Millennium Declaration report recommendations clearly have Africa in mind. The report calls on African states to adopt development strategies that are bold enough to meet the Millennium Development Goals' targets by 2015. It appeals to donors and Africans alike to identify funding gaps, and to address these through significant debt relief measures and Official Development Assistance (ODA). The report suggests that at least a dozen MDG fast-track countries be designated for a rapid scale-up of ODA, with an increased number of countries granted such status as soon as they are ready. The report also stresses the need for a major breakthrough in the Doha trade round at the World Trade Organisation (WTO) and urges the immediate launching of a set of "quick win" actions: the free mass distribution of malaria bed-nets, the expansion of school meal programmes utilising locally produced foods, an end to fees for primary schools and improvements in essential health services.[9]

A further shortcoming of the High Level Panel's report was the lack of attention to Africa's special needs. The UN Millennium Declaration and UN General Assembly resolution of September 2000 both make reference to the special needs of Africa. Moreover, in its resolution on NEPAD in December 2004, the UN General Assembly invited "the High-level Plenary meeting which is to be held on the commencement of the 60th Session of the General Assembly, to address the special needs of the African continent".[10]

In addressing the special needs of Africa, there is a critical need for increased financial commitment by the United Nations system, which is in turn contingent on the organisation receiving additional financial resources for its joint programmes and new initiatives from the donor community. The High-level Panel report did not fully articulate means of increasing financial resources for the UN system and its agencies to assist African countries more effectively. Furthermore, the report did not address the issue of mutual accountability whereby both the donor community, on the one hand, and developing countries in Africa and elsewhere, on the other, would honour their respective commitments on resources for development. However, these omissions were addressed in the Sachs' report which should be seen as a compliment to the High-level Panel report. Both reports form the central message of the UN Secretary-General's *In Larger Freedom* report of March 2005.

A further omission of the High-level Panel report was not to have spelt out the precise mandate of the Peacebuilding Commission and the sources of funds for peacebuilding operations and post-conflict reconstruction in war-torn countries in Africa and elsewhere. It was not stated whether the funding for the Peacebuilding Commission would come from UN-assessed contributions or voluntary contributions. In addition, the institutional home for the proposed Peacebuilding Commission was the subject of vigorous debate with many member states questioning the UN Security Council as the appropriate location for the Commission.

Finally, the report of the High-level Panel failed to identify the urgent need for policy coherence in international assistance to Africa and the lack of complementarities in the debt, aid and trade policies of rich countries towards Africa. For example, for a period stretching back over 10 years, ODA to Africa has been almost offset by debt service payments by Africans. Another example of incoherence is evident in trade and ODA relief whereby, for nearly a quarter of a century starting from 1970, the dramatic decline in Africa's market share amounted to an estimated income loss of $70 billion per annum: almost five times the average annual ODA to Africa. The High-level Panel report has not adequately addressed how such policy incoherence can be remedied.

Nonetheless, it is fair to say that the High-level Panel's report was a start, and a good start, but not the end to the process of defining international collective threats and challenges and designing collective responses to meet them. Moreover, the future implementation of these recommendations depends on adequate follow-up mechanisms. As noted in the report, building a "more secure world" will require much more than a report or a summit. It will take long-term and sustained resources and commitments commensurate with the scale of the challenges. Most of all, it will need leadership – both within states and in intergovernmental bodies – to create future strategies to translate recommendations and expectations into reality.

The January 2005 AU summit in Abuja endorsed the decision made by the Executive Council of African foreign ministers which preceded the summit, to examine further the High-level Panel's report and to set up a committee of 15 members to prepare a common African position on it. Consequently, the meeting of the committee was convened in Swaziland in February 2005 and produced the "Ezulwini Consensus".[11] This was followed by an extraordinary session of the Executive Council to adopt Africa's position, which was then submitted to the UN Secretary-General for inclusion in his report to the UN General Assembly in March 2005. It was gratifying to note that a common African position was adopted, the African group of states being the only regional group in the UN to forge a common position.

NEPAD as the Core of the Report of the Commission for Africa

The release of the report of the UK-led Commission for Africa (sometimes referred to as the Blair Commission) in March 2005 generated considerable debate over the significance of its findings on African development and for international support of this effort. The report recommended, *inter alia*, an additional $25 billion per annum in ODA, to be implemented by 2010; fairer international trade agreements for Africa; debt cancellation or relief for impoverished African countries; and enhanced capacity for peacekeeping, conflict prevention and "good governance".[12] Much less discussion, however, has focused on the implications of the report for NEPAD or on the process of taking its recommendations forward. These are both equally important.

One of the five outlined objectives of the Commission for Africa was to support existing structures in Africa – in particular, NEPAD and the AU – and to help ensure that their goals are achieved. This objective, no doubt, allayed the concerns of those who feared that the work of the Commission might divert attention from NEPAD. There were also other significant ways in which the efforts of the Commission complemented those of NEPAD.

First, the Commission's report underlined many of the stated priorities of NEPAD. For example, it places considerable emphasis on the need for effective governance and capacity building, peace and security, investing in human development, poverty reduction, fairer trade and increased aid to Africa. With respect to aid, it is significant to note that when the NEPAD document first estimated that Africa would need transfers of about $64 billion per annum to achieve an estimated seven per cent annual growth rate, this figure was derided by many analysts as unrealistic. Yet the Commission for Africa advocated the doubling of aid to Africa in 2005, bringing it to about $50 billion per annum. Furthermore, the report estimates that Africa will need around $75 billion by 2010 to meet the various developmental needs that the Commission identified.

Second, since NEPAD was created in July 2001 and adopted as a programme of the African Union in July 2003, one major international event has dominated the global agenda every year, effectively eclipsing much international attention from Africa's development. Fortunately, the UN General Assembly's annual debate on NEPAD, and the G-8's annual discussion on its Africa Action Plan have both ensured that Africa's development needs remain on the global agenda. The report of the Commission is thus a major contribution to efforts at international policy dialogue and actions in support of Africa.

Finally, the report's recommendation that an effective independent governance monitoring mechanism should be created and supported by a small unit within an existing African or international institution, is consistent with NEPAD's orientation for periodically evaluating progress both by Africa and by its development partners. The idea of such a unit calls for an AU/UN partnership to ensure both regional legitimacy and international credibility.

Just as there was much scepticism initially over the establishment of the Commission, great expectations have since emerged due to the bold and imaginative recommendations that the report has outlined. The challenge now is to build both international consensus and to generate action around the report's key recommendations.

In this regard, four steps can assist this process. First, leadership by example. If African governments embrace and enact some of the key recommendations of the Commission, this can help to galvanise more international support for them. The British government decided in 2005 to ease conditionality in its aid policy, to double its bilateral aid to Africa, and to write off 100 per cent of debts to the poorest countries. Second, the G-8 and the EU should adopt the report's main recommendations. This will be consistent with the support that these two organisations have expressed for African development and for NEPAD, in particular. Third, the process of implementing the report will be helped greatly by some ranking of the various recommendations directed at Africa's development partners. Such a process would contribute to a more productive dialogue. A review of these recommendations indicates that they could be classified into three main categories. First, those that entail financial commitments; second, those that require changes in legislation, for example in dealing with repatriation of illicitly acquired state funds and assets from rich countries to Africa; and finally, those that require goodwill and a change of attitude by giving, for example, greater voice in multilateral institutions to African countries. The Commission's report can provide encouragement for African governments to deepen their policy commitments on enhancing productive capacity, strengthening administrative capability, and promoting accountable governance: all essential ingredients for sustained growth and poverty reduction.

Concluding Thoughts

In his 2004 commencement address at Harvard University in the US, UN Secretary-General Kofi Annan argued that "the UN offers the best hope of a stable world and a broadly equitable world order based on generally accepted rules". Events since 2003 have proved this statement to be prophetic. In his Harvard speech, the Secretary-General went on to say, "in devising and applying the rules, the legitimate interests of all countries are accommodated and decisions are reached collectively; that is the essence of multilateralism and the founding principle of the United Nations".[13]

Concerted action on these issues is required on the part of Africa and its international partners to help overcome the current obstacles to Africa's development. This will in turn pave the way for an Africa that depends more on its own competence and productive capacity than the world's compassion to survive and succeed: in short, we must build a strong and prosperous Africa which is in our common interest.

Notes

[1] *A More Secure World: Our Shared Responsibility:* Report of the United Nations Secretary-General's High-level Panel on Threats, Challenges and Change. Published by the United Nations Department of Public Information DPI/2367, December 2004.

[2] Sachs, J: *The Millennium Development Project: Practical Action Plan to Combat Poverty* available at www.unmilleniumproject.org/reports/fullreport.htm (accessed 11 November 2005).

[3] *In Larger Freedom: Towards Development, Security and Human Rights For All,* Report of the UN Secretary-General; follow-up to the outcome of the Millennium Summit. 21 March 2005, A/59/2005.

[4] Statement by Kofi Annan on the 4th Ordinary Session of The Assembly Of African Union 30 January 2005, Abuja, Nigeria. Available at: http://www.africa-union.org/summit/jan2005/Assembly/SPEECH%20KOFI%20ANNAN.htm (accessed 7 February 2006).

[5] *A More Secure World,* p.16.

[6] *A More Secure World,* p.96.

[7] *A More Secure World,* p.xi.

[8] Sachs, J: *The Millennium Development Project: Practical Action Plan to Combat Poverty.*

[9] Sachs, J: *The Millennium Development Project: Practical Action Plan to Combat Poverty.*

[10] Paragraph 31 of UN Resolution (A/59/L.33) of 21 December 2004. See http://www.un.org/africa/osaa/speeches/ReflectionsReptofSCF189.pdf

[11] See http://www.africa-union.org/News_Events/Calendar_of_%20Events/7th%20extra%20ordinary%20session%20ECL/Ext%20EXCL2%20VII%20Report.doc (accessed 31 March 2006).

[12] Commission for Africa: *Our Common Interest: Report of the Commission for Africa* (London: Penguin Books, 2005).

[13] UN Secretary-General Kofi Annan's commencement address at Harvard University: "Three Crises, and the Need for American Leadership" in Cambridge, Massachusetts (June 2004). Available at http://www.commencement.harvard.edu/annan.html (accessed 7 February 2006).

Section Two

©Cape Argus/Trace Images

Sovereignty as Responsibility

5

Africa's Responsibility to Protect

Musifiky Mwanasali

THIS CHAPTER[1] CONTRIBUTES to the debates over sovereignty, non-interference and responsibility in light of Article 4(h) of the Constitutive Act of the African Union (AU) of 2000 and the emerging international consensus over the "responsibility to protect" populations from genocide, war crimes, ethnic cleansing and crimes against humanity.[2] The idea of the "responsibility to protect" was adopted by the United Nations (UN) World Summit in September 2005. I seek to analyse the implications for Africa of this evolving international norm in light of the AU's Article 4(h), and to explore some of the issues that could confront African governments as the international community strives to give substance to the idea of the "responsibility to protect".

In his 2004 speech to commemorate the tenth anniversary of the genocide in Rwanda (See Anyidoho in this volume) at the Human Rights Commission in Geneva, Switzerland, UN Secretary-General Kofi Annan announced his intention to launch a UN action plan to prevent future acts of genocide. The plan consisted of five related facets: first, the prevention of armed conflicts; second, the protection of civilians in armed conflicts; third, the strengthening of judicial systems to end impunity; fourth, information analysis and early warning; and fifth, swift and decisive action, including military intervention.[3] Kofi Annan, mindful of the widespread – and what some deem unfair – criticism of his role during the tragedy in Rwanda in 1994 reflected:

> When we recall such events and ask, 'Why did no one intervene?' we should address the question not only to the United Nations, or even to its member states. No one can claim ignorance. All who were playing any part in world affairs at that time should ask: 'What more could I have done? How would I react next time – and what am I doing now to make it less likely there will be a next time?' [4]

In Annan's own words, "the risk of genocide remains frighteningly real". Such a risk was present in the mind of the founders of the African Union as well. Not only does its Constitutive Act proclaim the organisation's commitment to the sanctity of human life, it also grants the AU "the right to intervene in a member state pursuant to a decision of the Assembly in respect of grave circumstances, namely: war crimes, genocide and crimes against humanity, as well as a serious threat to legitimate order to restore peace and stability to the member state".[5]

The AU Constitutive Act – and before it, the 1999 Algiers decision on unconstitutional changes of government – constitutes a normative revolution in the history of the continental organisation and a significant review of the principles of sovereignty and non–interference as defined in the Charter of the Organisation of African Unity (OAU).[6] In a clear break with the past, African leaders recognised that "good governance", transparency and human rights are essential elements for building representative and stable governments and for contributing to conflict prevention efforts on the continent. Building on the "spirit of Harare" during the summit of June 1997 in Zimbabwe, and the 1999 summit in Algiers, Algeria, the AU Constitutive Act enshrined the right of the continental body to intervene in the internal affairs of member states to protect human rights and constitutional order. In so doing, African leaders unanimously agreed to transform the old principle of sovereignty as non–interference and to infuse it with the new meaning of "sovereignty as responsibility".[7] (See Deng in this volume).

Such a transformation occurred as a result of a drive on at least three fronts. First were the international norms created by the treaties relating to the protection of civilians in the fields of human rights, humanitarian, refugee and international criminal laws. Second, the global democracy movement of which many African governments are members and whose agenda includes the enhancement of democratic governance, the rule of law, as well as the promotion of democratic freedoms, institutions and practices as agreed in the context of new and restored democracies. Finally, demands "from below" for broadened participation, equitable representation and transparency in the management of public affairs.

This triple force created a convergence of views in Africa and elsewhere; between treaties, norms and principles entered into at the international level, and legal and constitutional norms and judicial practices enacted at the national level. As a result democracy, for example, has become more than a universal principle: the right to democracy is now a human rights concern. Freedom of the press, as another example, is no longer just a requirement of democracy, it has now become a human right: the right to a free press.

The "responsibility to protect" is another such emerging international norm.[8] Kofi Annan has advocated that the "responsibility to protect" is consistent with the notion of "sovereignty as responsibility". According to him:

> Sovereign states are the basic and indispensable building blocks of the international system. It is their job to guarantee the rights of their citizens, to protect them from crime, violence and aggression, and to provide the framework of freedom under the law in which all individuals can prosper and society develop… Therefore, one of the great challenges of the new millennium is to ensure that all states are strong enough to meet the many challenges they face.[9]

While recognising the need to strengthen states, civil society, the private sector and the international system at large in enhancing collective security and providing freedom for all, Kofi Annan emphasised "the accountability of states to their citizens, of states to each other, of international institutions to their members and of the present generation to future generations".[10] In Annan's view, where there is accountability, there is advancement.

Sovereignty as responsibility and accountability is at the core of this international intervention consensus.[11] First and foremost, it implies that the primary duty of the state apparatus is to ensure the well-being and safety of all people under its jurisdiction. Second, by virtue of their commitment to human rights and democratic governance, and by virtue of their membership in the global community of nations, all states and their personnel undertake to abide by international norms. This includes taking into account their actions towards their own citizens and towards the rest of the world, either internally through the legal system, or externally through international institutions set up for that purpose.[12] These obligations have increasingly challenged the old notion of sovereignty as non-interference in the internal affairs of other governments and have focused the minds of governments on the fact that the international community can take action against members whose actions are in gross violation of the international obligations that they have freely entered into.

"Responsibility to Protect": AU and UN Perspectives

Advocates of the "responsibility to protect" usually associate it with three distinct but interconnected sets of responsibilities: "the responsibility to prevent, the responsibility to react, and the responsibility to rebuild".[13] Although the language in the AU Constitutive Act of 2000 and the 2005 UN World Summit document are strikingly similar, there was such a misunderstanding among UN member states – including African governments – about what "protection" meant, that the effort to include this proposal in the 2005 summit's final resolution was in danger of being dashed.

During the discussions leading up to the adoption of the AU Constitutive Act in Lomé, Togo in July 2000, delegates generally accepted the principle of, and the need to, protect civilians against war crimes, genocide and crimes against humanity. After all, it was at the same summit in Lomé that the Organisation of African Unity's *Panel on the Rwandan Genocide* unveiled its report, which contained among other things, scathing criticism of the OAU and the international community for not having intervened to stop the massacre of nearly one million innocent Rwandans in 1994. Discussions and debates in Lomé focused largely on two issues: the authorisation of the intervention, and the need to add the preservation of political stability to the reasons to intervene. In time, both issues were resolved.[14]

At the 2005 UN World Summit, the process was not as smooth. A number of government delegations questioned the whole notion of the "responsibility to protect" on the grounds that "the vision... for a future United Nations should not be filled with vague concepts that provide an opportunity for those states that seek to interfere in the internal affairs of other states."[15] President Robert Mugabe of Zimbabwe, whose views resonated with many heads of state from the developing world such as Algeria and Malaysia, further cautioned the 2005 World Summit that:

> Concepts such as humanitarian intervention or responsibility to protect need careful scrutiny in order to test the motives of their proponents...We need to avoid situations where few countries, by virtue of their privileged positions, dictate the agenda for everybody else. We have witnessed instances where the sovereignty and territorial integrity of small and weak countries have been violated by the mighty and powerful, in defiance of agreed rules of procedures and the provision of the United Nations Charter.[16]

In Mugabe's view, the international community "needed to rediscover, reassert and pursue in a practical manner, the agenda for peace, security and development for all through fostering genuine cooperation based on respect for the sovereignty, equality and territorial integrity of all states".[17] For President Abdelaziz Bouteflika of Algeria, Africa should be able to participate in this debate "with serenity and conviction", based on the commitment expressed by African people and governments "from the Algiers decision of the Organisation of African Unity rejecting access to power by unconstitutional means through the Constitutive Act of the African Union and the guiding principles of NEPAD on the promotion of democracy, the rule of law and good governance".[18]

The views of the United Nations members on the "responsibility to protect" are reflected in two relatively short paragraphs in the World Summit document of 2005. Paragraph 138 recognises that "each individual State has the responsibility to protect its populations from genocide, war crimes, ethnic cleansing, and crimes against humanity", and encourages the international community to help states – especially small and weak nations – to build their capacity to exercise this responsibility.

Paragraph 139 of the document, on the other hand, points out the responsibility of the international community, the United Nations and its 15-member Security Council, "to use appropriate diplomatic, humanitarian and other peaceful means, in accordance with Chapter VII and VIII of the Charter, to help protect populations from genocide, war crimes, ethnic cleansing and crimes against humanity". The World

Summit document further prescribes collective action as in the case of Article 4(h) of the AU Constitutive Act. The World Summit document also prescribes recourse to Chapter VII of the UN Charter to be carried out "on a case by case basis and in cooperation with relevant regional organisations as appropriate, should peaceful means be inadequate and national authorities manifestly fail to protect their populations from genocide, war crimes, ethnic cleansing and crimes against humanity".[19]

However, any action by the international community, including the AU, which purports to exercise the commitments entailed in the "responsibility to protect" should take into consideration at least three elements: first, collective action and, particularly, cooperation with regional organisations in conflict and crisis prevention; second, concern, especially by weak states, over intervention and in particular the use of force; and third, the emphasis by societies emerging from conflicts on reconstruction and peacebuilding as priorities in the post-intervention phase. These three elements will now be examined in more detail.[20]

Crisis Prevention and Collective Action: The Tragic Case of Darfur

Collective action to respond to emerging crises is the cornerstone of the notion of the "responsibility to protect", according to the Canadian-sponsored International Commission on Intervention and State Sovereignty (ICISS) of 2001, which stated that "the responsibility to protect implies an accompanying responsibility to prevent".[21] However, while justifying the emphasis on prevention and the need to exhaust peaceful options before resorting to forceful intervention, the international community should guard against complacency and pious invocations of internationally agreed norms and principles on prevention while failing to implement these obligations. As the ICISS put it: "it is more than high time for the international community to be doing more to close the gap between rhetorical support for prevention and tangible commitment".[22]

The commitment by African leaders to "the promotion of a stable, secure, peaceful and developed Africa" and their "desire to assume a greater role in the maintenance of peace and security in Africa" cannot be questioned.[23] This is why they created the 15-member African Union Peace and Security Council (PSC) in May 2004 as a standing decision-making organ to facilitate timely and efficient responses to security threats and adopted protocols that regulate the efforts of the organisation, alongside other members of the international community, to promote peace and security in Africa.

The "responsibility to protect" is central to the mandate of the AU. Yet no AU legal document explicitly mentions it,[24] even though Articles 2(4) and other key provisions of the PSC Protocol reflect the ideas embodied in this norm in its three dimensions: prevention, intervention and reconstruction. It is thus reasonable to assert that, even in the absence of a specific reference by AU policy organs to the "responsibility to protect", the Constitutive Act and the PSC Protocol provide a sufficient legal basis for the AU to make this norm operational.

In an earlier study devoted to the relevance of "non-indifference" as the core of the AU's new conflict prevention doctrine,[25] I highlighted three conditions under which prevention could be effective: first, the enforcement of agreed norms and principles; second, the harmonisation of mandates and division of labour between the UN and the AU; and third, the availability and predictability of funding to sustain prevention initiatives.[26] The crisis in Sudan's Darfur region illustrates what can go wrong with the "responsibility to protect" concept when the rhetoric on international norms is not translated into robust action on the ground to uphold them; when means are not commensurate with ends; and when mandates are not effectively synchronised with what needs to be done to exercise the responsibilities entailed in such norms.

The international community belatedly awoke from its indifference to the long-festering crisis in Darfur in 2004, only to find itself powerless in the face of the heavy toll in human suffering and the immensity of the task needed to prevent the escalation of the crisis in a territory the size of France. By default, the AU was catapulted to the frontline with the blessing of powerful members of the UN Security Council. But this was soon to become a case of "mission impossible" for the continental organisation which eventually forced the PSC to shed all pride and call for a transition to the UN in March 2006. (See Anyidoho in this volume).

The AU Peace and Security Council took on the momentous responsibility to deploy African troops under the banner of the African Union Mission in the Sudan (AMIS) for a very short period – one-year renewable, if need be – and with a very soft mandate:

to monitor and observe compliance with the humanitarian ceasefire agreement of April 2004 and all other such agreements; to assist in the process of confidence building; and to contribute to a secure environment for the delivery of humanitarian relief and, beyond that, the return of refugees and internally displaced persons, in order to assist in increasing the level of compliance of all parties with the humanitarian ceasefire agreement and to contribute to the improvement of the security situation throughout Darfur.[27]

Protection was part of the AMIS mandate. Its Peace and Security Council further decided that:

Within the framework of its mandate, AMIS shall, among other tasks, (i) protect civilians whom it encounters under imminent threat and in the immediate vicinity, within resources and capability, it being understood that the protection of civilian population is the responsibility of the Government of the Sudan; (ii) protect both static and mobile humanitarian operations under imminent threat and in the immediate vicinity, within capabilities.[28]

But the conditions for exercising this aspect of the mandate were so restrictive that protection ultimately amounted to no protection at all.

Initially, AMIS deployment – often erroneously dubbed as the first-ever African peacekeeping force and thus ignoring earlier efforts in Chad in the 1970s – was met with some exhilaration as a demonstration of how Africans could take care of their own problems. This was despite the knowledge that the government of Sudan had resigned itself to the deployment in Darfur of an AU force as a lesser evil than a UN-led international force. Soon, however, this enthusiasm waned as an ill-prepared AU began to encounter a host of problems with respect to troop generation, financial sustainability, logistical support, as well as increased violence and a deterioration of the security situation on the ground. These developments seriously impeded AMIS capacity to ensure proper protection of civilian populations and humanitarian relief workers even within the limited confines of its area of responsibility.

A donor's conference co-hosted by the AU and the UN in Addis Ababa, Ethiopia, in May 2005, and subsequently, the decision of the AU Peace and Security Council to augment AMIS troop strength in September

2005 provided little relief to an over-spent mission which, in the minds of many observers, was not up to the task. Increasing calls began for a robust, larger and better-equipped UN force. When, in January 2006, the AU's Peace and Security Council expressed its support – in principle – to a transition from AMIS to a UN operation "within the framework of the partnership between the AU and the United Nations in the promotion of peace, security and stability in Africa", the belief became widespread among non-governmental organisations and the international media that the AU had failed in Darfur.

For the proponents of "African solutions to African problems", AMIS is the symbol of Africa's growing maturity and ability to exercise its "responsibility to protect". For the naysayers, however, AMIS exemplifies the limits of collective action through cooperation with regional organisations that lack the requisite capabilities. The jury may still be out on AMIS, but whatever the verdict, one should not underestimate the ability of member states to frustrate initiatives by AU policy organs and their disquiet over the organisation's standing in relation to its membership. Nor should one minimise the reluctance by AU member states to accept decisions by intergovernmental bodies – especially those they belong to – on matters that concern them directly as parties to a conflict or crisis situation.

Article 4(h) of its Constitutive Act of 2000 implies that the AU has authority over its membership, that its decisions are binding, and that whatever is agreed at the regional level has primacy over policy considerations or political pragmatism at the national level. Furthermore, the legal framework provided by the Constitutive Act and the PSC Protocol upholds – with some ambiguity – the principle of non-interference in the internal affairs of others, while defining a bold vision that allows the AU to intervene in the internal affairs of member states, although only in clearly defined circumstances. In reality, African governments, like governments elsewhere, tend to agree with external involvement in their internal affairs if it can help them consolidate their hold on power; generally governments oppose such interference when they are seen as the culprits in crisis situations.

Given the centrality of state security in the AU's security architecture and the great influence of its membership on its decision-making processes, it is not surprising how difficult it has been for AMIS to exercise a protection mandate in Darfur. In several communiqués, the Peace and Security Council has repeatedly requested the government of Sudan to disarm the government-supported *Janjaweed* militia and to facilitate the deployment of AMIS in accordance with its stated commitment. But very often, Khartoum did not heed such calls.

Still, the Constitutive Act's Article 4(h) constitutes an essential feature of the AU's "responsibility to protect" in that it establishes a broad prevention framework while suggesting the need for the organisation to secure the full support and cooperation of national governments and the international community. For now, though, such cooperation remains uncertain, owing in part to the reluctance of national governments to cooperate, and in part due to the fact that the support of the international community and the UN Security Council has hardly extended beyond rhetorical pronouncements. The World Summit document of 2005 proclaims the responsibility of governments to ensure the safety of their citizens and to create conditions favourable to the peaceful resolution of differences. The AU has agreed to exercise the right to intervene in a country in order to restore internal peace and political stability. This is certainly an innovation, but for now, and looking at the AU experiment in Darfur, one is left to wonder whether, on its own, the AU can really enforce Article 4(h).

Chapter VII, the Use of Force and the Authority to Intervene

Article 4(h) and the PSC Protocol designate the AU as the legitimate authority to authorise interventions. In the Constitutive Act, this decision is the exclusive prerogative of the Assembly of Heads of State and Government, while the PSC Protocol confers on the PSC – presumably at the head of state and government level – the authority "to use its discretion to effect entry into", and take appropriate action, to address potential or actual conflict situations. The PSC Protocol also authorises the Chairperson of the Commission – in 2006, former Malian President, Alpha Oumar Konaré – to bring to the attention of the PSC any matter s/he deems to be a threat to internal peace and stability. The chair of the Commission is also mandated to undertake "good offices" to prevent or resolve conflicts and to engage the organisation in peacebuilding activities.

The UN Charter lays on the Security Council the responsibility for the maintenance of international peace and security, but also encourages regional arrangements to deal with peace and security issues in their regions. However, the Charter subjects this responsibility to two conditions: no enforcement action should be taken by regional organisations without the Security Council's authorisation, and the Council should, at all times, be kept fully informed of the activities undertaken or contemplated by regional organisations in the maintenance of regional peace and security.

The AU's Constitutive Act takes due account of the UN Charter, and the PSC protocol is mindful of these provisions. However, frustrated by what it considers to be the UN Security Council's indifference or tardiness in responding to African conflicts – despite the fact that about 70 per cent of its time is taken up by deliberations on threats to international peace and security in Africa – the AU has taken some liberty with the UN Charter by deciding that the Assembly shall be the only source of authority with respect to the enforcement of Article 4(h): a posture that actually means no prior UN Security Council authorisation is needed before taking action. The Libreville decision of the PSC of January 2005 to undertake forcible disarmament of the *Interahamwe* in eastern DRC was a case in point.

Kofi Annan's March 2005 report *In Larger Freedom* considers the use of force as a necessary element of the UN's role as a forum for resolving international conflicts. He is of the view that "the UN Charter, as it stands, offers a good basis" for our understanding of when to use force.[29] The 2005 World Summit document which devotes four paragraphs – agreed upon after a bitter debate – to the use of force, also underscores "the obligation of all member states to refrain in their international relations from the threat or use of force in any manner inconsistent with the Charter of the United Nations".[30]

The AU's position on the use of force is articulated in its Ezulwini Consensus of March 2005, which states that any recourse to force by an African country against another, outside the framework of article 4(h) of the AU Constitutive Act, is illegal.[31] The Ezulwini Consensus does not ignore the UN Charter. However, while it stresses that the UN should not abdicate its responsibility for the maintenance of international peace and security, Ezulwini recognises that the AU and sub-regional organisations should be able to intervene with the approval of the UN Security Council, although in certain situations – notably in circumstances requiring urgent action – such approval could be granted "after the fact".The rationale for this position is that since the UN Security Council is often far from the scene of conflicts, it may not be in a position to undertake effectively a proper appreciation of the nature and development of conflict situations. Evidently, the UN Charter does not envision this exception. Nor does Kofi Annan, who considered illegal any use of force outside the Charter framework and forcefully argued that "the task is not to find alternatives to the Security Council as a source of authority".[32]

The use of force by Africa's sub-regional organisations raises its own set of questions. If the AU Peace and Security Council is responsible for the maintenance of continental peace and security, it should be the only organ to authorise the use of force by sub-regional peace and security mechanisms. The problem, however, is that sub-regional organisations such as the Economic Community of West African States (ECOWAS) which have threatened, used or have the capabilities to do both (including imposing sanctions) against their member states, have not always bothered to consult either the UN Security Council or the AU's Peace and Security Council before resorting to these measures.The ECOWAS Ceasefire Monitoring Group (ECOMOG) interventions in Liberia and Sierra Leone in the 1990s represent examples of this trend. For now, the AU Commission and Africa's sub-regional organisations are quiet about this, preferring to leave to African heads of state and government the authority to decide on the threat or use of force. But the issue may soon come to a head as sub-regional organisations are increasingly involved in peace enforcement operations.[33]

While Article 4(h) consents to the possibility of using force, the AU has yet to develop clear measures in this area. Following the work of the International Commission on Intervention and State Sovereignty, Kofi Annan proposed five conditions for the use of force. These are: "(i) the seriousness of the threat; (ii) the proper purpose of the proposed military action; (iii) whether other means short of the use of force might plausibly succeed in stopping the threat; (iv) whether the military option is proportional to the threat at hand; and (v) whether there is a reasonable chance of success".[34] In the context of the AU, one would be well advised to add a sixth criterion: whether the military option is enforceable and sustainable.

Reconstruction in the post-Intervention Phase

Since the adoption of the Millennium Declaration in 2000, the UN undertook to review its approach to conflict prevention by requesting UN agencies to develop an integrated approach and to move closer to addressing the root causes of crises and conflicts. The Millennium Declaration reaffirms the commitment of UN member states to the core values of freedom, equality, solidarity, tolerance, respect for nature and shared responsibility.

In the section devoted to the needs of Africa, the Millennium Declaration affirms the following: "We [the international community] will support the consolidation of democracy in Africa and assist Africans in their struggle for lasting peace, poverty eradication and sustainable development, thereby bringing Africa into the mainstream of the world economy".[35] Four key measures are spelt out in the declaration: (i) full UN support to emerging democracies; (ii) encouraging and sustaining regional and sub-regional mechanisms for conflict prevention and the promotion of political stability, and ensuring reliable resource flows for peace support operations; (iii) adopting special measures for poverty eradication, including debt cancellation and increased flows of foreign direct assistance; and (iv) building capacity to tackle the spread of HIV/AIDS and other infectious diseases. (See Legum as well as Ndinga-Muvumba in this volume). These measures, coupled with adequate and sustainable assistance for post-conflict reconstruction and close working relationships with local actors and civil society organisations, constitute the core elements of a UN strategy for conflict prevention.

By establishing the Peacebuilding Commission in December 2005, world leaders reiterated the commitment and need for the international community to assist countries emerging from conflicts towards recovery, reintegration and reconstruction, and to help them lay the foundation for sustainable peace, security and development. The Peacebuilding Commission is not meant to become yet another layer of UN bureaucracy. Its mandate is "to focus attention on the reconstruction and institution-building efforts necessary for recovery from conflict and support the development of integrated strategies in order to lay the foundation for sustainable development". (See Murithi in this volume).

Kofi Annan first articulated the need for the Peacebuilding Commission in his March 2005 report *In Larger Freedom*, in which he

101

intimated that there could be no security without development, no development without security, and that neither would exist without human rights. In an explanatory note issued thereafter, Annan outlined the road map for the Peacebuilding Commission.

Much hope has been placed in the Peacebuilding Commission, particularly by states emerging from conflicts – such states see the body as the solution to the problem of scarcity of post-conflict reconstruction funds and development assistance. According to the World Summit document, "the main purpose of the Peacebuilding Commission is to bring together all relevant actors to marshal resources and to advise on and propose integrated strategies for post-conflict peacebuilding and recovery".[36]

UN experience in peacebuilding evolves around three clusters of issues: security sector reform, state-institution building and development. Security sector reform is broadly conceived to create a sufficiently secure environment for normal social and economic interactions. This includes disarmament and demobilisation, as well as the restructuring of security forces. One of the objectives in reforming the security sector is to create a professional corps, subject to the control of elected civilian rule and respectful of the human rights and the dignity of the citizenry at large.

State-institution building is another cluster of issues that covers a wide range of activities that are essential for the restoration of constitutional rule and the strengthening of the rule of law. UN involvement in this area has generally centred around the drafting of essential legislation, the organisation of elections, the building of state institutions (including an independent judiciary), and the extension of state authority throughout a previously war-torn country. Such assistance has had mixed results, much of it in elections and to a lesser degree in the drafting of essential legislation. Strictly speaking, the responsibility to rebuild state institutions and to strengthen the capacity of national authority to rule the country effectively is the primary responsibility of national elected officials, and UN efforts in this regard are generally too new and sparse to be assessed in a definitive manner.

The third cluster of issues – development – covers short-term initiatives such as "quick-impact" projects that intend to provide small incomes and to allow post-conflict countries a gradual return to normal economic life. This also covers short-term budgetary support to enable governments to meet their most pressing needs while negotiating substantial development assistance with the Bretton Woods institutions – the World Bank and the International Monetary Fund (IMF) – and other international donors. The Special Representative of the Secretary-General (SRSG) usually leads the state-institution building aspect in UN mission areas. In mission and non-mission areas, the United Nations Development Programme (UNDP) and UN country teams (depending on the mandate of their respective agencies) take the lead with the other aspects of post-conflict reconstruction.

In his explanatory note on the Peacebuilding Commission in 2005, UN Secretary-General, Kofi Annan, indicated that the Commission "should support, not attempt to replace, effective country-level planning for recovery". He added that "the core of the work of the Peacebuilding Commission must be in country-specific activities". Much of the existing post-conflict assistance is provided directly through field efforts, or through bilateral agreements of governments with the Bretton Woods institutions or donor countries. The UN is often involved in these negotiations, and usually plays a major if not determining role, in particular, through aid advocacy. This has generally been effective in securing critical short-term resources for activities like disarmament, elections and economic recovery.

The experience accumulated over the years by UN country teams is therefore valuable, and should be at the core of post-conflict reconstruction efforts if the Peacebuilding Commission is to be practical and useful in this field. Three sets of questions need to be addressed in this respect: What comparative advantage would a unit based at UN headquarters have over UN country teams and other donors' local initiatives? What value would such a unit add – and in what areas – if it is to complement field-based recovery initiatives? And how best can the actions of the UN Security Council and its Economic and Social Council (ECOSOC) be coordinated to avoid duplication and delays in delivering much critical assistance that could prevent the recurrence of violence, especially if the conflict has at its root economic grievances?

The Security Council is mandated under the UN Charter primary responsibility for the maintenance of international peace and security. On the other hand, ECOSOC is the only principal UN organ explicitly invested by the Charter with responsibility over socio-economic matters.

One important aspect of ECOSOC's work is to address the economic and social dimensions of conflicts. In the case of Africa, ECOSOC has set up *ad hoc* advisory groups on specific African countries emerging from conflicts to assess short-term economic needs such as budgetary support and help in elaborating long-term development programmes. Article 65 of the UN Charter also stipulates that ECOSOC may furnish information to the Security Council and will assist it upon request.

Various institutional arrangements are currently under discussion at the UN on how the two organs – the Security Council and ECOSOC – can work closely together to further the objectives of the Peacebuilding Commission. Regardless of the eventual relationship established between both bodies, it should be stressed that *ad hoc* arrangements will no longer suffice to deal with the challenges of short-term recovery and long-term reconstruction. The Peacebuilding Commission should therefore fill this institutional deficiency since one of its key functions is to ensure the sustained international attention vital for countries moving from transitional recovery towards development. The UN Security Council and ECOSOC would have to agree on when a country on the agenda of the Security Council is ripe to move to ECOSOC for a discussion of its long-term needs for post-conflict economic recovery.

For example, while a country is on the agenda of the UN Security Council, ECOSOC could advise the Council on the challenges and options for long-term socio-economic recovery. As this country moves into the post-conflict phase, the Security Council could ensure that the vast resources that were used during peacekeeping efforts are gradually shifted to give ECOSOC a predictable and reliable source of funding for socio-economic development. In this case, the role of the Peacebuilding Commission would be one of a bridge between the Security Council and ECOSOC. Working closely with the UN country team and other local stakeholders, the Peacebuilding Commission could serve as an advisory board to both organs while making sure that it reinforces the efforts of, rather than substitute for, UN country teams and local partners.

The Peacebuilding Commission is set to work closely with regional and sub-regional organisations on post-conflict reconstruction and development efforts. UN experience in this area will therefore be valuable to the AU and Africa's sub-regional organisations as they endeavour to develop their own post-conflict reconstruction capacity. Experts convened by the AU in Durban, South Africa, in September 2005, adopted a draft framework for post-conflict reconstruction and development, which was subsequently discussed at the AU Commission in Addis Ababa. The draft framework covers a wide range of aspects including humanitarian, governance, DDR (Disarmament, Demobilisation and Reintegration), human rights, socio-economic recovery and gender.[37] The UN system took part in these discussions.

It is premature to comment on a framework for post-conflict reconstruction and development that has yet to be implemented. However, it is possible to foresee some of the obstacles that may hinder its effectiveness. These include the perennial lack of resources, limited institutional capacity to formulate and implement national development programmes or to absorb external support, and the absence of a proven tradition of transparency and "good governance" in many recipient countries. Furthermore, poverty and weak economic growth will continue to impede progress towards sustainable peace and political stability in Africa despite the efforts by the AU and its international partners to reverse these negative trends.

I have dwelt at some length on post-conflict reconstruction because it presents a most daunting challenge to the "responsibility to protect". Democracy, as the saying goes, cannot be preached to, or embraced by, empty bellies. The Peacebuilding Commission is one element of the UN reform process that received the strongest support from member states. All have emphasised its vital importance for Africa, and this is clearly reflected in the World Summit document, which highlights the centrality of the peace and development nexus as well as the need to meet Africa's special needs. The Peacebuilding Commission could make a significant contribution to predictable financing and a more development-based approach to peace consolidation.

Most African countries are unlikely to meet the Millennium Development Goals by 2015. According to experts, Africa is the most marginalised continent in this globalised world. With a share of total world trade declining from 4 per cent in the 1990s to less than 2 per cent at present, the continent is often said to have been bypassed by globalisation. Africa is now host to the largest UN peacekeeping missions in the world. (See Adebajo in this volume). It should not be allowed to be at the receiving end of interventions related to the "responsibility to protect". The challenge facing Africa is therefore how to catch up with the rest of the world or, at the very least, how to create conditions that are conducive to sustained economic growth, poverty alleviation and, most importantly, the harnessing of domestic resources and energies to ensure successful transitions from violent conflicts to stable peace.

Transitions from war to peace represent the greatest challenge to the international community. This is an era in which external assistance is critical to sustaining fragile cease-fires and peace processes and to help create the conditions for long-term political stability and human security. The UN's missions and country teams around the world are investing large amount of resources in "quick impact" initiatives, short-term budgetary support, and other forms of assistance to transitional or newly elected governments. But such resources are still not enough.Very often, countries emerging from war or a severe armed conflict are confronted with enormous challenges in the form of salary arrears, dilapidated social and health infrastructure, massive unemployment among youth populations and widespread destitution. Such countries need immediate assistance from the international donor community to address their most pressing social problems and to gain a temporary respite to undertake the arduous and long-term task of macro-economic restructuring. Failure by the international community to assist these countries at this critical juncture is a sure recipe for a relapse into conflict. Examples abound in Africa to support this proposition.

Concluding Reflections

Over the years, the AU – with the support of the UN and the rest of the international community – has taken steps to push protection, conflict prevention, mediation and peacekeeping higher up the agendas of its member states. With the proposal to establish a framework for post-conflict reconstruction and development following the creation of the Peacebuilding Commission in December 2005, the institutional set-up for the "responsibility to protect" in its three dimensions is now in place at the international and regional levels as an intrinsic component of collective efforts towards peace and development. There are therefore no more excuses for the failure of the international community to implement this emerging international norm.

In Africa, peace and development must go hand in hand if the "responsibility to protect" is to make a difference. The onus is now on us as African citizens, individual African countries, the United Nations and the international community at large, to help the peace and development nexus become a reality on our continent.

This chapter has attempted to identify some key issues, ranging from prevention to reconstruction through intervention, which the AU will have to address in order to implement Article 4(h) of its Constitutive Act effectively. This and other legal provisions define the circumstances under which the AU has an obligation to intervene and to identify the source of authority in such situations. Although the words "responsibility to protect" is not clearly mentioned in any AU key legislative documents, the emerging international consensus around this idea is nonetheless becoming clear.

This chapter has further argued that, in order to retain their collective nature, any action by the AU to prevent, intervene and rebuild should be consistent with the UN Charter and be undertaken in cooperation with the rest of the international community. Although the legality of such actions is generally accepted by the AU to be in accordance with its legislative mandate, their legitimacy may be questioned if cooperation between the AU membership and the international society at large is lacking. This essay has also contended that, while the use of force is implied in Article 4(h) of the AU's Constitutive Act and may sometimes become necessary, the AU is well advised to reflect on the AMIS experience in Darfur in setting strict criteria for military operations in order to ensure their effective enforceability and sustainability.

The chapter has dwelt extensively on post-conflict reconstruction efforts because this is the litmus test of the relevance of the "responsibility to protect". Upgrading the role of ECOSOC as a strategic forum to coordinate socio-economic activities appears to be a *sine qua non* since the body is well placed to address the socio-economic grievances at the root of violent conflicts. (See Jonah in this volume). Enhanced cooperation between the UN Security Council and ECOSOC (as anticipated in the context of the Peacebuilding Commission), and between the Peacebuilding Commission and such similar institutions that may be established at the regional and sub-regional levels, could go a long way to enhancing peace and development efforts in Africa.

It is therefore advisable that resources for post-conflict reconstruction be directed to the local level. It is the responsibility of national governments to provide security and to create the necessary conditions for economic recovery. Simply put, the responsibility to prevent, to act and to (re)build should be owned by national and local actors. The role of the international community – whether the AU or the UN – should be to advise and support national efforts and to contribute to the mobilisation of sustainable and predictable resources to help societies recover from the scourge of violent conflicts.

Notes

[1] The views expressed herein are the author's sole responsibility.

[2] United Nations Resolution A/60/L.1, also referred to as the 2005 World Summit Document (or, simply, the Outcome Document).

[3] United Nations Press Release SG/SM/9197 AFR/893, HR/CN/1077 of 7 April 2004 at http://www.preventgenocide.org/prevent/UNdocs/KofiAnnansActionPlantoPreventGenocide

[4] United Nations Press Release SG/SM/9197 AFR/893, HR/CN/1077, p.1.

[5] Protocol on Amendments to the Constitutive Act of the African Union, Article 4(h) available at www.africa-union.org/ (accessed 7 July 2006).

[6] Decision AHG/Dec.141 (XXV) was adopted by the 35th ordinary session of the Assembly of Heads of State and Government of the Organisation of African Unity (Algiers, Algeria, 12–14 July 1999).

[7] See Deng, F *et al.*: *Sovereignty as Responsibility: Conflict Management in Africa* (Washington, DC: The Brookings Institution, 1996).

[8] For the genesis of this concept, see International Commission on Intervention and State Sovereignty (ICISS), *The Responsibility to Protect: The Report of the International Commission on Intervention and State Sovereignty* (Ottawa: International Development Research Centre, 2001).

[9] Annan, K: *In Larger Freedom: Towards Development, Security and Human Rights for All* (New York: United Nations, 2005), UN document A/59/2005, 21 March 2005, p.7.

[10] Annan, K: *In Larger Freedom*, p.7.

[11] ICISS, p. 13.

[12] ICISS, p. 13.

[13] ICISS, p. 13.

[14] At the Lomé summit, delegations agreed to defer to the Assembly of Heads of State on the legal authority to authorise intervention. Preservation of political stability was added at the AU's Maputo summit of 2003.

[15] Statement by President Robert Mugabe to the High-level Plenary Meeting of the General Assembly, New York, 14 September 2005.

[16] Statement by President Robert Mugabe at the World Summit. Prime Minister Abdullah Ahmad Badawi of Malaysia echoed similar views when he indicated that the existing provisions of the UN Charter are sufficient to address the full range of security threats, including the question of the responsibility to protect civilian populations from crimes against humanity. However, he added, "any intervention must give due recognition to Charter principles pertaining to sovereignty, territorial integrity and non-interference". See his statement to the High-level Plenary Meeting of the 60th Session of the United Nations General Assembly, New York, 14 September 2005.

[17] President Robert Mugabe's statement to the High-level Plenary Meeting of the 60th Session of the United Nations General Assembly, New York, 14 September 2005.

[18] *Intervention de S.E. Abdelaziz Bouteflika, Président de la République algérienne démocratique et populaire à la Réunion plénière de Haut niveau de l'Assemblée générale des Nations unies*, New York, September 2005.

[19] Resolution A/60/L.1, p. 31.

[20] In this chapter, "African Union" designates all 53 members of the regional body, including sub-regional organisations that are part of its overall security architecture. "AU Commission" is used to describe the Addis Ababa-based operational arm of the AU, in contrast to sub-regional security mechanisms located in Africa's five subregions.

[21] ICISS, p. 19.

[22] ICISS, p. 19.

[23] African Union: "Statement of Commitment to Peace and Security in Africa issued by the Heads of State and Government of Member States of the Peace and Security Council of the African Union", Addis Ababa, 25 May 2004, see http://www.africa union.org/News_Events/Calendar_ of_%20Events/Lancement%20PSC/Statement.pdf (accessed 21 April 2006).

[24] On the margins of a seminar on the "responsibility to protect" organised by Canada's Ploughshares in Addis Ababa in October 2005, AU Commissioner Said Djinnit, although recognising that the "responsibility to protect" was relevant to the AU's security architecture and work, indicated that, since the wording does not appear in any AU legal document, the Commission could not take active part in any discussion on the matter unless specifically mandated to do so by AU policy organs.

[25] Mwanasali, M: "'From Non-interference to Non-indifference': Emerging Doctrine in Conflict Prevention in Africa" in Akokpari, J, Murithi, T & Ndinga-Muvumba, A (eds.): *Building an African Union For the Twenty First Century: Relations with the RECS, NEPAD and Civil Society* (forthcoming).

[26] Mwanasali, M: "'From Non-interference to Non-indifference.'"

[27] African Union: *Report of the Chairperson of the Commission on the Situation in Darfur*, 12 January 2006, classified as PSC/PR/2(XLV).

[28] African Union: *Report of the Chairperson of the Commission on the Situation in Darfur*.

[29] Annan, K: *In Larger Freedom*, p. 43.

[30] Resolution A/60/L.1, para 77 to 80.

[31] The AU summit in Abuja, Nigeria, in January 2005 set up a committee of 15 member states to elaborate a common African position on the UN reform proposed by the High-level Panel on *Security, Threats and Challenges* created by Secretary-General, Kofi Annan in 2003. The committee met in Swaziland at the end of February 2005 to agree on a draft that was submitted to the AU Executive Council a month later for approval. The document is officially known as "The Common African Position on the Proposed Reform of the United Nations: 'the Ezulwini Consensus' ". It was approved by the 7th extraordinary session of the Executive Council of the African Union held in Addis Ababa from 7–8 March 2005 (Ext/EX.CL/2(VII). The following citations are drawn from the section on collective security and the use of force.

[32] "The Common African Position on the Proposed Reform of the United Nations: 'the Ezulwini Consensus'": p.43.

[33] Once constituted by 2010, the intention is that the African Standby Force will serve as a continental peacekeeping force that could be deployed in various operational theatres under a single, pan-African command. The role of sub-regional mechanisms will then be solely to provide troops to the force. How this development will affect the relevance of the sub-regional organisations remains a matter of conjecture.

[34] Annan, K: *In Larger Freedom*, p.33.

[35] http://www.un.org/millennium/declaration/ares552e.htm (accessed 2 April 2006).

[36] United Nations Resolution A/60/L.1

[37] African Union: *"Report of Proceedings: The 4th Brainstorming Retreat of the Peace and Security Council and other AU Member States" Permanent Representatives to the African Union on Post-Conflict Reconstruction and Development in Africa*, 4–5 September 2005, Durban, South Africa.

6

The International Challenge of State Failure and Internal Displacement

Francis Deng

STATE FAILURE IS A matter of degree. A successful state is one that lives up to an optimum degree of responsibility to protect its citizens (and those under its jurisdiction) and to provide for their general welfare. This should entail containing violence, managing diversity, developing and implementing sound economic policies that balance growth with equitable distribution, respecting democratic values and fundamental rights, and forging cooperative relations at the regional and international levels. Failure begins to manifest itself when a state cannot manage conflicts to minimise violence, ensure physical security, protect human rights, and to provide essential services and development opportunities. In particular, failure to meet the survival needs of its citizens, to respond effectively to man-made or natural disasters, and to provide emergency protection and assistance are all symptoms of a failed or failing state. Viewed in this light many, if not most, states experience varying degrees of failure to achieve the optimal standard of "good governance" and the best possible management of the affairs of state. At the extreme end of failure is the total collapse of the state, when its capacity to respond to crises disappears or diminishes to a minimum standard.[1]

Whatever the extent of state failure, the international community has historically been called upon to step in to assist. It should be noted that the emphasis remains that the state is the cornerstone of the international system and that the concept of state sovereignty continues to be a fundamental norm within the international order. Human rights and humanitarian principles, of course, provide a basis for international involvement, which can take a variety of forms and intensity, ranging from diplomatic dialogue on behalf of the affected population to more coercive measures, culminating in military action. Yet, international access to needy populations can be significantly impeded by the negative exercise of state sovereignty, as long as a semblance of the state still exists. The paradox of the situation is that it is generally assumed that the responsibility to enforce the rule of law and to provide protection and assistance to needy populations falls first and foremost on the states concerned. Even when these states are undergoing degrees of failure and possible collapse, there is often reluctance on the part of the international community to step in and take appropriate action. Whether or not this reluctance is due to the potential material and human costs involved, respect for sovereignty often provides a convenient shield. In any case, a disaster that is already underway, rather than the need to prevent such events, is what often drives effective international responses.

This chapter investigates the experience of the international community over the global crisis of internal displacement. First, I analyse the nature of the conflicts and human rights violations that generate displacement, especially the identity crises in these conflicts that create voids of moral responsibility, and the necessity for the international community to take remedial action. The chapter then considers the ways in which the international community has reacted to this challenge and the obstacles that still constrain international responses to crises. This is followed by a brief outline of more recent global developments intended to improve the response of the international system to crises.[2] The chapter then draws attention to the dilemmas and ambivalences taken up by all parties when state failure makes humanitarian intervention imperative. Finally, I conclude the chapter by stressing the need to address the root causes of crises in order to evaluate more effective responses, solutions and ideally, prevention.

The Crisis of Internal Displacement

Internal displacement is a microcosm of broader challenges facing the state and the international system. Some 25 million persons in over fifty countries have been uprooted and forced to flee their homes as a result of internal conflicts, communal violence, or flagrant violations of human rights. These internally displaced persons (IDPs) have however remained within their national borders.[3] As a result of their forced displacement, they are deprived of essentials such as shelter, food, medicine, education, community and a resource base for self-sustaining livelihood. Worse, internally displaced persons remain within borders of a country at war with itself, and even when they move to safer areas, are viewed as outsiders, discriminated against and often harassed. Although whole communities are affected by displacement, those uprooted from their homes are especially vulnerable to physical attack, sexual assault, abduction, disease and deprivation of basic needs. They suffer higher rates of mortality than the general population, sometimes as much as 50 times greater.[4] While this crisis is global, Africa – with 12.7 million internally displaced persons in 20 countries – is the worst affected continent.

What is most disturbing about this phenomenon is that the conflicts, the generalised violence, and the human rights violations that cause internal displacement are often characterised by acute crises of national identity. This serves as both cause and effect as well as being a factor in official responses to the consequent humanitarian tragedies. This phenomenon is particularly obvious in countries in which ethnic or religious factors are a dominant feature in the conflict. Often, identity issues such as race and ethnicity combine with economic marginalisation, manifested through poverty, as corresponding aggravating factors.[5]

Although state responsibility to guarantee the protection and general welfare of its citizens has been increasingly accepted in international law, this still poses practical problems in countries experiencing cleavages among the various groups with differentiated identities based on race, ethnicity, religion, language or culture. Often, the groups most affected by conflicts are minority or marginalised groups who are peripheral to the dominant identity group and, in most cases, elements of these peripheral or marginalised groups are in conflict with the dominant group. Either because they support rebels or dissidents, are sympathetic to their cause, or simply by association, these groups tend to be identified as part of the enemy, if not being tagged the enemy itself. Rather than be protected and assisted as citizens, these groups tend to be neglected and even persecuted. Under these circumstances, citizenship becomes only of paper value and marginalisation becomes tantamount to statelessness.[6]

The irony is that, if these victims of conflict had crossed international borders, they would be classified as refugees for whom the international community has a well-established framework through the 1951 Refugee Convention, a 1967 Protocol and the Office of the United Nations High Commissioner for Refugees (UNHCR). While refugees constitute about half of displaced populations, and, having fled across international borders are outside the danger zone, they are the subject of international concern, while IDPs are often victims of contested or divided sovereignty.

In many countries experiencing conflict, the internally displaced are not only dispossessed by their own governments, but are also outside the reach of the international community due to the appeal to sovereignty to prevent international involvement. While international humanitarian and human rights instruments offer legally binding foundations for international protection of needy populations within their national borders, these populations are at the mercy of their national authorities for their security. (See Scanlon in this volume). Diplomacy and the art of persuasion can however assist in allowing international access and, in extreme circumstances, more assertive intervention may be imperative.

The basis for diplomatic dialogue is to advance sovereignty as a concept of a state's responsibility to protect and assist its citizens in need and not as a barrier against international involvement and cooperation. Where inadequate resources and operational capacities necessitate, states could invite or at least welcome international assistance to complement national efforts. While this is a persuasive argument, there is an implicit assumption of accountability behind responsibility. This means that, where large numbers of populations suffer extreme deprivation and are threatened with death, the international community – obligated by humanitarian and human rights normative standards – cannot be expected to watch passively and not respond. Humanitarian intervention then becomes an imperative. The best assurance for maintaining sovereignty is, therefore, to establish at least minimum standards of responsibility, if need be with international cooperation. (See Mwanasali in this volume).

The principle of "responsibility to protect" disadvantaged populations within state borders (including internally displaced persons), though by no means new, has been more assertively advocated over the last decade. The crisis of internal displacement on the international scene that emerged in the late 1980s made necessary some response by the international community. During the Cold War, most domestic and regional conflicts around the world were perceived as part of the confrontation between the two superpowers: the US and the Soviet Union. Internal or regional crises were managed through the bi-polar control mechanisms of the superpowers, who provided effective support to their less capable ideological allies. The outcome of this system was such that domestic crises such as internal displacement were often not visible to the outside world.

With the end of the Cold War and the demise of the superpowers' strategic concerns, these conflicts began to be seen in their proper national or regional contexts. Except for essential humanitarian assistance, the support of the major powers disappeared, leaving former superpower allies with diminished capacity to manage conflicts and to respond to the humanitarian consequences of these wars. Worse, the post-Cold War era witnessed the proliferation of internal conflicts which have tended to target women, children and the elderly. Indeed, the overwhelming majority of those internally-displaced globally are women and children. Without external support either in the management of conflicts or in addressing their humanitarian consequences, governments were confronted with mounting crises that they could scarcely manage. In 1982, there were 1.2 million internally displaced persons recorded worldwide.[7] Today, as noted earlier, this figure has risen to about 25 million.[8]

Concomitantly, human rights and humanitarian concerns began to replace strategic national interest as norms in international politics. Human rights, humanitarian, and developmental organisations also began to intensify their activities as watchdogs over the extent to which these universal standards were adhered to within national borders. To enhance their capacities, non-governmental organisations (NGOs) began to receive additional support for their new responsibilities of meeting humanitarian needs, since the international donor community increasingly saw them as more transparent and credible than governments. In light of these developments, the observance of sovereignty as a barrier to international scrutiny came under increasing pressure. The international media began to focus attention on the human tragedies within state borders and exposed the plight of millions who fell prey to the new types of wars being fought internally. It was under these circumstances that the crisis of internal displacement became evident on the international scene.

International Response to Crises

In 1992, in response to the growing phenomenon of internal displacement, the United Nations Commission on Human Rights decided to put the issue on its agenda and requested the then UN Secretary-General, Boutros Boutros-Ghali, to appoint a Representative on Internally Displaced Persons. I was appointed to this mandate.

A fundamental guiding principle in my approach to governments was to recognise that internal displacement is inherently sensitive, since it touches on matters of national sovereignty. Because of this sensitivity, this issue requires a unique approach that is significantly different from the usual human rights mechanisms of the UN system. In my experience, it does not help IDPs to confront governments through an adversarial promotion of human rights. This is not to say that there is no room for an adversarial role on human rights issues; instead, while making use of the information available from various monitoring sources, including NGOs and human rights advocates, a constructive and cooperative dialogue with the authorities often promises better results.

Given the sensitivity of the issue of internal displacement, I began to focus the work of my mandate on the need to balance conventional notions of sovereignty and invoking the responsibility of the state to provide for the protection and general welfare of citizens and all those under state jurisdiction, if necessary with the complementary support of the international community.[9] In my own opinion, this approach has proved to be most effective in dialogue with governments. Of the 30 missions I have undertaken around the world, no government authority has ever argued, "I don't care how irresponsible or irresponsive we are, this is an internal matter and none of your business".

Another guiding principle in this work is that the problem of IDPs affects the entire UN system and the international community at large, linking human rights, humanitarian, development and security issues. Therefore, although the mandate on IDPs was created by the Commission on Human Rights under the Special Procedures Mechanism, we have operated across all UN agencies and the wider international community in collaboration with humanitarian, human rights and development organisations – governmental and non-governmental. Sometimes, this mandate is even more closely identified with the UN's Office for the Coordination of Humanitarian Affairs (OCHA) and other humanitarian agencies instead of with the UN's Office of the High Commissioner for Human Rights (OHCHR). This means broadening the scope of inter-agency cooperation. In addition, I have from the start found it appropriate not to limit my scope of operations to the UN system. We therefore developed an approach that keeps one foot within the UN system and another foot outside the system. This approach has been carried out through the Washington DC-based Brookings–School of Advanced International Studies (SAIS) Project on Internal Displacement, which I co-direct with Roberta Cohen, a Senior Fellow at the Brookings Institution.

This arrangement affords us the opportunity, in a sense, to divide roles. There are certain things one can do more effectively within the UN system; and there are things better done outside the system. Our work has, of course, been defined by various resolutions of the Commission on Human Rights and the UN General Assembly, but we have also interacted with the drafters of the resolutions, so that over the years the pillars of the mandate have tended to increase with the kind of work we do, and with our reports to the Commission on Human Rights and the General Assembly. Initially, this work focused on four key pillars: developing and promoting a normative framework, developing improved institutional arrangements, undertaking country missions and conducting research on the causes and consequences of internal displacement. Since then, the reports of the mandate and the project have tended to specify awareness-raising, placing this issue among the four pillars. In addition, helping to build the capacity of regional, national and local partners – particularly civil society – has been added to the list of priorities.

Raising consciousness about the problem of IDPs is a function of an advocacy strategy that can be pursued through a wide variety of approaches including reports to UN bodies, scholarly and popular publications, speeches, seminars, workshops and conferences, as well as direct dialogue with governments, non-state actors, and all those concerned with the problems of internal displacement. Much progress has been made in raising awareness as a result. When we started 14 years ago, if one spoke of IDPs, almost certainly one would have had to explain what one meant. Today, not only would most people in the international community recognise IDPs, virtually all governments now also recognise this as a legitimate area for international concern.

Developing what was initially defined by the UN Commission and the General Assembly as an "appropriate framework" has resulted in the Guiding Principles on Internal Displacement, based on existing standards in human rights law, humanitarian law and analogous refugee law.[10] We decided that, instead of considering the Guiding Principles as a legal document and giving it a binding status, we would simply restate the fundamental principles, making them persuasive rather than binding, and therefore potentially threatening and controversial. In a sense then, the framework we adopted was in line with the persuasive approach underlying constructive dialogue with governments and all pertinent actors.

Even though they are based on existing law, the Guiding Principles were initially considered very sensitive when first presented to the UN Commission on Human Rights in 1998. For this reason, we did not ask that they be "adopted" by that body, but rather that it "take note" of them, and also that it note my plans to use them in dialogue with states and other actors. Even before their formal submission to the Commission, the Inter-Agency Standing Committee (IASC) – comprised of the heads of the operational agencies of the UN system, the International Committee of the Red Cross (ICRC), the International Organisation for Migration (IOM), and representatives of non-governmental organisations – endorsed the Guiding Principles and decided to bring them to the attention of their governing bodies and field staff to guide them in their work. The Commission also took note of the action taken by the IASC. In subsequent years, the Commission and the UN General Assembly have gradually grown more supportive in their descriptions of the Principles. In their 2003 resolutions, both bodies "express[ed] appreciation of the Guiding Principles on Internal Displacement as an important tool for dealing with situations of internal displacement" and "encourage[d] all relevant actors to make use of the guiding principles when dealing with situations of internal displacement".[11]

These resolutions also "welcome[d] the fact that an increasing number of states, United Nations agencies, and regional and non-governmental organisations are applying them as a standard".[12] Indeed, the growth in acceptance of the Guiding Principles at all of these levels in the last five years has been remarkable. Supportive resolutions and decisions have been adopted by the Organisation of African Unity (OAU) – now the African Union (AU), the Commission on Refugees, the Commonwealth, the Economic Community of West African States (ECOWAS), the Intergovernmental Authority on Development (IGAD), the Inter-American Commission on Human Rights, the Organisation for Security and Cooperation in Europe (OSCE) and the Council of Europe's Parliamentary Assembly. A number of governments have adopted policies and/or laws based, at least in part, upon the Guiding Principles, and several other states such as Uganda and Mexico, are currently considering plans to follow suit. Even some non-state actors have begun to make active use of them. United Nations agencies, non-governmental organisations, local civil society representatives, and internally displaced persons themselves around the world are making increasing use of the Guiding Principles in their own programmes and in advocacy with governments for better conditions for the internally displaced. It is particularly significant that the principles have been a source of empowerment to the internally displaced who are now able to demand their rights rather than see themselves as recipients of humanitarian favours.

In parallel with the development and promotion of a normative framework for internal displacement, the international community has become more active and coherent in its own operational or institutional response to internal displacement over the last decade. However, much progress remains to be made.

Early in the work of the mandate, I identified three options for solving this "mandate gap" for internally displaced persons: first, the creation of a new agency focused on internally displaced persons; second, the designation of an existing agency (such as the UNHCR) to assume responsibility for them; or third, collaboration among all relevant agencies. The third option has been favoured over the last decade, and institutions and policies have been put in place to enhance its potential.

In 1990, the UN General Assembly assigned "Resident Coordinators" (who are UN officials otherwise charged with coordination of development activities) the responsibility for coordinating assistance to IDPs in the field. In 1991, the General Assembly created the post of Emergency Relief Coordinator (ERC) at the level of Under-Secretary-General to coordinate the system-wide response to emergency situations. The following year, the General Assembly established the Inter-Agency Standing Committee in which all the major humanitarian and development agencies and organisations and NGO umbrella groups participate. As part of UN Secretary-General Kofi Annan's reform programme in 1997, the ERC was formally entrusted with overall responsibility for the coordination of assistance and protection of IDPs, and the post of "Humanitarian Coordinator" was created (and frequently delegated as a second "hat" to Resident Coordinators) and assigned the task of ensuring coordination for IDPs at the country level.

At UN Headquarter-level in New York, a senior Inter-Agency Standing Committee on Internal Displacement was formed with the support of a Working Group to facilitate inter-agency cooperation on the issue and, in 2002, a dedicated "IDP Unit" was created within the Office for the Coordination of Humanitarian Affairs to assist the ERC in his duties with regard to IDPs. The IASC also remained engaged, generating policy and guidance for field collaboration such as the 2000 Policy Paper on the Protection of Internally Displaced Persons, which carefully laid out the responsibilities of UN agencies and their partners in the field.[13] Moreover, other human rights organs of the United Nations – including the bodies that interpret the major human rights treaties and a number of human rights rapporteurs, experts and working groups – have increasingly addressed issues of IDPs as relevant to their various mandates.

Country missions are another area where the work of the IDP mandate has focused. These missions are the litmus test of what is being achieved on behalf of the internally displaced. Statistics become human faces, and one witnesses the protection and assistance needs of displaced populations. Dialogue with governments comes into focus and is often quite gratifying. Of all the missions that I have undertaken, in nearly all cases, the results have been positive. In some instances, we have found that as governments begin to change their policies and as dialogue begins to produce results, humanitarian and development agencies which are often fearful of internal displacement as an area that touches on the sensitive issue of sovereignty, tend to lag behind the changing policy environment. However, performance in this regard is improving. I am finding increasingly that UN agencies on the ground are responding faster to the opportunities of changing policies. This is further evidence that the international community is becoming progressively more alert to the problems of internal displacement.

There are, of course, difficult countries; either because they are in denial of the problem of IDPs or simply because they are jealously guarding their narrow view of sovereignty. It took me a number of years to secure invitations from some countries, but once I was invited and undertook the missions, dialogue with the authorities was constructive and the outcome often positive. The challenge confronting me then was to move the operational agencies to catch up with the positive developments on the ground and to cooperate with governments in responding to the needs of the internally displaced. And then there are problems of the implementation of recommendations. Sometimes we believe positive feedback on implementation, but quite often there is a gap between the encouraging results of missions and the level of implementation and follow-up activities. This, I fear, is quite common to all human rights mechanisms. Nevertheless, the fact that governments initially respond positively to the recommendations of the missions means that there is common ground for on-going dialogue to bridge the gap of understanding with governments and the level of implementation.

Through the Brookings–SAIS Project on Internal Displacement, we have also conducted studies in this area. Among these was the request by the then UN Secretary-General, Boutros Boutros-Ghali, in 1994, for me to carry out research on internal displacement in an independent institution to address such questions as what displacement is, how many people are affected, where they are, who is meeting their needs, what gaps exist, and how these gaps can be bridged, including by mobilising not only the UN system but also other intergovernmental and non-governmental organisations. Since then, we have produced volumes on various aspects of internal displacement.[14] We have also recently began to probe into more difficult and controversial issues such as the role of peacekeepers in protecting IDPs; measuring national responsibility; dealing with non-state actors; voting rights; access to education; property rights; criteria for when displacement ends; development-induced displacement; and efforts to develop a more comprehensive protection regime for IDPs and refugees. It is important to stress that these are policy-oriented studies whose findings are capable of practical application in the field.

An important aspect of what we have found in our work so far is the linkage of various levels of action. When we remember that the problem is inherently internal, then the distance between global concerns and local conditions becomes obvious. Working through regional organisations and local communities down to the ground level is critical. For example, the Brookings–SAIS project has worked with the Consortium of Humanitarian Agencies (CHA), based in Sri Lanka, to develop a tool kit and a practitioner's kit on return and resettlement for use in work with IDPs at the local level by governments and non-state actors. The project not only conducts and commissions research on various aspects of the problems of internal displacement, but also organises seminars at the national and regional levels, and cooperates with community leaders, research institutions, academics and other experts globally. In addition, the project has assisted the work of the mandate in forging cooperation with regional organisations.

Recent Developments in Response to Crises

During the 2004 session of the UN Commission on Human Rights, the delegation of Austria introduced a resolution to end the IDP mandate of the Commission on Human Rights, and called on the UN Secretary-General to establish a new mechanism to mainstream the human rights of internally displaced persons into the humanitarian and development activities of the UN system. The resolution was adopted by consensus.

The need to create a new mechanism while building on the achievements of the Commission's mandate will mean making use of the six pillars that have guided our work as well as strengthening and sharpening them in various ways. Future work should, however, emphasise that the responsibility for addressing the needs of the internally displaced is first and foremost that of national authorities. The role of the international community is to render complementary protection and assistance to those in need and to hold governments accountable in the discharge of their national responsibilities. This is the essence of "sovereignty as responsibility" which I have consistently advocated and which has been enhanced and mainstreamed by the report of the Canadian-sponsored Commission on Intervention and State Sovereignty of 2001.[15] This principle needs to be more forcefully reaffirmed, particularly through intensified dialogue with governments and increased monitoring and advocacy, to focus attention on the national context as the first layer of apportioned responsibility.

Since the consequences of the conflicts and the human rights violations that generate displacement often spill over national borders and create a flow of refugees, the immediate neighbours in a region, whether or not they are organised into a sub-regional association, share a mutual concern about developments within their common border, and should therefore logically form the second layer of joint responsibility. In other words, they should be their brothers' and sisters' keepers. This regional approach should be given added emphasis.

The third layer of responsibility is the international community as the custodian and protector of universal human rights and humanitarian standards, with the capacity to uphold and enforce the principles they embody. While the international community is now seized with its responsibility to the internally displaced and, especially in recent years, has undertaken a number of important steps to fulfil it, more focused attention is still needed to ensure a comprehensive and effective international response to crises, especially with regard to protection. It will also be necessary to increase reporting on specific situations to support accountability measures at all levels of responsibility.

These three layers do not envisage monolithic organisational structures or modes of operation, but a multiplicity of actors. Even within a state, a wide variety of actors are involved beyond the government, including national human rights bodies, non-state actors, NGOs and external actors with internal mandates and operational activities. Likewise, there are also multiple regional actors. Of course, the international community is inherently diverse. There is a need to link these layers so that they are not viewed in isolation, whether with respect to causes and consequences, or required responses. Indeed, analytically, it is through observing the impact of internal displacement across national borders in creating refugees and asylum seekers that the ultimate mutuality of interests can be demonstrated.

The principle of sovereignty will continue to provide a powerful basis for dialogue. The real question is how the international community can reinforce, strengthen and make effective the application of the principle, building on the national, regional and international apportionment of responsibility. With respect to IDPs, the question is whether governments, in partnership with the international community, are effectively and comprehensively addressing the crisis of internal displacement and meeting the needs of affected populations. There is clearly still a major gap between what "ought" to be and what "is".

The challenge that postulating "sovereignty as responsibility" poses for the international community is that it implies accountability.

Obviously, the internally displaced themselves – marginalised, excluded and often persecuted – have little capacity to hold their national authorities accountable. Only the international community – including sub-regional, regional and international organisations – has the power to persuade governments and other concerned actors to discharge their responsibility or otherwise fill the vacuum of irresponsive sovereignty. However, increasingly, rather than being passive recipients of humanitarian assistance, IDPs are beginning to assert their rights as citizens. In fact, as a result of democratic progress around the world, citizens are holding their governments responsible for respecting human rights. Often, the fact is that governments of affected countries, even if they wanted to discharge the responsibility of assisting and protecting their needy populations, lack the resources and the capacity to do so. No government worthy of the title can request material assistance from the outside world and reject concern with the human rights of the people on whose behalf it requests such assistance.

Ambivalence and Dilemmas of State Failure and Foreign Humanitarian Intervention

When a state fails to meet the basic needs of its population, and the international community is called upon to fill the vacuum, a range of ambivalence and dilemmas are set in motion that need to be carefully managed, or interventions are bound to be, at best, controversial. For example, evaluations of the drought-related relief operations and "Operation Lifeline Sudan", conducted by independent researchers in the 1980s, revealed four sets of dilemmas resulting from these interventions, from which both the international community and the recipient countries have much to learn.[16]

The first dilemma relates directly to the reality that the government has failed and needs foreign assistance. This in itself creates a situation injurious to national pride, particularly on the part of those who are not directly affected by the famine – the urban population, the intellectuals and the middle-class. In the case of the Sudanese operations, one professor spoke with outrage, "We should have been left alone". The number of relief workers who were operating in the country, representing governmental organisations and NGOs, was overwhelming: it was like an invasion. Humanitarian help had turned into humiliation. The presence of these humanitarian interveners was greatly resented, at least by the urban population or more precisely the middle-class. Considering that these relief workers were living much better than even the country's well-established middle-class, it is easy to understand the local response.

The failure of the government in Khartoum to discharge its responsibility to its citizens which led to this external involvement, created ambivalent feelings of needing help and resenting such help at the same time. Foreign donors and relief workers were equally outraged; they had come to help because the country had failed to provide for its citizens and yet they were regarded as intruders and treated with hostility. Feelings ran high on both sides.

The second source of dilemma and ambivalence has to do with the limited degree to which external assistance makes use of the country's existing structures, institutions, resources, and the resourcefulness of local populations. In the case of Sudan, the external assumption was that the Sudanese were incapable of managing their own problems; the emergency operations were not seen as an exercise aimed at enhancing the future emergency management capacity of the country. There were individuals on both sides who disapproved of this approach, but that was the operating assumption.

Third, in most serious emergencies literally hundreds of NGOs want to be involved and to operate independently or autonomously, even when they recognise the necessity of coordination. Quite apart from not wanting to be coordinated by local government officials as a matter of principle, the NGOs suspect coordination to be an undesirable impediment to their work since speed and results are the objectives of their operations.

Fourth, emergency operations tend to be externally focused, in that logistics, management and accountability are controlled through foreign authorities with a limited role for national actors. Observers in the Sudan case wondered in the end whether what had been done had ultimately strengthened or weakened the nation's capacity to respond to future emergencies. Some experts argued that, while lives had been saved, relief operations had also been a source of weakness since they encouraged long-term dependence on the part of those receiving assistance.

Does this argue against external assistance? Of course not. What it means however, is that prevention, as the old saying goes, is better than cure. Putting one's house in order is the best way of protecting one's sovereignty. During emergency operations, all sides must realise the complexities and dilemmas involved and work hard to provide needed relief while minimising its negative consequences.

Africans are increasingly being told by the international community that, given the scarcity of resources in the world and the tendency toward isolationism on the part of rich western countries, they will have to rely primarily on themselves and that whatever help they can expect from the outside world will be targeted selectively. This limited assistance will naturally be motivated by the values of those who are coming to help. Accordingly, the degree to which a country values human rights, humanitarianism, democracy and the market economy will determine the degree to which it receives external support. However, this promise, too, poses a paradox since the cases of greatest humanitarian need are often those in which national governments are neglectful of their population. Africans are responding to this challenge not only because they are being told by outsiders to shape up, but also because they have begun to scrutinise their own performance and are sharpening their own sense of responsibility, especially in the areas of conflict prevention, management and resolution.

Recent developments that are noteworthy are the Conference on Security, Stability, Development and Cooperation in Africa (CSSDCA), the New Partnership for Africa's Development (NEPAD), and the AU, which has transformed the OAU into an organisational framework that embraces the various initiatives that postulate an even more ambitious vision for Africa. There is a tendency to see the AU as a mere change of name from the OAU, but the AU, both conceptually and normatively, stipulates and promises a more robust response to crises on the continent, especially in conflict management. It is noteworthy that while the classic principles of respect for sovereignty, territorial integrity and non-interference in the internal affairs of other states are still upheld, the AU principles provide for a more assertive role in preventing, managing and resolving internal conflicts and promoting democracy, human rights and fundamental freedoms. (See Mwanasali in this volume). It is also significant that the CSSDCA, NEPAD and the AU have much in common, not only because of their commitment to the fundamental norms of security, democracy, human rights and responsible economic and financial management, but also in terms of mechanisms for peer review, scrutiny and correction.

It should be reiterated that while these initiatives are still largely prescriptive, they indicate incremental progress in the response of African governments to the plight of their people. The magnitude of this plight and the need for Africans to assume responsibility was dramatically demonstrated by the genocide in Rwanda in 1994 in which an estimated one million people were killed. (See Anyidoho in this volume). The United Nations withdrew at precisely the time of the country's greatest need for humanitarian intervention in the face of genocide, and then, as though to compensate for this gross failure to meet an urgent humanitarian challenge, the international community returned with a massive emergency assistance programme, especially for refugees and internally displaced populations, costing hundreds of millions of dollars.[17] What was particularly striking was that humanitarian operations were being conspicuously conducted by expatriates, well equipped with vehicles, communications systems and other supplies in an atmosphere in which the newly established Rwandan government lacked the basic needs – authority, infrastructure and resources – for running a state. The inevitable outcome was that the Rwandan government responded ambivalently to international humanitarian operations to a degree that began to threaten the continuation of relief assistance programmes – a scenario reminiscent of the Sudanese experience of the mid-1980s.

Concluding Thoughts: Opportunity in Crises

This chapter has argued that state failure is relative and that, in terms of ensuring peace, stability and welfare for all citizens, a degree of failure is common. Where countries suffer from internal conflicts, rampant communal violence and human rights violations, a heightened degree of state failure becomes evident. Whatever the degree of failure, governments often lack the capacity to provide adequate protection and assistance to all their citizens. In many cases, the response to the needs of the affected population becomes selective. In a divided country, some groups are favoured, while others are discriminated against, grossly neglected and perhaps even persecuted. International human rights and humanitarian standards as well as global solidarity call for international humanitarian intervention on behalf of the affected population, ranging from diplomatic intercession to varying degrees of pressure, which might culminate in military action in extreme cases.

This chapter has also focused on the internally displaced as an example of a particularly vulnerable group which nevertheless represents a microcosm of the wider population affected by conflict, communal violence and human rights violations. In my capacity as Special Representative of the UN Secretary-General on IDPs between 1992 and 2004, I have always stressed the need to see crises as offering opportunities for remedial action by addressing the root causes of conflicts. Displacement is only a symptom of the causes reflected mostly in conflicts and human rights violations, which are themselves symptoms of deep-rooted problems. These are characterised by acute disparities or inequalities in the shaping and sharing of power, national wealth, public services and development opportunities. Discrimination on the basis of race, ethnicity, religion, culture or gender means that there are those who are "in," enjoying the dignity of full citizenship, and those who are "out," marginalised to the point of virtual statelessness.[18] Unless these inequities are firmly addressed, the countries plagued by these ills will have difficulty achieving peace, security, stability and development.

Internal displacement challenges the international community with the need to develop ways of preventing the arbitrary displacement of populations, to respond to the protection and assistance needs of those already displaced, and to find durable solutions in the form of safe return with dignity, alternative resettlement, and social reintegration and development. Whatever the degree of state failure, it challenges the state – if need be with the support of the international community – to create conditions for peace, security, stability and the general welfare of its people. This would, in turn, prevent or discourage further conflict, human rights violations, and resulting displacement. In other words, internal displacement is not only a humanitarian and human rights crisis; it is also a political and security issue – a challenge to nationhood and international solidarity with those dispossessed within their own countries, requiring cooperation with governments to discharge the responsibilities of sovereignty.

Notes

1 See Zartman, I W: *Collapsed States: The Disintegration and Restoration of Legitimate Authority* (Washington, DC: Lynne Rienner, 1995).

2 This chapter builds on other works by the author that have appeared elsewhere. These include, Deng, F: "Sovereignty and Humanitarian Responsibility: A Challenge for NGOs in Africa and the Sudan" in Rotberg, R. I: (ed.): *Vigilance and Vengeance, NGOs Preventing Ethnic Conflict in Divided Societies* (Brookings: The World Peace Foundation, 1996); Cahill, K (ed.): "Trapped within Hostile Borders: The Plight of Internally Displaced Persons" (Forthcoming: Fordham University Press); and "The Plight of the Internally Displaced: A Challenge to the International Community," United Nations High Level Panel on Global Security, March 2004, http://www.un-globalsecurity.org/pdf/deng.pdf (accessed 12 March 2006).

3 *The Guiding Principles on Internal Displacement* (New York: OCHA, 2000) defines internally displaced persons as "persons or groups of persons who have been forced or obliged to flee or to leave their homes or places of habitual residence, in particular as a result of or in order to avoid the effects of armed conflict, situations of generalised violence, violations of human rights or natural or human-made disasters, and who have not crossed an internationally recognised state border."

4 See Cohen, R & Deng, F: *Masses in Flight: The Global Crisis of Internal Displacement* (Washington, DC: Brookings, 1998), pp. 23–29; see also United Nations High Commissioner for Refugees: *The State of the World's Refugees* (UNHCR, 1998), pp. 112–15; and World Health Organisation, *Internally Displaced Persons: Health and WHO*, paper presented at the humanitarian affairs segment of the substantive session of the ECOSOC, 2000, p. 5.

5 See Deng, F: "Identity in Africa's Conflicts" in *American Behavioural Scientist*, 40, 1, September 1996, pp. 46–65; "War of Visions for the Nation" in Voll, J (ed.): *Sudan, State and Society in Crisis* (Bloomington: Indiana University Press, 1991); "Identity Factor in the Sudanese Conflict" in *Conflict in Multi-Ethnic Societies* (Foreign Service Institute, 1989); Deng, F: "Negotiating a Hidden Agenda: Sudan's Conflict of Identities" in Zartman, W (ed.): *Elusive Peace: Negotiating an End to Civil Wars,* (Washington DC: Brookings, 1995).

6 See Deng, F: "Ethnic Marginalisation as Statelessness: Lessons from the Great Lakes Region of Africa" in Aleinikoff, T. & Klusmeyer, D (eds.): *Citizenship Today: Global Perspectives and Practices* (Washington, DC: The Carnegie Endowment for International Peace, 2001), pp. 183–208.

7 Cohen, R & Deng, F (eds.): *The Forsaken People: Case Studies of the Internally Displaced* (Washington, DC: Brookings Institution Press, 1998), p.1.

8 The Norwegian Refugee Council: "Internal Displacement: A Global Overview of Trends in 2003" in *Global IDP Project* (February 2004), p.26.

9 For my various contributions to the normative theme of the responsibility of sovereignty, see the following books, chapters, and articles: *African Reckoning: A Quest for Good Governance,* (ed.), with Lyons, T (Washington, DC: Brookings Institution Press, 1998); Rotberg, *Supra* note 2, *Sovereignty as Responsibility: Conflict Management in Africa*, co-authored with Kimaro S, Lyons T, Rothchild D, & Zartman I W, (Washington, DC: Brookings Institution Press, 1996); "Reconciling Sovereignty with Responsibility: A Basis for International Humanitarian Action" in Harbeson, J & Rothchild, D (eds.): *Africa in World Politics* (Boulder, Colorado: Westview, 1995); and "Frontiers of Sovereignty: A Framework of Protection, Assistance and Development for the Internally Displaced" in the *Leiden Journal of International Law*, vol. 8, no. 2, 1995.

10 See Kälin, W: *Guiding Principles on Internal Displacement: Annotations* (Washington, DC: American Society of International Law & The Brookings Institution Project on International Displacement, 2000); Kälin, W: *The Handbook For Applying the Guiding Principles on Internal Displacement* (Washington, DC: The Brookings Institution Project on Internal Displacement

and OCHA, 1999); Kälin, W: *Recent Commentaries about the Nature and Application of the Guiding Principles on Internal Displacement* (Washington DC: The Brookings-CUNY Project on Internal Displacement, 2002).

[11] UN DOC:E/CN.4/RES/2003/51http://ap.ohchr.org/documents/E/CHR/resolutions/ E-CN_4-RES-2003-51.doc and at http://www.unhchr.ch/Huridocda/Huridoca.nsf/0/ ad204056757dc5f8c1256d20002da65f (accessed 20 February 2006).

[12] ibid.

[13] Inter-Agency Standing Committee: *Policy Paper Series No. 2* (United Nations: New York, 2000).

[14] See for example, Mishra, O (ed.): *Forced Migration in the South Asian Region* (Manak, Dehli: Centre for Refugee Studies, Brookings-SAIS Project on Internal Displacement, 2004); *Guiding Principles on Internal Displacement and the Law of the South Caucasus, Georgia, Armenia and Azerbaijan,* jointly published with the American Society of International Law (ASIL), the Organisation for Security and Cooperation in Europe (OSCE) and the Georgian Young Lawyers Association (GYLA) (Washington, DC: 2003); Korn, D A: *Exodus within Borders: An Introduction to the Crisis of Internal Displacement* (Washington, DC: Brookings Institution Press, 1999); Cohen, R & Deng, F: *The Forsaken People: Case Studies of the Internally Displaced* (Washington, DC: Brookings Institution Press, 1998); Deng, F: *Protecting the Dispossessed: A Challenge for the International Community* (Washington, DC: Brookings Institution Press, 1993).

[15] *The Responsibility to Protect: Report of the International Commission on Intervention and State Sovereignty* (Ottawa: International Development Research Center, 2001).

[16] For an appraisal of these emergency operations, see Deng, F & Minear, L: *Challenges of Famine Relief* (Washington, DC: Brookings Institution Press, 1992).

[17] "The Endless Wait for Justice" in *World Press Review* (March 1995), p.12. In this article, Shahryar Khan, the UN Secretary-General's special representative in Kigali, is reported as saying: "The world has spent $700 million on emergency aid to Rwanda – milk, power and jerry-cans. By contrast, the Justice Ministry has received two payments – $27,000 from the Germans and $1 million from the Belgians – and two typewriters."

[18] Cohen, R & Deng, F: *The Forsaken People: Case Studies of the Internally Displaced* (Washington, DC: Brookings Institution Press, 1998); Deng, F: *Protecting the Dispossessed: A Challenge for the International Community,* (Washington, DC: Brookings Institution Press, 1993), *supra* note 6.

7

The UN Human Rights Council: From Rights to Responsibility?

Helen Scanlon

> If the United Nations is to meet the expectations of men and women everywhere – and indeed, if the Organisation is to take the cause of human rights as seriously as those of security and development – then Member States should agree to replace the Commission on Human Rights with a smaller standing Human Rights Council.
>
> *Kofi Annan, 2005*[1]

The UN and Human Rights

THE ESTABLISHMENT OF the United Nations Human Rights Council in March 2006 to replace the discredited Human Rights Commission has been hailed by international human rights groups and many pundits as a landmark development. While the protection of human rights, alongside peace and security, is one of the three pillars of the UN's mandate, this goal has generally been deemed to be one of failure and inaction by the organisation in the last 60 years. Emanating from UN Secretary-General Kofi Annan's call for the replacement of the Commission in his March 2005 report *In Larger Freedom*, the creation of an autonomous and efficient international human rights instrument could potentially bring an end to international impunity for human rights abuses, as well as encourage the greater recognition of human rights standards internationally. Although this represents one of the few significant outcomes of Annan's 2005 drive for UN reform, the ability of the Human Rights Council to be insulated from the politicisation that occurred with its predecessor remains uncertain. The new body will suffer from the same inherent limitations of the old organisation as an association of sovereign governments in which the political and security agendas of western governments are generally deemed as paramount. (See Jonah in this volume). The Council also faces the question of how it will define human rights concerns unanimously and whether it will acknowledge development as intrinsic to the support of human rights in many parts of the world.

This chapter seeks to explore the creation of the Human Rights Council within the context of the growth of human rights concerns by the United Nations since its inception, as well as the relevance of these developments for Africa. It seeks to examine some of the failures of the Council's predecessor – the Human Rights Commission – and the reasons for its politicisation; what its recent metamorphosis can potentially offer to Africa; and to provide an analysis of the need for human rights institutions in Africa. The significance of the protection of human rights for Africa's long-term security and development has been gaining widespread recognition since the 1994 Rwandan genocide. (See Anyidoho in this volume). Increasingly, Africa's national and intergovernmental institutions are taking up human rights issues as essential to development concerns. As a result, the mandate and powers of the Human Rights Council must be an urgent priority for key actors on the continent.

Global Human Rights Initiatives

Among the UN's founding fathers' declared set of goals was the commitment that:

> We the peoples of the United Nations determined to save succeeding generations from the scourge of war…[pledge] to reaffirm faith in fundamental human rights, in the dignity and worth of the human person, in the equal rights of men and women and of nations large and small, and to promote social progress and better standards of life in larger freedom.[2]

In order to uphold the commitments of the UN Charter, the

Commission on Human Rights was created in 1946 by the UN Economic and Social Council (ECOSOC) – a subsidiary body of the General Assembly – to "examine, monitor and report" on human rights issues in member states and to establish legal norms to protect human rights and freedoms worldwide. The Commission's mandate included: "promoting respect for human rights globally, fostering international cooperation in human rights, responding to violations in specific countries and assisting countries in building their human rights capacity".[3] The body subsequently developed into a forum in which states and civil society could express concerns over human rights issues in specific countries. As the primary human rights body in the UN system, the Commission on Human Rights was tasked with holding "public meetings to review the human rights performance of states, to adopt new standards and to promote human rights around the world".[4] The work of the Commission was supported by the sub-Commission on the Promotion and Protection of Human Rights, as well as through the engagement of individual experts, representatives and special rapporteurs who investigated allegations of human rights abuses.

However, when it was created, the Commission had no real power to respond to complaints relating to human rights violations. As Human Rights Watch's Kenneth Roth has noted, initially the Commission "didn't do much of anything. Because it never condemned governments, it didn't matter much and therefore was largely ignored".[5] This situation was slightly improved by two amendments made to the Commission's mandate by ECOSOC. Resolution 1235 of 1967 permitted the Commission to investigate situations of gross human rights violations which were brought to its attention, while Resolution 1503 of 1970 instituted a system for investigating complaints that "appear to reveal a consistent pattern of gross and reliably attested violations of human rights".[6] The process was confidential, however, and thus not accessible to concerned human rights activists. It was also limited due to the criteria of "gross violations". This limitation was dramatically apparent in the case of Rwanda, which was discussed by the Commission under the 1503 procedure confidentially in 1992 and 1993. However it was not until seven weeks after the outbreak of the Rwandan genocide of 1994 that a special rapporteur was appointed to investigate human rights abuses.[7]

From 1946, ECOSOC held annual votes to elect the Commission's members – whose numbers grew from an initial 18 members to 53 by 2005 – to serve three-year terms. These members were proposed by the UN's five regional groups: Africa, Asia, western Europe and other states, Latin America and eastern Europe. There were no qualifications for membership, and members could serve unlimited consecutive terms. This has allowed Russia to continuously serve on the Commission from its foundation. The Commission met annually for six weeks every March and April in Geneva, Switzerland. Among the body's achievements was the development of a number of international human rights treaties such as the Universal Declaration on Human Rights of 1948, which remains the foundation of international standards for human rights. The Declaration was explicitly motivated to help prevent the future occurrence of atrocities such as the Nazi genocide against six million Jews during the Second World War by establishing international standards for human rights. Although member states of the UN had wide-ranging political systems and ideologies at that time, the Universal Declaration of Human Rights was said to represent a statement of aspirations for the protection of ordinary citizens globally. Despite the fact that, as a declaration, it is not a legally binding instrument, the Declaration is generally perceived to be part of international customary law. Each UN member state is currently a signatory of at least one of the seven major human rights treaties.[8] The Commission also prepared international standards over torture, "disappearances", executions and, according to the international non-governmental organisation (NGO) Human Rights Watch, made a significant impact in the protection of "the victims of the dictatorial regimes of Latin America".[9]

Since the Commission's creation, however, there have been enormous shifts in the world's political geography as well as in international perceptions of human rights. When the Universal Declaration of Human Rights was signed in 1948, racial segregation remained enshrined in the constitution of the United States, while Britain, France, Portugal and Belgium were still major colonial powers in Africa. The membership of the UN has since mushroomed from 51 members in 1945 to 192 by 2006, incorporating former African and Asian colonies as well as the successor states in central and eastern Europe. The development of human rights rhetoric to support the needs of various "minorities" have since been the result of the pressures and demands emanating "from below" – civil society and disaffected communities – instead of initiatives derived by the dominant powers within the UN system.[10] Political analyst, Timbaya Zeleza and others have argued that the phrasing of the Universal Declaration of Human Rights itself, while stating high principles, was loose enough to leave the matter of enforceability of human rights issues unresolved in order to protect the powers who created it from scrutiny of their own human rights abuses.

This disjuncture between policy and practice has been at play at the national level. Washington has been a constant denouncer of human rights violations in many countries, but was also instrumental in ensuring that the Universal Declaration on Human Rights was not binding. It has failed to ratify all major UN human rights treaties levied by the Commission and only in 1988 did the US finally sign the 1948 Genocide Convention. Similarly, it took America 28 years to ratify the 1966 Convention on the Elimination of all Forms of Racial Discrimination. This ratification was done with "reservations", thereby limiting its impact on US domestic law. America's approach to human rights has thus been described as a "kind of superpower rights narcissism".[11] (See Baregu in this volume).

In recent years, the UN's Human Rights Commission has faced increased criticism that certain countries have used membership of the organ to prevent scrutiny of their own human rights abuses and to block international action against them, provoking allegations that it was an "abuser's defence society".[12] In UN Secretary-General Kofi Annan's 2005 report *In Larger Freedom*, he argued that the Commission has been undermined by "declining credibility and professionalism".[13] Detractors of the body often cite the fact that 6 of the 53-member Commission on Human Rights in 2005 – China, Cuba, Eritrea, Saudi Arabia, Sudan and Zimbabwe – were considered to be among the world's "worst of the worst" abusers of human rights by the US-based Freedom House.[14] China has been accused of regularly defeating efforts to discuss its human rights record within the Commission. One of the structural defects of the body was perceived to be the ability of blocs of states to act together both to propose and to prevent action, which according to some analysts allowed members to vote on the basis of ideological solidarity instead of on human rights issues. This was clearly illustrated in 2005 when, on the one hand, African countries opposed the interrogation of Zimbabwe's human rights records, while on the other, the West blocked calls to investigate events at the US prison camp at Cuba's Guantánamo Bay.[15]

The Commission has thus come under mounting fire, particularly over the election of Libya as its chair in 2003, in what was deemed to have been part of the unofficial *quid pro quo* that Libya had negotiated with African members in return for financing the newly-created African Union. Of particular concern was the fact that in 2004, the Commission failed to take action against Sudan despite frequent reports of human rights abuses in the country's Darfur region. (See Anyidoho in this volume). Sudan was elected to the Commission for three years shortly after this, causing the US to walk out of the body. The reform of the Commission has consequently been considered to be a vital component in restoring the UN's damaged credibility during the recent drive for the reform of the organisation. While there have been a number of attempts within the Commission itself to reform its procedures and to broaden the definition of human rights, these have proved to be largely ineffective. The most recent bid for reform instigated by South Africa's Jacob Selebi in 1998, foundered due to the failure of the Commission's members to reach agreement.[16]

In its December 2004 report on UN reform, the High-level Panel on *Threats, Challenges and Change* voiced concerns that: "Standard-setting to reinforce human rights cannot be performed by States that lack a demonstrated commitment to their promotion and protection... The Commission cannot be credible if it is seen to be maintaining double standards in addressing human rights concerns".[17] As a result, the Panel recommended that the Commission be restructured to include all 191 UN member states in a bid to show that its commitment to the promotion of human rights bound all members. The report further suggested that all members of the Commission should designate prominent and experienced human rights figures as the heads of their delegations and that the body should prepare an annual report on the state of human rights worldwide.[18]

The subsequent March 2005 report *In Larger Freedom* by Kofi Annan, went further and urged the replacement of the Commission with a smaller, permanent Human Rights Council with stricter criteria for membership.[19] The UN Secretary-General noted that "states have sought membership of the Commission not to strengthen human rights but to protect themselves against criticism or to criticise others. As a result, a credibility deficit has developed, which casts a shadow on the reputation of the United Nations system as a whole".[20] Annan further argued that membership of a smaller Human Rights Council should be confined to those governments who abide by what he called "the highest human rights standards" and that the proposed Council should meet throughout the year and not for just six weeks like its predecessor.[21]

Support for a UN Human Rights Council?

At the 60th meeting of the UN General Assembly in September 2005, a diluted proposal for a new Human Rights Council was accepted. While a decision to create the Human Rights Council was made in theory, there was disagreement among states over the specifics of its functions, size, the criteria for membership and its status within the UN as a whole. The US Ambassador to the United Nations, John Bolton, vigorously opposed the body's creation and argued that Annan's proposal did not go far enough to keep what he described as "repressive states" off the Council. American officials demanded more assurances that states with poor human rights records would be excluded from the body and that the election of members to a smaller body should be done by a strict two-thirds majority vote in the General Assembly. Washington further argued that a Human Rights Council should be composed only of democracies and even demanded that all permanent members of the Security Council – including Russia and China – automatically receive seats: a position from which the administration later retreated. When asked for the reason for the United States' lack of support for Annan's recommendations during negotiations, Bolton declared, "We want a butterfly. We're not going to put lipstick on a caterpillar and declare it a success".[22]

The Group of 77 (G-77) – the group of developing countries within the UN – on the other hand, lobbied for measures eliminating tough membership criteria for the Council. Developing countries questioned less the size of the body but more what they saw as the hypocrisy applied to criteria for membership and the use of country-specific resolutions. A number of governments decried the fact that developing countries appeared to be the ones targeted by human rights resolutions and, as such, they felt that the Commission was subject to the application of double standards and politicisation. Governments from the south argued that those powerful countries who had most strongly argued for the creation of the

Human Rights Council had a specific target in mind, namely to exclude certain countries like Zimbabwe, Sudan and Libya from the Council. Fears were also voiced over the use of country-specific resolutions, which some member states argued were often used as a stick to beat opponents as a result of bilateral disputes with powerful countries rather than originating from a desire to uphold human rights. Further, countries such as the US were accused of posing qualifications for other countries for membership of the Council, while being guilty of human rights abuses themselves, for example in Iraq and at the US prison camp at Guantánamo Bay, Cuba.

The African Union reached a common position in response to Annan's report *In Larger Freedom* in Addis Ababa, Ethiopia in March 2005. The resultant Ezulwini Consensus argued that measures were necessary to address the selective nature and politicisation of the agenda of the Human Rights Commission and that any new body should pay equal attention to economic, social and cultural rights as to civil and political rights.[23] The Ezulwini Consensus also noted that the proposal to universalise the membership of the Commission on Human Rights was not tenable, especially since the body reported to ECOSOC, which itself had limited membership. AU members thus argued that the status quo on the composition and location of the Commission should be maintained. The African Group also argued vehemently that there should be no third consecutive term for members of the Council, with the aim of providing wider participation through rotation in order to prevent the domination of the body by certain member states.

UN member states did, however, agree that the Council "should address situations of violations of human rights, including gross and systematic violations and make recommendations"; they also agreed that the body should "promote effective coordination and the mainstreaming of human rights within the United Nations system".[24] After five months of wrangling, in March 2006 draft resolution A/60/L.48 was adopted by the UN General Assembly replacing the 53-member Human Rights Commission with a 47-member Human Rights Council. The resolution was adopted by a vote of 170 countries in favour, four against – the US, Israel, the Marshall Islands (population 59 000) and Palau (population 20 000) – and three abstentions.

The newly-created Human Rights Council is mandated to promote universal respect for the protection of human rights and to make recommendations in situations where those rights are violated. The Council also derives its authority from the United Nations but differs from the Commission in six significant details. First, the Council's institutional standing has been elevated to make it a subsidiary body of the General Assembly rather than of ECOSOC. Second, the Council awards its seats in accordance with equitable geographical distribution, and members are ineligible for re-election after two consecutive terms. Third, members of the new Human Rights Council, in contrast to the Commission, are to be elected by an absolute majority of the 192-member UN General Assembly – that is at least 97 members. Fourth, members of the new Council are to serve for three years and, diverging from its predecessor, the council will meet throughout the year and hold at least three sessions for a total duration of at least ten weeks with the option for one-third of the Council's members to request additional sessions "when needed".[25] This is to counter the frequent criticism that, when serious human rights situations arose in the past, it could take 11 months before there was a session of the Commission to address the issue. Fifth, a key difference from the Commission is a clause that requires members of the Council to undergo a review of their human rights records, which did not previously exist. Finally, the UN General Assembly can suspend any members of the Council committing "gross and systematic" human rights violations if agreed by a two-thirds majority.

The new membership criteria means that the size of the western group – which traditionally had a higher percentage of members – has been reduced, and there has been an increase in the percentage of members from the African and Asian regional groups. Asian and African states now form a majority of the Council with 26 seats, leaving the other regions with 21 seats thus better reflecting the geographical distribution of the world. Latin America now has eight seats; Africa has thirteen; Asia has thirteen; western Europe and other countries have six; and eastern Europe seven. The new rotation of states off the Council every two terms would mean the end of the dominance of countries such as the United States and Russia that have been almost permanent members of the Commission since 1946.

Africa and the UN Human Rights Council

The support of African states for the creation of the Human Rights

Council is indicative of the fact that many African governments – acting nationally and also collectively through the AU – are confronting what some observers have depicted as the "culture of impunity" that exists for those guilty of human rights abuses on the continent. (See Mwanasali and Deng in this volume). Since the birth of the UN, the evidence of the link between gross human rights violations and the emergence of conflicts has become increasingly apparent and this is of particular relevance to the continent. Through the AU, African heads of state have recently expressed their "determination to address the scourge of conflicts in Africa in a collective, comprehensive and decisive manner" as well as the need to address human rights violations on the continent in order to achieve this.[26]

Africa's human rights record has tended to mirror political developments on the continent.[27] The European colonial powers' repudiation of the human rights of Africans in the nineteenth and twentieth centuries proved critical in provoking demands for self-governance in the 1950s and 1960s. However during the Cold War era, many of the first wave of democratically elected post-colonial governments were substituted by one-party states and autocratic regimes under which the protection of human rights proved low on the list of priorities. White governments clinging to colonial rule in southern Africa further perpetuated flagrant human rights abuses. The failure of other leaders on the continent to react in circumstances of obvious human rights abuses by their neighbours was often condoned by the Organisation of African Unity's (OAU) promotion of "non-interference in the internal affairs of member states".[28] Although the African Charter on Human and Peoples' Rights was adopted by the OAU in 1981 enshrining the same principles as those in the UN's Universal Declaration of Human Rights, critics often dismissed the organisation as a "dictator's club" which failed to respect the human rights of citizens on the continent.[29] Nonetheless, events during the 1994 Rwandan genocide and the failure of the international community to intervene provoked calls for a more cohesive and systematic approach to human rights in Africa.

In the wave of democratisation across Africa in the 1990s, coupled with the overthrow of white minority rule in southern Africa, the importance of human rights for Africa's long-term security and development prompted changes in official understandings of, and approaches to, human rights. The proliferation of national and intergovernmental institutions reflected this new approach. The birth of the AU in Durban, South Africa in 2002 to replace the discredited OAU and the subsequent commitment to an African Peer Review Mechanism (APRM) – which over 23 AU governments have since subscribed to – shows an increasing willingness by many African governments to support human rights protections at the continental level. Unlike its predecessor's Charter, the AU's Constitutive Act of 2000 includes a number of provisions placing human rights firmly on the agenda of the organisation. Within the Act, it is stated that African leaders are "determined to promote and protect human and peoples' rights, consolidate democratic institutions and culture, and to ensure good governance and the rule of law".[30] Article 3(g) of the Act also notes that the "promotion and protection of human and peoples' rights in accordance with the African Charter on Human and Peoples' Rights and other relevant human rights instruments" is an objective of the Union. Other guiding principles of the AU have implications for the protection of human rights in Africa. These include the promotion of gender equality – the AU Commission has mandated a 50 per cent representation of women,[31] the endorsement of social justice and the support of "good governance" through the rejection of unconstitutional changes of government.

The AU's Constitutive Act has also made provision for the participation of civil society through structures such as the Pan-African Parliament (PAP) and the Economic, Social and Cultural Council (ECOSOCC), as well as the New Partnership for Africa's Development (NEPAD).[32] The hope is that the creation of these organs will promote the involvement of civil society in continental institutions and provide for the greater protection and monitoring of human rights. To augment these developments, the AU created the African Court on Human and Peoples' Rights in 2004, which analysts consider demonstrates its growing commitment towards advancing human rights. The Court enhances existing human rights institutions on a continent not generally recognised for the defence of the human rights of its citizens.[33]

There have also been some significant developments at the national level. In 2005, the number of national human rights commissions in Africa had grown in the previous 15 years from just 1 national agency to 24, with an additional two countries in the process of creating such commissions.[34]

The large number of these bodies illustrates the growing acceptance that human rights protection is the responsibility of national governments. However, while some national human rights commissions have been established in an effort to promote human rights, critics point to the fact that in many contexts, governments wishing to deflect international attention away from their human rights record have established these commissions.[35] In March 2006, for example, the Zimbabwean Human Rights Commission was created in the face of criticism of flagrant human rights violations within the country. Nonetheless, commissions established in Ghana, South Africa and Uganda, among others, have been praised by observers for their independence and their protection of the rights of their citizens.[36]

Despite these substantial advancements in Africa's human rights architecture, there still remains great uncertainty over the commitment to these principles by some governments. The current conflict in Sudan's Darfur region has resulted in an estimated 180 000 deaths since 2003 and the displacement of a further two million people from their homes.[37] (See Anyidoho and Deng in this volume). Nonetheless, the Khartoum government has so far not been called to account for the violence, nor its failure to protect its citizens. While the premise of finding local solutions to addressing human rights abuses in Africa is preferable to external solutions, there nevertheless remains a need to strengthen the role of the UN in promoting a culture of human rights on the continent. Since the tragedy of the Rwandan genocide in 1994, a more cohesive conflict management mechanism has been developed but in order to achieve the full protection of human rights in Africa, the new UN Human Rights Council must play a key role.

Concluding Thoughts

Following the adoption of the 2006 resolution establishing the Council, UN Secretary-General Kofi Annan noted: "Now the real work begins. The true test of the Council's credibility will be the use that member states make of it".[38] Prominent international NGOs such as Human Rights Watch and Amnesty International have backed the creation of the Human Rights Council, while twelve Nobel Peace laureates, including South Africa's Archbishop Desmond Tutu, have released a letter saying that they believe the proposed Council will be more responsive to human rights violations.[39] While the body has been hailed as a significant improvement on the Commission, others have slated the new Council as inadequate. Many human rights groups and governments supported the new Council on the grounds that it was better than the previous organ, or more bluntly, that it was better than none at all.

Some observers have reasoned that, since the Human Rights Council is being taken out of ECOSOC, there is a risk that the protection and promotion of social and economic rights will suffer and not be upheld by the new Council. Others have raised concerns that since Kofi Annan has levelled so much criticism at the Commission, it has lost all credibility and the Human Rights Council may be similarly tarnished.[40] Furthermore, some experts argue that the lack of a shared interpretation of human rights values by UN members will continue to thwart any attempt to reform the UN's human rights structures. Fundamental questions remain over the interpretation of the meaning of "human rights". (See Asmal in the volume). Since there exists no fixed definition of what constitutes "human rights" member states differ greatly over whether the traditional civil and political rights should be prioritised, or the more inclusive economic, social and cultural rights. Developing countries have called for the mandate of the Human Rights Council to accept all human rights as indivisible, in contrast to the tendency among richer members of the UN to emphasise civil and political rights. Many African governments have argued for the need to prioritise the right to development on the same basis as other political and economic rights in the mandate of the Council.[41] The US, however, opposed the proposal that the "right to development" be viewed as equal to the rights to peace and security as an "inalienable human right". Although Kofi Annan has stated that "Human rights are as fundamental to the poor as to the rich, and their protection is as important to the security and prosperity of the developed world as it is to that of the developing world", the level of this commitment in the light of the Washington Consensus and an inequitable global economic order is difficult to see.[42] (See Legum in this volume).

A further criticism levelled at the Council is that since members remain government representatives rather than independent individuals, the body remains at risk of the politicisation that occurred to its predecessor. After the Human Rights Commission's creation in 1946, its delegates tended to be key actors in the human rights arena and thus often had expertise in human rights work. However, this practice has lapsed and if not revitalised may perpetuate accusations of delegates being led primarily by political interests. Concerns have also been voiced as to whether the new Council will retain active NGO participation and the use of independent experts and special rapporteurs, as occurred with the Human Rights Commission. This system will be under review after the Council has completed its first year. Women's NGOs particularly have regularly used these mechanisms to advance women's rights as fundamental human rights, and it is deemed that the participation of NGOs remains crucial for the successful functioning of the Council.

The creation of the Human Rights Council holds great promise for the improvement of the capacity of the United Nations to promote and protect human rights. An effective human rights body could greatly bolster efforts to strengthen representative government in Africa and elsewhere. Nonetheless, the new body has the same innate limitations of the old body as an association of sovereign governments that have multiple issues with each other. To expect countries to discard their own interests, and to perform objectively over human rights over whose very definition they disagree, is highly unrealistic. The expectation that the creation of the Human Rights Council generates, however, is that it will make it harder for governments to continue to deny their obligation to protect and promote human rights. As a result, the new Human Rights Council could make a significant contribution to bolstering and supporting Africa's evolving human rights architecture.

Notes

[1] *In Larger Freedom: Towards Development, Security and Human Rights For All*, Report of the UN Secretary-General; follow-up to the outcome of the Millennium Summit, A/59/2005 (21 March 2005), p.45.

[2] United Nations, *Charter of the United Nations*, 24 October 1945.

[3] See Alson, P: *The United Nations and Human Rights: A Critical Appraisal* (Oxford: Clarendon Press, 1992); Bailey, S & Daws, S: *The United Nations: A Concise Political Guide* (Basingstoke: Macmillan Press, 1995); Farer, T & Gaer, F: "The UN and Human Rights: An End of the Beginning" in Roberts, A & Kingsbury, B (eds.): *United Nations, Divided World: The UN's Role in International Relations* (Oxford: Oxford University Press, 1993), pp.240–96; Weschler, J: "Human Rights" in Malone, D (ed.): *The UN Security Council: From the Cold War to the 21st Century* (Boulder & London: Lynne Rienner, 2004); Roth, K: "The UN Reform Agenda and Human Rights" in Heinbecker, P & Goff, P (eds.): *Irrelevant or Indispensable? The United Nations in the Twenty-First Century* (Ontario: Wilfred Laurier University Press, 2005), pp.131–39.

[4] http://www.un.org/Overview/brief3.html (accessed 18 April 2006).

[5] Roth, K: "The UN Reform Agenda and Human Rights" in Heinbecker, P & Goff, P (eds.): *Irrelevant or Indispensable? The United Nations in the Twenty-First Century* (Ontario: Wilfred Laurier University Press, 2005), p.134.

[6] See Donnelly, P: *Universal Human Rights in Theory and Practice* (Ithaca and London: Cornell University Press, 2003), p.129.

[7] Donnelly, P: *Universal Human Rights in Theory and Practice*, p.133.

[8] These include the International Covenant on Economic, Social and Cultural Rights (ICESCR); the International Covenant on Civil and Political Rights (ICCPR); the International Convention on the Elimination of All Forms of Racial Discrimination (ICERD); the Convention on the Elimination of All Forms of Discrimination against Women (CEDAW); the Convention against Torture and Other Cruel, Inhuman or Degrading Treatment or Punishment (CAT); the Convention on the Rights of the Child (CRC); and the International Convention on the Protection of the Rights of All Migrant Workers and Members of their Families.

[9] Brody, R.: "Will the New UN Council get serious about Human Rights?" in *Mail & Guardian*, 11 April 2006.

[10] Zeleza, T & McConnaughay, P J: "The Struggle for Human Rights in Africa" in Zeleza, T & McConnaughay, P J (eds.): *Human Rights, the Rule of Law, and Development in Africa* (Philadelphia: University of Pennsylvania Press, 2004), p. 8.

[11] Zeleza, T & McConnaughay, P J: "The Struggle for Human Rights in Africa", p. 8.

[12] "Creation of the Human Rights Council" http://www.globalpolicy.org/reform/topics/hrcindex.htm (accessed 12 April 2006).

[13] *In Larger Freedom: Towards Development, Security and Human Rights For All*, Report of the UN Secretary-General; follow-up to the outcome of the Millennium Summit. 21 March 2005, A/59/2005.

[14] Press release: "World's Worst Regimes Revealed" Freedom House, March 31, 2005, www.freedomhouse.org/template.cfm?page=70&release=255 (accessed 4 February 2006).

[15] See http://hrw.org/english/docs/2006/04/12/global13170.htm (accessed 16 April 2006).

[16] ibid.

[17] *A More Secure World: Our Shared Responsibility,* Report of the United Nations Secretary-General's High-level Panel on Threats, Challenges and Change. (United Nations Department of Public Information DPI/2367, December 2004), p.102.

[18] *A More Secure World: Our Shared Responsibility*, p. 102.

[19] *In Larger Freedom:* p. 45.

[20] *In Larger Freedom:* p. 45.

[21] *In Larger Freedom: Towards Development, Security and Human Rights For All*. See also "Creation of the Human Rights Council" at http://www.globalpolicy.org/reform/topics/hrcindex.htm (accessed 9 March 2006).

[22] Schaefer, B D: "The UN Human Rights Council is Not Enough: Time for a New Approach to Human Rights" in *Talking Points* No. 1910, 8 February 2006.

[23] African Union: *The Common African Position on the Proposed Reform of the United Nations: The Ezulwini Consensus*, Seventh Extraordinary Session of the Executive Council, Ext/EC.CL/2 (VII) (Addis Ababa: African Union, 7–8 March 2005).

[24] http://www.un.org/apps/sg/sgstats.asp?nid=1951 (accessed 18 April 2006).

[25] See for example "UN Human Rights Council at a Glance" The *Associated Press*, 16 March 2006.

[26] www.africa-union.org/Official_documents/ Decisions_Declarations/Maputo%20decisons.pdf (accessed 15 April 2006).

[27] Fleshman, M: "Human Rights Move up on Africa's Agenda: New African Court to Promote Rule of Law, End Impunity for Rights Violators" in *Africa Renewal* 18, 2 (July 2004), p. 10.

[28] Fleshman, M: "Human Rights Move up on Africa's Agenda: New African Court to Promote Rule of Law, End Impunity for Rights Violators", p. 10.

[29] Fleshman, M: "Human Rights Move up on Africa's Agenda: New African Court to Promote Rule of Law, End Impunity for Rights Violators", p. 10.

[30] Constitutive Act of the African Union. Full text available at http://www.africa-union.org/ organs/pan%20african%20parliament/AbConstitutive_Act.htm (accessed 18 April 2006).

[31] See Centre for Conflict Resolution: "Women and Peacebuilding in Africa" (Cape Town: Seminar Report, 27–28 October 2005), available at http://ccrweb.ccr.uct.ac.za

[32] See Centre for Conflict Resolution: "Building an African Union for the Twenty First Century" (Cape Town: Seminar Report, 20–22 August 2005) available at http://ccrweb.ccr.uct.ac.za

[33] Fleshman, M: "Human Rights Move up on Africa's Agenda: New African Court to Promote Rule of Law, End Impunity for Rights Violators", p. 10.

[34] These include Algeria, Benin, Cameroon, Central African Republic, Chad, Ethiopia, Ghana, Kenya, Liberia, Malawi, Mali, Mauritania, Morocco, Niger, Nigeria, Rwanda, Senegal, Sierra Leone, South Africa, Sudan, Togo, Tunisia, Uganda and Zambia.

[35] Human Rights Watch: *Protectors or Pretenders? Government Human Rights Commissions in Africa*. (New York, Brussels, London, Washington: HRW, 2001), p. 2.

[36] http://www.hrw.org/reports/2001/africa/overview/summary.html (accessed 18 April 2006).

[37] "Behind the Scenes at the UN" in *The Guardian* (London), 15 April 2006.

[38] See http://www.un.org/apps/sg/sgstats.asp?nid=1951 (accessed 18 April 2006).

[39] Signatories include former President Jimmy Carter, United States; José Ramos Horta, East Timor; Archbishop Desmond Tutu, South Africa; Oscar Arias, Costa Rica; Bishop Carlos Ximenes Belo, East Timor; Norman E. Borlaug, United States; Former President Kim Dae-jung, Republic of Korea; Adolfo Perez Esquivel, Argentina; John Hume, Northern Ireland; Mairead Maguire, Northern Ireland; David Trimble, Northern Ireland; and Jody Williams, United States.

[40] "Creation of the Human Rights Council" at http://www.globalpolicy.org/reform/topics/ hrcindex.htm (accessed 9 March, 2006).

[41] See for example Ambassador Boniface Chidyausiku, the Permanent Representative of Zimbabwe to the United Nations in New York in Singh, S: "Will the Human Rights Council Do Better than the Commission?" in *South Bulletin*, 15 February 2006.

[42] *In Larger Freedom*: p.37.

8

A Tale of Two Tragedies: Rwanda and Darfur

Henry Anyidoho

APRIL 2006 MARKED the twelfth anniversary of the genocide in Rwanda during which over 800 000 mostly Tutsi and moderate Hutu died. The events of April 1994 stunned the world. Books have been written, countless interviews have been conducted and journalists have revealed horrifying pictures. The Best Practice Unit of the United Nations (UN) Department of Peacekeeping Operations has carried out a post-mortem, the Organisation of African Union (OAU) instituted separate investigations, and institutions of higher learning have carried out in-depth research. Still the question lingers: What went wrong? The answer in brief is that the international community could not protect the Rwandans, let alone prevent genocide. Nevertheless, while the world continues to condemn this 1994 tragedy, the African continent is still confronted with multiple conflicts.

As a consequence of the horrors of the events that transpired in Rwanda in 1994, the African Union (AU) – established in 2002 – has been compelled to adopt a more practical approach to finding "African solutions to African problems". (See Mwanasali in this volume). For example, the idea of an African Standby Force (ASF) was conceived by the AU as a result of the inaction of the UN, the OAU and the international community as a whole during the 1994 genocide in Rwanda. The thinking was that, if Africa had forces ready to intervene in conflicts within the continent, perhaps another Rwanda could be prevented. As fate would have it, however, Africa has not had sufficient breathing space over the internal conflicts that have surfaced since Rwanda to realise this idea. From east to west, from south to north and across its middle belt, Africa continues to suffer the scourge of internal conflicts. This generation of Africans are still conscious of the seemingly endless conflict in Somalia which erupted in 1991, even before Rwanda.

In 2004, the international community "discovered" the internal conflict in Sudan's Darfur region. The conflict between the government of Sudan and the Sudanese People's Liberation Movement (SPLM) was already well publicised, but little was known about the events unfolding in Darfur, until civil society activists and journalists started to detail the human right abuses occurring there. Two important international personalities then decided to visit Darfur in 2004: UN Secretary-General Kofi Annan, and the then US Secretary of State, General Colin Powell. This finally put Darfur firmly on the map.

In this chapter, I will examine some of the failed strategies of the international community leading to the genocide in Rwanda in 1994, and the manner in which the ongoing atrocities in Darfur have been addressed. My intention is to identify the possible links between events leading to the Rwandan genocide and the current crisis in Darfur, with the aim of drawing attention to the failings of international response to both conflicts. By charting these connections, it is possible to see the extent to which lessons learnt from Rwanda have been effectively applied to Darfur in the area of humanitarian interventions. This requires an analysis of the peace agreements implemented in both cases, the responses emanating from the international community, as well as the reaction from the AU and the difficulties encountered by that organisation in the case of Darfur.

Agreements

The Arusha peace agreement between the Rwandan government forces and the Paul Kagame-led Rwandese Patriotic Front (RPF) signed on 4 August 1993 led to the creation of the UN Assistance Mission for Rwanda (UNAMIR) to assist with the peace process. I was serving as UN deputy force commander under General Roméo Dallaire at this point. Both parties had previously approached the UN and requested the establishment of the mission to take the country through a period of transition to democratic governance. The UN Security Council subsequently passed Resolution 872 in October 1993, which mandated the Secretary-General at the time,

Boutros Boutros-Ghali, to deploy UNAMIR to Rwanda to undertake specific tasks such as overseeing a power-sharing deal that could create a new army and demobilise ex-combatants.[1]

Did all the parties involved honour the 1993 Arusha peace agreement? Did the UN carry out an adequate assessment of the situation in Rwanda? The answer to both questions is "no": the key participants in the Arusha peace accord – particularly the government of Rwanda – did not demonstrate sufficient faith in the agreement. The UN's assessment of the situation was also incorrect and inadequate.

In the case of Darfur, a Humanitarian Ceasefire Agreement (HCFA) was signed between the government of Sudan, the Sudan Liberation Army/Movement (SLA/M) and the Justice and Equality Movement (JEM) in the capital of Chad, N'djamena, on 8 April 2004.[2] Following the strengthening of the HCFA, the AU deployed an observer mission of 60 military observers with a protection force of 300 troops to Darfur. The mission, named the AU Mission in Sudan (AMIS), began operations on 9 June 2004. No sooner had the mission commenced, than the AU discovered that the serious security situation in Darfur had been grossly under-estimated. As the AU observer mission attempted to deploy in Darfur, attacks on villages continued unabated. The AU had clearly not intended to establish a full-scale peace support operation in Darfur. Instead, the intention was for the observer mission to facilitate the maintenance of political dialogue, on the assumption that all parties would respect the cease-fire.

At its meeting on 20 October 2004, the 15-member AU Peace and Security Council (PSC) decided that it was necessary to increase the size of the mission in Darfur to 3 320 personnel, including 670 observers, a protection force of 1 703 troops, 132 civilians and 815 civilian police (CIVPOL). The mission was renamed AMIS II and eventually increased to 6 170 military personnel and 1 560 CIVPOL. The inclusion of CIVPOL was – incredibly – an afterthought in a region in which law and order remains difficult to enforce. The Chairman of the Humanitarian Ceasefire Commission, Major-General Festus Okonko, was tasked with the role of Force Commander, while Chief Military Observer, Colonel Antony Amedo, became the chief of staff of AMIS II. A number of military observers had to metamorphose into staff officers in order to rapidly create the semblance of a force headquarters.

Mandates

UN Security Council Resolution 872 of October 1993 mandated UNAMIR, among other things, to contribute to the security of the capital city of Kigali within a weapons-secure area, to monitor observance of the ceasefire agreement, to observe the security situation during the final period of the transitional government's mandate prior to elections, to investigate instances of alleged non-compliance with the provisions of the Arusha peace agreement and to investigate and report incidents regarding the activities of Rwanda's *gendarmerie* (security force) and police. A force, numbering a mere 2 548 troops, proved slow in being deployed due to the general apathy of the international community in responding to the Security Council's call. The small size of the force also meant that it could not possibly fulfil its mandate. As it was, UNAMIR was hardly at full capacity before the events of April 1994 unfolded.

In Darfur, the tasks assigned to AMIS by the AU included monitoring and observing compliance with the humanitarian ceasefire agreement; assisting in the process of confidence-building; contributing to a secure environment for the delivery of humanitarian relief; assisting with the return of Internally Displaced Persons (IDPs) and refugees to their homes; and improving the security situation throughout Darfur. However, questions were asked over how a force of just 3 320 troops (and now even 6 170) could provide security throughout Darfur, a region the size of France.

Poor assessment of the situation in Rwanda by the international community, coupled with flagrant disregard for the Arusha Accord by its signatories, led to a gradual escalation of the conflict in Rwanda and the eventual shooting down of the presidential aircraft on 6 April 1994, killing both the Rwandan president, Juvenal Habyarimana, and the Burundian president, Cyprien Ntaryamira. As is well documented, this event sparked the dormant civil war and culminated in the genocide of over 800 000 people within Rwanda's borders.

In the case of Darfur, it remains unclear why the AU began by only deploying an observer mission when reports at the time had extensively detailed the plight of IDPs and shown that refugees were pouring into Chad's Abeche region. Why do mediators in conflicts believe what they are told by warring factions during the negotiating and signing of ceasefire agreements? Has the world not witnessed enough violations of these agreements? Will the persistent violation of ceasefire agreements be a sufficient basis to reconsider how to hold responsible those "spoilers" who mislead negotiators? What can be done about those countries that back the warlords? Can they be viewed as sincere at the negotiating table? Do these parties fulfil expectations when it comes to the implementation of such agreements? These questions must always be asked and addressed to avoid the future breakdown of peace accords, as occurred in both Rwanda and Darfur.

Response from the International Community

Rwanda was a victim of the international peacekeeping disaster in Somalia in October 1993. The west was reluctant to deploy troops in any part of Africa in 1994 and UNAMIR was deploying at the peak of the American debacle in Somalia. As a result, UNAMIR was poorly supported.

The atrocities which started soon after the crash of President Habyarimana's plane resulted in the RPF's Major-General Paul Kagame sending me a message at the UN headquarters in Kigali saying that he was dispatching a battalion to the capital to assist government forces in preventing a further bloodbath by renegade forces. Four days later, the RPF entered Kigali and the guns began to fire. Sustained small arms, heavy machine gunfire, multiple rockets and artillery bellowed over the city. A well coordinated attack had started in earnest. The sadness that dominated my mind at that time inspired the title of my 1997 book, *Guns Over Kigali*.[3]

Only a week after the signing of the Arusha Peace Accord, the UN published a report that provided a disturbing picture of the human rights situation in Rwanda. Why then did the UN Security Council establish such a small force, allowing for only three ill-equipped infantry battalions, and deploying under Chapter VI of the UN Charter, rather than the more robust enforcement powers of Chapter VII? There seemed to be no political will on the part of UN member states, especially the five permanent members of the Security Council – the US, Russia, China, France and Britain – to intervene seriously in Rwanda.

UN Security Council resolutions are often so ambiguously worded that the commander in the field sometimes has to improvise his own interpretation of his mandate. The 800 Ghanaians deployed in the demilitarised zone (DMZ) were too small a force to provide effective security for this area of several kilometres, and similarly, the 500-member Belgian and Bangladeshi battalions could not maintain security in Kigali. Simply put, there was insufficient manpower and equipment to match the tasks that had been assigned. Failure started from the outset of the mission because of the wrong assessment of the situation and improper synchronisation of troops and equipment to the task, especially when signs of danger were looming.

Those of us on the ground in Rwanda were well aware of the inadequacies in the composition of UNAMIR. There was a lack of vehicles and radio equipment (we had to wait for these to come from other UN missions that were closing down). Meanwhile, the relationship between the UN Special Representative, Jacques-Roger Booh-Booh, and the Force Commander, Roméo Dallaire, was conflictual. The Rwandans, especially the government of President Habyarimana, paid lip service to the Arusha Peace Accord. On 28 December 1993, UNAMIR accompanied 600 RPF troops to Kigali and installed some of them at Parliament House. This was to be followed by the installation of a Broad-Based Transitional Government (BBTG), paving the way for democratic elections. I arrived in Kigali in January 1994 and soon after began to participate in the lengthy negotiations, but the BBTG was not established. Both government forces and the RPF harassed UNAMIR soldiers. While this intransigence continued, there were reports of killings and massacres, which were duly reported to UN headquarters in New York.

Much has been said about the cable of 11 January 1994 in which UNAMIR communicated a looming danger in Rwanda to the Department of Peacekeeping Operations, then under current UN Secretary-General, Kofi Annan. Consider the following additional events: on 21 February 1994 Felicien Gatabazi, Rwanda's minister of public works and a moderate Hutu of the Liberal Party (PL) was shot and killed; on 22 February 1994, as a reprisal for Gatabazi's death, the president of the Christian Democratic Party, Martin Buchana, was also ambushed near Butare and killed; and on 3 March 1994, a grenade exploded at the home of a member of the Revolutionary National Movement for Development (MRND): his family and five other people were seriously injured. On the same day, at a meeting between the vice-chairman of the RPF, Patrick Mazimhaka (now deputy Chair of the AU Commission) and the prime minister, Agathe Uwiligiyimana, a Rwandan government soldier on guard fired two rounds from his rifle and referred to it as "accidental discharge". On 15 March 1994, an ambush was executed by an unknown group near Kinihira tea plantation and factory, killing the manager of the factory, his wife, the cashier and two other employees.

The conclusion from the UN's assessment indicated that all of the above incidents were politically motivated, and our views were duly communicated to New York. As a security precaution, UNAMIR withdrew an expanded company of the Ghanaian battalion from the demilitarised zone on 28 February to strengthen security in Kigali. The RPF then began to deploy some of its elements in the DMZ. Protests from UNAMIR led to greater restrictions on the patrol activities of our military observers. The RPF was building up forces in Uganda, an indication that preparations for a possible war were underway. The UN's work was becoming increasingly difficult and frustrating. One could smell danger everywhere in Kigali and beyond. Hell was about to break loose.

News of the crash of the presidential jet spread like wildfire. I received orders from the UN force commander, General Dallaire, to proceed to our headquarters immediately, and to take charge of affairs while he tried to contact the authorities in Kigali. On my tortuous route to the headquarters complex, I had to negotiate my way through many roadblocks, which were being fortified and manned by government soldiers and notorious *Interahamwe* militia. These armed groups also undertook violent actions throughout Kigali. They headed for the homes of political opponents and started mass killings. The RPF could not stand by: a military confrontation had begun.

Within a couple of days of the presidential plane crash, France, Belgium and Italy carried out evacuation operations. During this period, the warring factions observed a cease-fire – even though the roadblocks were still aggressively manned. UNAMIR requested reinforcements, but instead, the international community, due to pressure from Belgium, contemplated the total withdrawal of UNAMIR. The Belgian foreign minister, William Claes, told the UN Secretary-General, Boutros Boutros-Ghali, on 12 April 1994 that the Ghanaian contingent had fled Rwanda. This was false (it was the only contingent that stayed behind) and represented a duplicitous attempt to have UNAMIR withdrawn from Rwanda.

The Belgian and Bangladeshi contingents were already prepared to abandon the mission when the UN Security Council passed Resolution 912 on 21 April 1994, calling for a reduction of UNAMIR from 2 548 to 270 personnel, and changing the mission's mandate. A ship in distress had sent out an SOS (*save our souls*) message and the reply was to abandon ship in mid-ocean. Only the Ghanaian contingent was left, and we had to build our residual force from soldiers from this contingent. We actually kept a force level of 450, even though this violated the Security Council resolution. Every day that Ghanaian soldiers stayed in Rwanda, I held myself accountable for every officer and soldier. I was worried about their families back home, especially after one of my soldiers was killed.

We felt forsaken with the passing of Resolution 912, as we no longer had the capacity to stop the massacres or to negotiate with the warring factions. However, it was a daring effort on our part to save the few people found hiding or who ran to our locations in Kigali. To add insult to injury, the Security Council passed Resolution 929 on 22 June 1994 that authorised the multinational "Opération Turquoise", with a chapter VII mandate, to be led by France to the south-western sector of Rwanda. This force was stronger, better equipped and was deploying as the resolution was being passed, even as the UN mission was being depleted.

Commanders require intelligence to operate effectively in the field. The UN resisted using the phrase "intelligence", since it implied spying on member states. We had to rely on foreign envoys and unreliable volunteers as our main sources of information through this chaotic period. Even then we were not allowed to use this information fully.

One of the most taxing difficulties faced by UNAMIR was poor logistics support. The UNAMIR administrative support system could not regularly provide food and water. Individual members of the force supplied us with biscuits and *gari* – a typical west African food made out of cassava – but these rations lasted only six days. We had to share with each other and with some of the internally displaced people. In addition, we did not have a blood bank. The best we could do was to identify individual donors. Power supply and telecommunications were disrupted in Kigali with the outbreak of violence. UNAMIR also had very few generators and radio equipment since we were still waiting for supplies from the UN missions in Somalia and Cambodia.

Despite many complaints about the press, without the news reporters in Kigali we would have perished in Rwanda: a land-locked country in which the airport was closed and all main roads blocked. It was the media that reported our plight through satellite communication to the world. However, *Radio-Television Libre de Mille Collines* (RTLM) in Rwanda was responsible for inciting the population to kill, reflecting an ugly side of media power.

Fortunately for AMIS II in Darfur, the international environment had changed since 1994. In the early twenty-first century, there appears to be considerably more good will towards Africa from the west and, above all, the UN is keen to support the AU. The AU's initial 2004 deployment plan for Darfur was designed by the UN after a visit to the region by a team of experts from its Department of Peacekeeping Operations. In 2004, the AU-led assessment mission, including the UN, the European Union (EU) and the US, visited Darfur and compiled a comprehensive report calling for the expansion of the mission. Consequently, the United Nations assistance cell for Darfur operations was established in October 2004 in Addis Ababa, Ethiopia, under my leadership. The cell works closely with the EU, the US and Canada in supporting the AU Darfur Integrated Task Force (DITF). In 2005, the UN Security Council passed Resolution 1590 which requested the UN Secretary-General, Kofi Annan, to report to the Council within 30 days about ways through which the UN mission in Sudan (UNMIS) could reinforce the efforts of AMIS.

How well is the AU maximising all this good will? Does the organisation have the capacity to absorb the assistance being offered? Certainly, the international community does not wish to be negligent in Darfur, as it was in Rwanda. The international community has been supportive of the AU and provided much-needed financial and logistical support to AMIS from 2004. The British government, through the European Union, has provided over 400 vehicles, while the US provided accommodation for the entire force. Canada contracted 16 helicopters in support of AMIS operations, and the Netherlands also placed three helicopters at the disposal of the force. In 2005, Norway provided office accommodation for the AU's civilian police in IDP camps. However, the mission reported in 2005 that it was $200 million short of its needs.

How well has the AU utilised these facilities? Certainly the force component deployed in Darfur, albeit at a slow pace, gave a certain amount of protection and hope to the people of Darfur. However, organisational difficulties within the AU headquarters in Addis Ababa and the mission headquarters in Khartoum, as well as the lack of administrative support to the force, has created difficulties. For example, there was no civilian component of AMIS in El-Fasher, the capital of north Darfur, which is also the force headquarters of AMIS. The Chief Administrative Officer is located in the country's capital, Khartoum, together with his finance and procurement officers, to address the day-to-day needs of the force. Initially, no senior political affairs officer was deployed to give guidance to the force commander. The March 2005 AU-led Assessment Mission report identified some of these deficiencies, several of which were subsequently corrected.

The OAU and the AU's Bold Decision

The OAU took the lead in establishing an observer mission in Rwanda before the establishment of UNAMIR. As the international community was clearly failing in the face of genocide in Rwanda, what did the OAU do? I enjoyed the support of my Ghanaian contingent and that of African officers from the OAU observer mission. However, I felt and still feel that the OAU could have done more than just calling on its member states to provide troops. Certainly, some members responded by providing troops, but at a very slow pace. We did not have a visit from the OAU headquarters during the crisis. No African religious leader visited Rwanda until long after the genocide. Similarly, there were no journalists representing the media in Africa.

With this background, one must praise the AU for its decision to deploy a mission to Darfur. In October 2003 AU Commission chairman, Alpha Konare, requested that the New York-based International Peace Academy (IPA) assist the AU in organising a seminar in Addis Ababa to outline a vision for the new organisation. The meeting included eminent participants from various professional backgrounds and from all over Africa, as well as the AU's key partners. The intention of the meeting was to provide useful guidelines for building the capacity of the African Union to respond to the circumstances on the continent into which it had been born. At the meeting, which I attended, participants expressed their views about the urgent need to build a strong human resource base within the AU in order for the organisation to be able to confront the challenges it faces in a new century. Unfortunately, thus far, the transformation of the OAU into the AU has been very slow, making it practically impossible for the new organisation to keep pace with the complex challenges that are engulfing the continent. Decisions taken are often not followed up or implemented swiftly. The AU continues to grapple with an old administrative structure that allows little room for the immediate operational action that is needed in critical circumstances, as clearly evidenced by the mission in Darfur.

With reference to Darfur in particular, the AU made crucial decisions. One of these was the establishment of the Darfur Integrated Task Force (DITF) at the headquarters in Addis Ababa to direct operations at the strategic level. From October 2004, however, various key posts within the DITF remained vacant. For example, the position of Logistics Officer remained vacant for over a year before being filled. It is therefore not surprising that important documents such as Standing Operating Procedures (SOPs), Rules of Engagement (ROE), Memorandum of Understanding (MOU) between the AU and troop-contributing countries were not finalised with the haste they required. Documents have often been drafted without final copies being distributed. Force generation has been another key challenge. AU members, having agreed to send a mission to Darfur, were reluctant to provide the troops needed to participate in the operations on the ground. Rwanda, Nigeria, Senegal, Gambia, Kenya and South Africa have been the main contributors of troops, while Rwanda and Nigeria have provided the bulk of the protection force. The development of the force has, however, been slow and, as a result, has created gaps for the warring factions to blatantly violate the Humanitarian Ceasefire Agreement.

Regarding military observers, some of the AU members did not provide even the ten pledged officers to participate in this operation. Observers to the Darfur peace process include the EU, the US, Chadian mediators, representatives of the warring factions and the AU's own observers. The inclusion of the warring factions in the observer group has both advantages and disadvantages. The main advantage is that the warring factions felt that they "own" the process, but the disadvantage is that the representatives of the parties sometimes leaked information to their principals on pending investigations or operational plans. At times, representatives of the warring factions also refused to sign investigative reports. These attitudes created doubts about the wisdom of including these factions in the various observer teams. These difficulties also influenced the work of the Ceasefire Commission, causing undue delays in the submission of its reports.

A further concern is the motives of some African countries in not providing officers or troops to the mission in Darfur. Some of these countries even claim to be playing the role of mediators in trying to revive the Abuja ceasefire talks. For example, the government of Libya engaged with the rebel movements to convince them to return to the Abuja talks. However, Tripoli did not provide the ten military observers to serve with AMIS as requested by the AU. The Abuja talks were instituted on 9 November 2004 when there was a complete breakdown in the peace process between the government of Sudan and the rebel movements in Darfur. While the rebels insisted that the government of Sudan must disarm the *Janjaweed* (Arab militia) in accordance with UN Security Council Resolution 1556 of 2004, the government demanded that the rebels first reveal their locations and disarm. Another bone of contention was the possible trial of those suspected of having committed crimes against humanity in Darfur. The rebels insisted that these suspects must be tried before the resumption of the Abuja talks. The UN Security Council passed Resolution 1591 authorising the trial of these suspects by the Hague-based International Criminal Court (ICC). The government of Sudan disagreed with this decision, and suspicions remain about the orchestrators of the demonstrations in North Darfur and Khartoum against the choice of the ICC for the trials. Meanwhile, the role of Chad as a mediator in the conflict in Darfur is ambiguous. It is the people of Darfur who are bearing the brunt of all this wrangling and who continue to suffer as the Sudanese government, the rebel movements and the "mediators" continue to employ delaying tactics. The attempted coup in Chad in April 2006 further poisoned relations between Ndjamena and Khartoum, as the Chadian government accused Sudan of backing the rebels.

Humanitarian Assistance

The Office of the UN High Commissioner for Refugees (UNHCR) and the United Nations Children's Fund (UNICEF) were two agencies that stood by us in Rwanda. In addition, the International Committee of the Red Cross (ICRC) and NGOs such as Adventist Development Relief

Agency and *Médecins Sans Frontières* (MSF) stayed with us throughout the genocide and beyond, delivering humanitarian aid. These agencies and NGOs are useful as long as they cooperate with peacekeeping efforts and support the interests of populations in distress. The military must also learn to understand and liase with UN agencies and NGOs.

In Rwanda, we did not have access to resources for humanitarian aid. Rwanda was a "failed state" at the time of, and immediately after, the genocide. Of what use was a bunch of soldiers with blue helmets to a community that was badly in need of food, medicine, shelter, clothing, hospitals and schools for their children? The government that was established immediately after the civil war had no resources for the administration of the country. All offices and ministries had been looted. Banks did not exist. The presence of troops under these circumstances gave the population a sense of security, but when they saw no concrete efforts in repairing the ruins of war, Rwandans began to question the usefulness of international peacekeepers. The communities that were most appreciative were those in which UNAMIR gave assistance such as daily medical care and establishing day-care centres for orphans. When the international community urges a failed state that has passed through a bitter civil war to respect human rights, and for internal factions to reconcile with each other, it is incumbent on the same international community to lend urgent assistance to this recovery.

A visit to Darfur and to the camps of internally displaced persons will shock any visitor. The largest camp – Kalma camp near the capital of South Darfur, Nyala – is sprawling and crammed with women, children and old men. They are living under appalling conditions despite the relentless efforts of UN agencies and NGOs. However, if it were not for these humanitarian actors, most of these IDPs would have died miserable deaths long ago. The question is: how long will the people of Darfur have to remain under these conditions? Brick walls are being erected in most of the camps to replace temporary structures, suggesting that these camps are turning into permanent homes. People are far away from their farmlands, and their animals have nowhere to graze. In fact, the animals are competing with humans in the camps for food and water. Repeatedly, many women have been raped when they venture out to look for firewood to cook. Men are also abducted from the IDP camps and killed. In light of these depressing events, what is the future of Darfur?

The Assessment Mission

In March 2005, an AU-led assessment mission, including the UN, the EU and the US, visited Darfur, Khartoum and Addis Ababa to investigate ways of strengthening the AMIS II operation in Darfur. The report of this mission recommended many corrective measures including the recruitment of essential staff; establishing correct budgetary, accounting and contract management procedures; and the eventual expansion of the force to up to 6 000 troops, with a strong logistics base supported by an effective intelligence unit. Meanwhile, AMIS II, which called for 3 320 troops, continued deploying amidst the sad news that some African countries were withdrawing their contribution to the civilian police component. If countries such as South Africa, Nigeria and Ghana are willing to provide civilian police in large numbers, why can other countries not follow suit? This calls into question whether there is sufficient political will among AU member states to see the end of the crisis in Darfur. Where is the African Standby Force that is building five sub-regional brigades? Could part of this force not have been deployed in Darfur? Former American Secretary of State, Colin Powell, referred to the situation in Darfur as "genocide" during testimony before the US Senate Foreign Relations Committee in September 2004.[4] The UN's own human rights investigation did not conclude that genocide was occurring in Darfur, though government militias persistently attack certain elements of the population in the region. What should the AU do about this tragic situation? What should Africa do about the situation in Darfur when help from the international community appears to be readily available?

UN Security Council Resolution 1590 of 24 March 2005 mandated a 10 000-strong United Nations Mission force in Sudan between South and North Sudan, following the Comprehensive Peace Agreement (CPA) between the government of Khartoum and the Sudan People's Liberation Army (SPLA). The same resolution requested that the UN Secretary-General, Kofi Annan, report to the Council on strategies for UNMIS to reinforce peacemaking efforts in Darfur through the provision of logistical and technical assistance to AMIS. However, without a clear identification of financial commitments for this assistance, very little can be done by the UN mission to support the AU mission. At the time of writing, the AU had requested that the UN take over its mission in Darfur by September 2006, amidst financial and logistical difficulties.

Concluding Thoughts

The case of Rwanda has become a tragic part of Africa's contemporary history. If there is anything Africa and the international community can learn from this event, it is that such an episode must never be allowed to happen again. Significantly, Rwanda was the first African government to deploy a protection force to Darfur as part of the AU mission. However, a lot remains to be done if genocide is to be avoided in Darfur. Rwanda's 1994 genocide was a result of the failed action on the part of the international community as a whole, and Africa in particular. The UN Secretary-General, Kofi Annan's assessment in April 2005 – like his earlier reports on Darfur – was gloomy about the situation in Sudan's troubled region. In the report, Annan deplored the fact that the Sudanese government has continued to pursue the military option on the ground with little or no regard for the commitments it had earlier entered into to end its attacks and to protect civilians.[5]

Darfur is a test case for the AU, and efforts should be concentrated on not allowing the situation to become another Rwanda. The complementary efforts of the AU, the UN, the EU, the United States and Canada should be increased. All AU members should become fully committed to the Darfur mission and not place the burden on a few countries and officials at the AU Commission in Addis Ababa. Ambassador Babagana Kingibe, the AU Commission Chairman's Special Representative on Darfur; the Force Commander General Festus Okonko; the CIVPOL Commissioner; Annand Pillay; and the entire AMIS deserve the support of both Africa and the international community. Let us avoid a repeat of the tragic events of Rwanda by acting decisively in Darfur.

Notes

[1] See, for example, Laegreid,T:"UN peacekeeping in Rwanda" in Adelman, H & Suhrke,A (eds.): *The Path of a Genocide:The Rwanda Crisis from Uganda to Zaire* (New Brunswick and London:Transaction Publishers, 1999); Organisation of African Unity, *The International Panel of Eminent Persons to Investigate the 1994 Genocide in Rwanda and the Surrounding Events* (July 2000); Prunier, G: *The Rwandan Crisis: History of a Genocide* (NewYork: Columbia University Press, 1995); Report of the Independent Inquiry into the actions of the United Nations during the 1994 Genocide in Rwanda, 16 December 1999, S/1999/1257; Suhrke,A:"UN Peacekeeping in Rwanda" in Sorbo, G &Vale P (eds.): *Out of Conflict: From War to Peace in Africa* (Uppsala: Nordiska Afrikainstitutet, 1997).

[2] For a background to the Darfur conflict, see Deng, F:"Specific Groups and Individuals: Mass Exodus and Displaced Persons" in Report of the Representative of the Secretary-General on Internally Displaced Persons Mission to the Sudan. UN Economic and Social Council. E/CN.4/2005/8 (27 September 2004). See also Prunier, G: *Darfur:The Ambiguous Genocide* (Ithaca: Cornell University Press, 2005) and Flint, J & de Waal,A: *Darfur: A Short History of a Long War (African Arguments)* (London: Zed Books, 2006).

[3] Anyidoho, H K: *Guns Over Kigali* (Accra:Woeli Publishing Services, 1997).

[4] See http://www.state.gov/secretary/former/powell/remarks/36042.htm (accessed 21 February 2006).

[5] Monthly report of the Secretary-General on Darfur, 12 April 2005 at http://daccessdds.un.org/doc/UNDOC/GEN/N05/303/55/PDF/N0530355.pdf?OpenElement (accessed 17 February 2006).

Section Three

©Adil Bradlow/Trace Images

Africa's Development and
Human Security Challenges

9

Nyerere's Challenge: Deconstructing the Washington Consensus

Margaret Legum

In 1998, FORMER TANZANIAN president Julius Nyerere met with top-level staff at the World Bank in Washington DC. This champion of African unity had governed Tanzania from its independence in 1964 until 1985. He had implemented economic policies based on bottom-up, rather than top-down, principles of rural agricultural development, social property and egalitarian self-determination. "Why have you failed?" the World Bank experts asked him. Nyerere answered:

> The British Empire left us a country with 85 per cent illiteracy, 2 engineers and 12 doctors. When I left office we had 9 per cent illiteracy and thousands of engineers and doctors. Our per capita income was twice what it is today. Now we have one-third less children in our schools and our public health and social services are in ruins. During these last thirteen years Tanzania has done everything that the World Bank and the International Monetary Fund (IMF) have demanded. So I ask: 'Why have *you* failed?'
> *Julius Nyerere, 1999*[1]

From Economic Development to Structural Adjustment

That story reminds us of two things that have been practically erased from the history books and from our collective memory. First, economics is not a science, but an aspect of political policy. One cannot separate economics and politics. There is no such thing as a political policy or programme that does not have economic ramifications and there is no such thing as economic policies that are not rooted in issues of political power. The pretence that economics is a science is only as old as the radical conservatives of the 1970s in the west. However, it has provided a spurious legitimacy – a kind of inevitability to the current world economic dispensation. This myth is the reason why it has lasted so long, despite its ill effects on more than half of humanity. That is why there has been collective amnesia about alternatives to this dispensation. I write not as an economist, but as a political economist. There is no other kind.

In the first ten to fifteen years of African independence – from about 1960 to 1975 – African economies were fairly successful judging by all practical social and economic indicators such as health, education, transport, per capita income and exports. A major cause of that success was that investment took place in the arena of infrastructure: physical infrastructure, and more importantly, human infrastructure. The long-term investment that matters is always in human capital and people's capacity to make a livelihood.

These fledgling political economies were broadly social–democratic, like their former colonial masters at that time. External aid, largely emanating from colonial powers, was primarily directed into investment in physical and human infrastructure. The countries' savings, which became capital available for local investment in the private sector, was subject to exchange control – like that of all sovereign nations. So it stayed where it was made. And emergent industries, born from the need to diversify colonial economies, were subject to strict protective controls. It was understood that, historically, all successful economies have grown through the protection of industries until they are strong enough to compete internationally. The difference between these macroeconomic priorities and the policies that dominate today is stark.

The well documented four-fold increase in oil price in 1973, after members of the Organisation of Petroleum Exporting Countries (OPEC) came together to determine the price of oil, had a number of damaging results for Africa.[2] First, the oil price increase led to the escalation of production and transportation costs everywhere. Since Africa largely exported raw materials and imported manufactured goods, it bore a disproportionate part of the burden of higher fuel costs. Second, internationally markets were reduced and as a result, prices for African commodities dropped. So Africa paid more for its imports and got less for its exports. Third, the OPEC financial sector was unable to cope effectively with the huge flood of money pouring in as a result of the oil price increase; so these countries turned to western banks for investment opportunities through providing loans. Western banks, seeking outlets for these loans, viewed Africa as an obvious recipient, being under-developed.

The result was the offer to African countries of huge loans, largely for projects aimed at strengthening infrastructure, at low interest rates. Banks, and their international financial counterparts, including the World Bank, offered technical advice which was taken, and which promised that the loans would pay for themselves within a few years. That erroneous advice is on record, but is seldom referred to. Nor do the institutions that gave the loans apologise for their mistake, or suffer the consequences. Loans were in effect foisted on inexperienced African governments, who through no fault of their own, found themselves suddenly facing unpredictable currency crises. In essence, these governments had agreed to accept credit on the basis of wrong advice. Between 1970 and 2002, African governments borrowed $540 billion and repaid $550 billion in interest and principal.

The original loans were granted with low interest rates, based on the then high liquidity of the banks, due to the surplus of savings created by the oil price increase. Then the whole global capital market was deregulated, resulting in the fact that savings could roam the world in search of profits. This enabled the scarcity of liquid capital through a range of financial instruments, the use and effects of which fall outside the scope of this chapter. Suffice to say, capital was enabled to command much higher prices and consequently interest rates rose dramatically worldwide.

So African governments became faced with much larger − later becoming compound[3] − interest rates for projects which had been confidently predicted to be self-financing. They failed, even without the increased interest rates. African countries were therefore unable to pay back these loans. Hence, under conditions of crisis and the interference of the World Bank and the International Monetary Fund in the 1980s, many African governments were unable to make their external account books balance. The IMF had been set up precisely to offer loans under such circumstances: bridging loans to enable governments to survive a crisis, while they set about introducing policies to correct the imbalance. The Fund and the Bank increasingly acted as debt-management institutions, lending in some cases as much as 50 per cent of a developing country's portfolio towards structural and/or sectoral adjustment lending. The primary rationale for this kind of lending was said to be the desire to restore a country's debt-servicing capacity by demanding, as a condition for the loans, that its government implement major economic reforms: the now notorious Structural Adjustment Programmes (SAPs). The problem was the nature of the policies that the IMF insisted upon as a condition of these roll-over loans – practically the polar opposite of the policies that had been successful in the first years of independence. Since then, African economies have nose-dived and drowned in the remaining debt, which currently stands at around $290 billion.

SAPs required first and foremost the end of tariffs and other means of protecting and promoting local enterprise. Local enterprise therefore had to compete on the open global market with those from mature capitalist nations; capital-rich, highly-educated and specifically skilled in innovation within markets, resourced over centuries and backed by rich sophisticated government institutions. The result was decimation of almost all budding private enterprise in Africa: output was easily undercut in terms of price and quality by exports from rich nations, and more recently by countries where labour is able or willing to accept wages below the poverty level.

This has been compounded by the condition that restrictions on the right of African capital to travel in search of more profitable investment options must end. Ironically, an argument used for the deregulation of capital is that it spreads capital from where it is abundant to where it is scarce. In reality, the opposite happens. Capital was and is siphoned from Africa, becoming a source of savings for Europe and America. An African entrepreneur could obviously make more money investing in those mature markets than at home. Economists who still advocate freedom for capital to travel – on the grounds that it spreads capital – are therefore out of touch with basic reality.

A further consequence of these events is that weaker governments became economically stagnant and as a result, much state enterprise was privatised. The theory was that the public sector is inevitably inefficient and corrupt while the private sector, conversely, is efficient and law-abiding. This approach thwarts the availability of resources for governments as well as their ability to carry out effective policy-making. This in turn directly affects their ability to offer any support for their poor and vulnerable populations. This has had tragic personal consequences. The most visible and tragic economic effect of SAPs was the diminished investment in human capital – education, health and subsidised food. The effect was referred to in Nyerere's response to the World Bank; a huge drop in the proportion of educated and healthy people in the population.

Additional consequences of the IMF loans for Africa came as a result of the insistence on export-oriented growth in order to maximise countries' foreign currency earnings. The effect was to promote large-scale export crops that are demanded in rich countries at the expense of local food production. IMF beneficiaries' economies were to be oriented to satisfy the needs of overseas customers, quite simply because that is where the money was. Food security, labour intensive production and rural community economies gave way to capital-based, large, export-oriented projects. These employed – often casually and always at low cash wages – people who used to own the land and make a livelihood from it. World Bank projects were particularly notorious for such endeavours that served to deepen rural poverty.

Some of the economic assumptions that lay behind the SAPs have often proved to be inappropriate in the African context.[4] One such assumption is that all African societies are fully monetised and market-oriented and, consequently, all individuals have the ability to respond to market forces.[5] This view fails to acknowledge the many social inequalities which hamper access to resources, the opportunities of particular groups and the importance of unpaid labour and mutual aid in all African economies.[6]

It is also clear that SAPs themselves are gender-biased in a number of ways and based on economic policies that ultimately increase the subordination of African women. The macroeconomic thinking on which SAPs are based takes little account of the gender-based division of labour prevalent in many African societies. For example, SAPs promote export-oriented crops, which tend to be grown by men. Women are left with little support, marginal land, and fewer resources to grow food crops to feed their families.[7] The advocacy of private capital and the relaxation of labour regulations also have implications for working conditions, especially for those concentrated in the least protected sectors of the workforce, the majority of whom are women. In addition, cuts to public services result in an increased workload for women as greater burden is placed on their role as caregivers and it is usually girls who suffer first when there are limited resources to pay for schooling.

The World Bank and IMF loans were contingent on the prioritisation of debt repayment over all other claims on foreign exchange. Despite this, and because of high and compound interest rates, African debt as a whole is widely recognised to be unrepayable. It is also accepted that the original loans have been repaid many times over and that debt repayment cripples the ability of governments to invest in education, social and health infrastructure. For example, between 2002 and 2004, Nigeria paid £3.5 billion sterling in debt service, but its debt burden increased by a further £3.9 billion.[8] The inflow of humanitarian aid and other transfers of resources from rich countries are directly contradicted by the repayment of this debt, so that resources are flowing steadily in the wrong direction from poor to rich countries. Moreover, domestic laws generally recognise that lenders have a responsibility to bear some of the costs of debt that cannot be repaid; hence bankruptcy laws are designed to clear past debt and allow the debtor to start again. In this case, it is crystal clear that the lenders bear a major share of responsibility for the debts, but there are no international bankruptcy provisions that could have that effect.

Nyerere was right. Since the 1980s, officials of the World Bank and IMF have ruled much of Africa. Elected governments did formally take policy decisions and passed laws through their own parliaments. However, the budgets of governments under SAPs had to be approved by officials of one or both of these international financial institutions, and there was often neither the expertise nor the confidence on the part of poor countries to protest against this perverse process. The omnipotence of the Bank and the Fund was such that opposition to their policies was apparently impossible. Moreover, it does not take long for aspiring politicians to understand what policies to propose in order to garner powerful foreign support. The global market ideology has consumed governments everywhere, especially since the fall of the Soviet Union in 1991.

The result of SAPs were rapidly declining economies, rising unemployment, the collapse of rural economies whose populations swell urban areas, the steady loss of African capital and the global perception that, "despite everything we do for them, Africans can't hack it". Concurrently, a new, very wealthy class of Africans developed, enabled by their exploitation of global market conditions. Their incomes distort Gross Domestic Product (GDP) figures, allowing misleading conclusions to be reached about the "growth" benefits of the global market. This group's own interests are served by the continuation of the current dispensation. Their position, however, as well as Africa's political stability, remains precarious while the growth of inequality undermines economic democracy and enrages excluded populations.

It is this economic history, and its consequences on current practice, that Africa lives with today. Africa is not alone since other regions of the world, including eastern Europe, have been forced into structural adjustment. The US has however avoided structural adjustment, despite having the largest external debt ever recorded – some $3 trillion, which is roughly equal to the debt owed by the whole of the developing world put together. American debt, unlike that of other countries, is being covered by the savings of the rest of the world because its currency is the world's reserve currency and the one in which oil is traded. Therefore, every nation must keep reserves in dollars, so they must use their capital to buy dollars, which helps service US debt.

Some of the other consequences of SAPs have included creating cultures of corruption and ethnic-fuelled conflict. Unfortunately, when people are forced to fight over scarce resources, conflict erupts and corruption becomes a reality of life. Research globally shows that economic constriction – and especially the collapse of economies – inevitably produces, as night follows day, a restriction in people's horizons in terms of who they view as friends and who they see as enemies. People who have co-existed happily will turn on each other when resources dry up, using identity and ethnicity as an excuse. Nobody enjoys seizing resources from neighbours, however necessary to their own survival, unless they can rationalise it by creating enemies. Ethnic feuds can start in that way. Rwanda was, and is, wracked by such a dynamic. (See Anyidoho in this volume).

Moreover, politicians whose room for policy action is restricted by factors outside their control often turn to ethnic difference as a means of separating themselves from their rivals. Thus, if there is no point in advocating alternative policies because powerful forces from outside the country would veto them, politicians will look around for other points of difference with their rivals. Regional and ethnic distinctions are easy, and Africa offers numerous examples.

Where Africa is concerned, it is especially frustrating that a racial explanation is often offered for its economic downfall. Stereotypes surrounding "tribalism" are easily triggered by conflicts that have arisen mainly since Africa was forced into SAPs. Africa is a "basket case" because Africans "can't run a bath, let alone a country". This analysis fits neatly with white, western stereotypes that enabled them to overrun the continent and enslave its people with a clear conscience. So why should we question these stereotypes? They are the reason why the economic history of the first phase of African independence has been erased from contemporary memory and why questions are not directed to whether the continent's failures derive from the decisions of the Bretton Woods institutions and not African governments'.

The contention is made more pointed when we realise that the collapse of the Soviet Union's economy and its political disintegration along ethnic lines is not described in the same terms as that of Africa – although its origins have close parallels. Indeed, Russia's plight is not widely publicised in western Europe and the United States; whereas "everyone knows" that Africa is a poverty-stricken shambles. That is because Russians are white, and if white people suffer poverty and collapse, there must be a good reason for it, whereas Africans bring it upon themselves by their intrinsic nature.

The significance of this understanding must lead to a questioning of how we begin the process of making recommendations for Africa's recovery and the UN Millennium Development Goals (MDGs) of 2000, which seek to halve poverty by 2015. How can prescriptions for Africa be valid without recognition of what has caused its current failings? How can you start to suggest what needs to be done if you start from today, and know nothing of the past?

Critiquing UN Reform Reports

Both the report of the UN High-level Panel and the UN Secretary-General's report to the General Assembly of March 2005, *In Larger Freedom*, are comprehensive and interesting documents.[9] The latter is actually inspiring. However, inevitably both read like a "wish list" because, without analysing the past, you cannot prescribe a direction of change to make a better future. Most pertinent, it seems the Panel bought into – without much examination – conventional neo-liberal economic theory and practice. But it was precisely this theory and practice that was used to create and enforce SAPs. Nowhere is the paradigm of the Washington Consensus questioned.

For example, six clusters of threats are defined as leading to a loss of collective security. This, in turn, is beautifully defined, *inter alia*, as an event or process that undermines the state as the basic unit of the international system. I would suggest that this also refers to states as the seat of sovereign democracy. Missing from the list of threats is the one at the root of most of the others: namely, the right that capital now has to move about the globe with little control or restriction. If investors with local capital can move their money from democratic states that do not do their bidding to ones that do, they call the shots. They can dictate the conditions under which their capital moves. Their influence with governments can outweigh that of a large majority of voters.

For instance, globally, capital owners now demand low taxes, little regulation of wages and work conditions, small government, privatisation and an eschewing of "pro-poor" policies. These measures deprive other citizens, whose votes against such policies are often ineffective. Capital owners are effectively beyond the democratic process, and this in turn severely limits the scope of policies that governments may adopt without risking losing the country's capital. All governments thus have to do the bidding of international capital.

There is no other explanation for the fact that governments in Africa, and indeed many other places, have not revolted against, for instance, unreasonable demands for debt-repayment. Why do nations in Africa not simply announce that none of them will repay debts – debts that were often taken out by tyrants and corrupt leaders, without popular consent, and the principal sum having long since been repaid? It is because capital owners have the right and the means to remove their capital from any country without warning or permission. These capitalists can incapacitate an economy by withdrawing from the market and selling their assets. They not only have additional influence within economies, but also the power to destroy them.

The situation is aggravated by the wrongly perceived need for Foreign Direct Investment (FDI), hence the aspiration to attract foreign capital. FDI is crippling the ability of sovereign governments to adopt certain policies, particularly those most sympathetic to workers and the poor. That poses a severe limitation on democracy and the sovereign right of governments, whether elected or not, to respond to democratic pressures. It is no coincidence that elected governments all over the world are introducing similar policies. This is a result of the fact that they come under the same pressures from international capital. So surely the unregulated right of capital to move from its country of origin should be seen as "an event or process that undermines states as the basis of the international system"? Democracy is surely part of that international system.

The question is raised as to why these factors were not discussed in either the High-level Panel's report of 2004 or the UN Secretary-General's report of 2005. They were ignored, I suspect, because the right of capital to move is the bedrock of the neo-liberal Washington Consensus. However, that unrestricted right is the most profound cause of the poverty that currently afflicts the world, and especially Africa. If you do not deal with this issue, you cannot deal with poverty.

In the annex of Kofi Annan's report *In Larger Freedom*, he urges state leaders "to reaffirm and commit to… the development consensus around the Millennium Development Goals".[10] Unfortunately, one of the aspects of this consensus is to make countries attractive to international private capital. The report states that:

> developing countries should recommit themselves to taking
> primary responsibility for their own development by strengthening
> governance, combating corruption and putting in place the
> policies and investments to *drive private-sector* [my emphasis]
> led growth and maximise domestic resources to fund national
> development strategies.[11]

A later paragraph ignores the history of Africa's current debt crisis by stating that "debt sustainability should be redefined as the level of debt that allows a country to both achieve the Millennium Development Goals and reach 2015 without an increase in its debt ratios".[12]

This statement effectively accepts the position of rich creditor nations on the whole issue of debt. Although it implies that more debt reduction is needed for most debtor nations, it ignores the history of the debt crisis. It overlooks the fact that many African governments were persuaded to take loans on false information; that they have all paid these loans back many times over; that any individual person owing such debts would by now have been offered solutions that acknowledge the lender's responsibility for injudicious lending; and that therefore by rights, they owe nothing. It is as though there were no controversy about the origins of the debt, its ethical dimensions as "odious" debt, or its gross effects on the perpetuation – even deepening – of debt. Surely, if Africa's claims around the debt issue were going to be rejected, they should at least have been argued. Kofi Annan's bland statement about the redefinition of sustainable debt allows such a wide range of outcomes that it is virtually useless. What level of debt would "allow a country both to achieve the MDGs and reach 2015 without an increase in its debt ratios"?[13] Is there no aspiration to reduce, or eliminate, those debt ratios?

Another of the UN Secretary-General's recommendations is based on the assumption that export-led growth and growing trade are automatically the best drivers for development.[14] With hindsight, we now know that the Doha round of the World Trade Organisation (WTO) did not succeed in getting rich countries committed to allowing developing countries access to their markets. Apart from that political failure, however, the whole concept of development through trade is by now controversial among economists – especially those committed to the MDGs. Surely the controversy should have been raised, and objections to the current orthodoxy addressed.

For instance, it is now widely accepted that private sector growth in itself provides no serious dent in unemployment, nor does it alleviate poverty. A recent New Economics Foundation (NEF) report in London, England, shows for instance that between 1990 and 2001, only 60 cents in every $100 generated by global economic growth contributed to poverty reduction.[15] This is 73 per cent less than in the 1980s, when the figure was $2.20 in every $100. This shows that *growth is not working* and that poverty is in fact growing. Today each $1 of poverty reduction requires $166 of extra growth. One further implication of these figures is that if the world continues to pursue the current type of growth in order to tackle poverty, not only will this fail, but the planet would be destroyed through global heating while fossil fuels would be depleted within a very short time.[16]

What is of concern is not that the theories of the Washington Consensus are articulated in these UN reports, but that those economic theories are apparently accepted as *sine qua non*. There is no debate over them. Surely by now, quite apart from historical lessons from Africa's own experience, we should at least have begun to have some doubts about these remedies. The theories are not being backed by facts. Clearly, questions need to be asked about the private sector's ability to address poverty and unemployment, about export-led growth as serving poor people, and about all trade driving growth that serves people. Surely these assumptions should be examined. Certainly, if development is an aspect of collective security, as these UN reports indicate, one should at least discuss what kind of development works, what kind does not, and for what reasons.

While these reports are depressing in their repetition of old solutions, there is no doubt that they reflect a new urgency and new awareness of the horrors of poverty – not only in Africa – and thus usher in a new period of enquiry. There are recommendations – including a series of "quick win" initiatives – that would make a real and immediate difference in the lives of poor people, which are desperately needed as long as poverty is perpetuated. In fact, I believe that the reason for the flaws in these reports is that, while more and more people know the current economic dispensation is not working, most have no conception of an alternative.

Thus we need a new paradigm. There are a number of influential economists who propose solutions short of a new paradigm. Some, including Jeffery Sachs and Joseph Stiglitz, left senior positions in the World Bank and the IMF because they considered their theories to be out of touch with reality. Sachs suggests that the MDGs could be met by transferring resources from rich to poor nations through dramatically increased flows of aid; unconditional grants, rather than loans. That would certainly make a dent in infrastructure shortfalls, which is important. Sachs' proposals are consistent with Kofi Annan's recommendation to heads of states, who are urged to "undertake to ensure that developed countries… establish timetables to achieve the target of 0.7 per cent of Gross Domestic Product for Official Development Assistance no later than 2015".[17]

The same effect could be achieved – on a more sustained basis – by the proposed "carbon trading" system. Under this proposal, according to the size of their population, countries would be allocated a proportion of the global warming emissions that the world can absorb, in the form of units of carbon. Those countries that need to burn more carbon than their allowance could buy more units from developing countries that do not use their full allocation. This would have the effect of making the transfer of resources from the rich to the poor a matter of international rights.

Similarly, when it becomes clear when the world will run out of cheap fossil fuels, a rationing system will have to be set up which could work in the same way as carbon trading: people and companies who use more oil than their allocation would have to buy them from people with a fuel-light lifestyle or mode of production. This is the only way to prevent shortages being solved by monopolisation for the already rich.

These suggestions, like those for ending all debt for developing countries, will have the effect of making more resources available to African (and other poor) nations. However, none of these ideas will, in and of themselves, change the way the world economy works on an ongoing basis to advantage rich countries and individuals at the expense of poor ones. If nothing changes, inequality and poverty will continue to be the outcome and the MDGs will never be realised. Therefore, what is needed is a critical analysis of how this current economic order creates impoverishment and how that can be challenged. That was not the brief of the UN High-level Panel, but it is urgently needed.

Finally, we need to understand what Africa's bargaining power is: what leverage do "we" have in negotiations with the west? First, we have markets that are needed by rich countries. Their own markets are saturated in some respects, and domestic markets are diminishing because of the growing poverty in these countries. Second, some African countries have oil and other commodities needed in Europe, the Americas and Asia. Third, African votes are needed in global institutions where decisions are taken that affect the interests of rich nations. The Doha round is a good example where African nations, together with other developing countries, simply refused to make any more agreements that the rich nations wanted until their own interests were attended to. Until 2005, Africa had accepted rich countries promises that they would progressively work towards reducing tariffs and other barriers to our access to their markets, and on that basis, had opened our markets to them. That stopped in 2005 when Africa required progress from rich countries before it made further concessions.

Beyond that, Africans will achieve very little unless they start to break some rules. That will take courage because as a continent we are poorer than others, and it is relatively easy to pick off one small nation and play it off against others. Solidarity is difficult to achieve when rewards are offered to countries that play the game. Our efforts will clearly only be realised by uniting as a continent to break the rules.

For example, Africans should as a continent refuse to repay any more of the debt stemming from the 1970s. It would be difficult for creditors to react effectively if it were a united move. The expected threat to end further lending is a hollow one, as Russia found when it declared the nation insolvent and stopped repaying debts. International financial institutions do not want to limit the areas in which they can operate. They would be more careful how loans are designed in future, and that is a good thing.

Second, African governments should re-introduce tariffs on imports that have been subject to subsidies of one kind or another. This is allowed by the WTO in certain circumstances, but Africa should act on our own principles in creating a level playing field for our own enterprise. Subsidies include not only providing financial underpinning for governments, but also subsidised transport, housing, education and basic infrastructure, which reduce the wage that workers in other countries can accept and still go to work. It also includes protection from the vagaries of currency markets that can destabilise the market for perfectly efficient and far-sighted enterprise.

Finally, Africans should declare the capital they create at home to be a resource to be used at home. Giving reserve banks the right to prevent our capital leaving – unless it is guaranteed to bring home more than it takes out – may well have some surprising results. It will stop the drain on African resources and will stimulate local enterprise. That may in turn attract foreign direct investment, which is currently warded off by our diminishing resources and markets. Courage will be needed to take the risks that will put Africa back on the path of growth necessary to challenge poverty on the continent, based on our own resources.

Notes

[1] "The Heart of Africa. Interview with Julius Nyerere on Anti Colonialism" in *New Internationalist* (Jan–Feb 1999), p. 309.

[2] OPEC was established in 1960 and was set up to coordinate the policies and prices of petroleum among member states, including Algeria, Iran, Iraq, Saudi Arabia, Kuwait the United Arab Emirates, Libya, Nigeria, Venezuela and Qatar, and to offset pressure from major (western) oil companies. The 1973 oil crisis emanated from OPEC's refusal to ship oil to western countries who had supported Israel in its Yom Kippur war.

[3] Compound interest is calculated not only on the initial percentage agreed but also the accumulated interest of prior periods.

[4] See Tsikata, D: "Effects of Structural Adjustment on Women and the Poor" at http://www.twnside.org.sg/title/adjus-cn.htm (accessed 21 February 2006).

[5] Tsikata, D: "Effects of Structural Adjustment on Women and the Poor".

[6] Tsikata, D: "Effects of Structural Adjustment on Women and the Poor".

[7] Tsikata, D: "Effects of Structural Adjustment on Women and the Poor".

[8] "Nigeria at Risk of 17 Billion Pound Default" in *The Guardian* (London), 26 April 2005.

[9] See *A More Secure World: Our Shared Responsibility*, Report of the United Nations Secretary-General's High-level Panel on Threats, Challenges and Change. Published by the United Nations Department of Public Information DPI/2367, December 2004; and *In Larger Freedom: Towards Development, Security and Human Rights For All*, Report of the UN Secretary-General; follow-up to the outcome of the Millennium Summit. 21 March 2005, A/59/2005.

[10] *In Larger Freedom* p.55.

[11] *In Larger Freedom* p.55.

[12] *In Larger Freedom* p.56.

[13] *In Larger Freedom* p.56.

[14] *In Larger Freedom* p.56.

[15] See www.neweconomics.org. (accessed 21 February 2006).

[16] www.neweconomics.org. (accessed 21 February 2006).

[17] Sachs, J: *The Millennium Development Project: Practical Action Plan to Combat Poverty*, January 2005. Available at www.unmilleniumproject.org/reports/fullreport.htm (accessed 11 November 2005).

10

Aligning HIV/AIDS and Security: The UN and Africa

Angela Ndinga-Muvumba

Introduction

IN SOUTH AFRICA'S PRISONS, HIV-positive inmates deliberately infect fellow prisoners. An act of sexual violence resulting in HIV infection is described as "slow puncture". Slow puncture serves as an unfortunate metaphor for the security implications of HIV/AIDS. The pandemic is indeed a slow puncture – over decades, and in wave upon wave of infection and death, the African AIDS epidemic is tearing apart families and communities, unlike any other infectious disease ever experienced in history. Without the promise of affordable treatment or delivery of a vaccine, without doctors and nurses, teachers and police, HIV/AIDS is a death sentence for the security of poor African countries.

AIDS is the number-one killer of adults in sub-Saharan Africa. In 2006 the African Union (AU) and the United Nations (UN) estimated that 22 million Africans have died due to AIDS-related illness in the last twenty years.[1] In December 2005, the Joint United Nations HIV/AIDS Programme (UNAIDS) confirmed that another 25.8 million Africans were living with the virus.[2] Although the region contains 10 per cent of the world's population, it is currently home to 60 per cent of all HIV infections. Finally, HIV/AIDS has orphaned over 12 million African children.[3] On a positive note, the HIV rates of infection in Kenya, Uganda, and Zimbabwe declined in 2004.[4] While estimates of HIV prevalence rates are only rudimentary measurements of average infection rates and approximates of the scale, variability and dimensions of multiple HIV epidemics, these numbers suggest an untold story about the links between the pandemic and insecurity. According to the executive director of UNAIDS, Peter Piot, HIV/AIDS "will transform some of the smaller countries, such as Lesotho, Swaziland and Botswana, which have already lost 30–40 years of life expectancy, into 'un-developing' countries."[5] While such statements are frequently brushed aside as alarmist they do reflect a reality that Africa's policymakers have to contend with: HIV/AIDS is a powerful phenomenon that must be urgently addressed to secure the future of the continent.

The UN High-level Panel's 2004 report, *A More Secure World: Our Shared Responsibility*[6] presented an opportunity to interrogate the relationship between non-traditional security issues such as poverty and health and collective international peace and security. (See Adebajo and Chinery-Hesse in this volume). In terms of HIV/AIDS, this opportunity came at a time when questions related to medium and long term repercussions for heavily-affected countries and regions needed further articulation, examination and analysis.

Since 2001, HIV/AIDS has emerged as a significant factor in the overall health of many African countries. This chapter examines the relevance of the UN High-level Panel's recommendation to explore the security dimensions of HIV/AIDS and the prospects for strengthening a new security consensus in response to the pandemic. I assess the theoretical aspects of HIV/AIDS as a human security threat and provide an overview on the debates relating to the pandemic's impact on defence forces and peacekeepers. A central preoccupation of this chapter is to raise awareness about the role of key actors in responding to HIV/AIDS in Africa. The chapter thus briefly provides an account of the roles and responses of UNAIDS and the Global Fund to Fight AIDS, Tuberculosis and Malaria (GFATM); addresses some successes, challenges and prospects faced by African governments; and assesses the promises and contributions made by rich governments. Finally, as an illustration of the nexus between health, development and security – which UN Secretary-General Kofi Annan has also articulated – this chapter stresses the urgent need to build effective health systems in Africa.

The Securitisation of AIDS

A recurrent theme in the "securitisation of AIDS" has been that the pandemic is a threat to human security. A second issue is that HIV/AIDS poses a specific threat to African defence forces and the continent's peacekeeping capacities. This chapter will examine both issues in turn.

HUMAN SECURITY AND HIV/AIDS

The term "human security" was first popularised in a 1994 UN Human Development Report, and encompasses economic, food, health, environmental, personal, community and political security. The AU's African Common Defence Pact of 2004 defines human security as social, political, economic, military and cultural conditions that protect and promote human life and dignity.[7] Human security provides a new framework for devising policies that address these interrelated threats in Africa. Human security differs from traditional or state-centric security because it places the safety of individuals, rather than the state, at the core of security. This re-working of priorities is not a total denunciation of state-centric security, but a more coherent articulation of the state's "responsibility to protect" and to promote the rights of people. (See Mwanasali as well as Deng in this volume). In Africa, where 32 wars have killed over 7 million people and spawned 9 million refugees since 1960, the birth of a concept that places the security of citizens above the survival of regimes could not be more radical and timely.

Current thinking often distinguishes between a narrow and broad concept of human security. The narrow concept of human security focuses on violent threats: human rights abuses; political repression; genocide; civil war; and attack from foreign state and non–state actors. The broader concept of human security encompasses non–violent threats: widespread diseases such as HIV/AIDS; environmental degradation; and poverty, social exclusion and inequality.[8] Narrowly defined, human security focuses on threats to freedom, while the broader concept also incorporates threats to human dignity. Despite these distinctions, the state is still viewed as the pivotal actor for securing both freedom and dignity for individuals.

The broad interpretation of human security has been criticised as being too unwieldy to assess and accomplish: it is often difficult to draw direct causal links between threats such as disease and poverty and overall societal stability and security. For example, the causes *as well as* the consequences of the African HIV epidemic include fragile health systems, poverty, gender inequality, competition over resources, and weak human rights regimes. It is especially difficult to untangle these root causes of HIV/AIDS from its impact on states and societies; it therefore becomes more challenging to devise replicable policy interventions. This difficulty in tracing HIV/AIDS to state instability has led to much backtracking among experts. Five years ago, debates about possible state failure and national crises characterised much of the discussion on the impact of HIV/AIDS on societies. In 2006, AIDS and society discourse has evolved to become more cautious and thoughtful.[9]

DEFENCE FORCES, PEACEKEEPING AND HIV/AIDS

Experts have speculated that HIV/AIDS poses a unique threat to the world's military forces. Paradoxically, this focus on defence forces has further "securitised" AIDS as a traditional security threat. Analysts have expounded on the potential impacts of HIV/AIDS in defence structures: a heavy toll on the decision-making command structure; rising costs in re-training highly skilled personnel; delayed deployment to international peace operations; and competition for resources with the civilian sector in order to meet the demands of expensive HIV/AIDS treatment. An additional concern has included the vulnerability of peacekeepers to HIV within conflict zones and the risk of these troops spreading the virus among civilian populations at home and abroad. The South African National Defence Force (SANDF) has openly stated that, if HIV and AIDS are not urgently addressed, the epidemic will have a negative impact on its combat readiness and the defence force will not be able to fulfill its mandate.[10] Consequently, in April 2001, the SANDF established a comprehensive HIV and AIDS management and mitigation programme. Most of Africa's defence forces have instituted HIV/AIDS prevention, care, support and treatment programmes.[11]

The genesis of this area of research and policy can be traced back to a 1998 UN report that stated that infection rates could be as much as two to five times higher in armies than in civilian populations.[12] Experts concluded that since soldiers were particularly vulnerable to sexually transmitted infections (STIs), they would have significantly higher rates of HIV than civilian populations. However, it is becoming increasingly clear that HIV rates within military populations may not be universally higher than in corresponding civilian populations.

As Tony Barnett and Gwyn Prins noted in their March 2006 report to UNAIDS, *HIV/AIDS and Security: Fact, Fiction and Evidence*, there has been a large amount of literature based on loosely interpreted data and little hard evidence to support many of the assertions made about HIV/AIDS and security.[13] Barnett and Prins assert that most of the current knowledge on HIV/AIDS and militaries has been based largely on newspaper articles. New knowledge must now be gathered which carefully considers the pathogenic characteristics of HIV, its effects at the individual level, and its impact on defence forces and societies. This level of analysis has been sadly absent in current assessments.[14] Barnett and Prins underscore that in the face of a threat such as HIV/AIDS, the greatest pressure to implement a response has coincided with a period when knowledge is at its lowest. Moreover, policymakers confronted with the need to raise funds and meet the demands of advocacy often rely on recycled data of poor quality.

The UN High-level Panel report of December 2004 recommended that the UN Security Council, in conjunction with UNAIDS, hold a second special session on HIV/AIDS as a threat to international peace and security in order to "explore the pandemic's future effects on states and societies, and generate research on the problem and identify a long-term strategy for diminishing the threat".[15] In response, Barnett and Prins have outlined a future research agenda that would include: integrated surveillance systems; a data-base of the demographic structure of armies; comparative perspectives; ethnographic studies of sexual behaviour among peacekeepers; and the response to HIV/AIDS within the security sector.[16] However, new research will meet old patterns of resistance. Researchers have faced particular challenges because military establishments generally view HIV prevalence and mortality data as too sensitive for outsiders. Military experts have resisted encroachment into their "territory" and continue to view the epidemic as a manageable public health problem (like malaria or any other preventable disease) that must be contained, if armies and peacekeepers are to do their jobs effectively. To many military brass hats, HIV/AIDS is not something those in the ivory tower or outside the state should meddle in.

The broader security policy issue that was raised by the High-level

Panel report is the threat that HIV/AIDS poses for African states and societies. HIV/AIDS raises the question of whether or not Africans will be able to contribute to, or enjoy, what Kofi Annan has described as freedom from fear, want and hunger. In effect, this question impacts state-centric as well as human security.[17] In the medium term, HIV/AIDS is transforming, in radical ways, the way people love, live, work, plan for the future, and participate in governance. There is a dynamic rationale for "securitising" HIV/AIDS which is much more indirect. On a continent ravaged by malaria, tuberculosis, and countless other diseases, HIV/AIDS seems to resemble other diseases of poverty and underdevelopment – indeed thousands of children die of malnutrition in Africa every day.[18] However, the long-term consequences of HIV/AIDS – which kills people in their most productive years – could have further-reaching implications than other important pandemics.

HIV/AIDS Unabated: Measures to Strengthen the New Security Consensus

From the beginning of the epidemic, the global response to HIV/AIDS was singularly relegated to the medical community. The UN's World Health Organisation (WHO) was thus seen as the most logical international actor to mobilise a response. However, beginning in January 1996, UNAIDS became the key international coordinator for addressing HIV/AIDS. In 2001, the Global Fund to Fight AIDS, Tuberculosis and Malaria was launched to mobilise and disburse the financial resources that are critical to addressing the pandemic effectively.

UNAIDS

UNAIDS was established out of a growing recognition that robust, interventionist activities by all UN agencies were critical to deploying a comprehensive development response to the accelerating AIDS pandemic. UNAIDS did not supplant the medical role of the WHO, but instead sought to devise coherent and coordinated policies through country-based "theme groups" that involved a broad group of international agencies. Consequently, UNAIDS coordinates ten other UN agencies by disseminating information and knowledge, conducting advocacy, and interfacing with governments and civil society actors across the globe.[19]

As a development partner, UNAIDS provides tracking and monitoring assistance and continues to mobilise political, technical and financial resources. The organisation also engages civil society organisations in country-driven approaches.

As the public face of the UN's response to HIV/AIDS, UNAIDS has struggled – but succeeded to some extent – to keep the pandemic as a prominent issue on the global policy agenda. The programme helped establish World AIDS Day on 1 December every year, and has launched campaigns to coincide with the UNAIDS/WHO annual report on the state of the pandemic. A major contribution to the global response to HIV/AIDS has been the programme's articulation of the links between human rights, gender inequality, socio-economic problems and HIV/AIDS. UNAIDS is thus responsible for expanding the involvement of political leaders in this battle. From its inception, the body argued that national AIDS programmes should not be based within health ministries but within the executive arm of governments. On the security front, UNAIDS has established an Office on AIDS, Security and Humanitarian Response and has been working with the UN's Department of Peacekeeping Operations (DPKO) in New York to implement an integrated approach to AIDS and security. This partnership has yielded some modest results: each major UN peacekeeping operation now has a full-time AIDS advisor, supported by trainers and counsellors, while all smaller missions have an AIDS focal point. UNAIDS also supports Africa's continental, sub-regional, and national HIV/AIDS management and mitigation initiatives.[20]

UNAIDS introduced a new lexicon to the health and development world with jargon such as "multi-sectoral approaches" and "mainstreaming HIV/AIDS" in order to push governments to involve all segments of society in the fight against the pandemic. In its ambitious efforts to organise national HIV/AIDS plans, UNAIDS has had mixed results. By 2002, over 40 African countries had produced AIDS programmes, and by 2005, almost all African governments had adopted one HIV/AIDS strategic plan; one national HIV/AIDS coordinating body; and one national monitoring and evaluation system. While these strategies have been more coherent than the disparate strategies adopted by African governments in the late 1980s and early 1990s, critics have highlighted the danger of writing policy from a single model. These plans are very useful to donors because of their uniformity and reliance on UNAIDS-sanctioned policies. However, an AIDS response blueprint may not include local strategies for coping with the disease such as: the demographics of HIV/AIDS' morbidity and mortality; HIV's capacity to recombine; its many viral subtypes; its multiple entry-points into society; and political, socio-economic and cultural differences on the ground. These all call for unique and innovative interventions. Standardised AIDS programmes have often failed to prioritise strategies according to specific country-level realities.[21]

The Global AIDS Fund

In April 2001, African leaders convened a special summit in Abuja, Nigeria, and declared HIV/AIDS to be an emergency.[22] That gathering, which produced the 2001 "Abuja Declaration and Plan of Action", also proposed the establishment of a special fund to combat the three pandemics ravaging Africa: HIV/AIDS, malaria and tuberculosis. A small but active group of AIDS activists in the north and south thereafter lobbied for a Fund which was finally agreed at the UN Special Session on HIV/AIDS in New York in June 2001. In many ways, the Global Fund represents a new way of doing business. The Fund's governance structure is composed of rich and poor governments as well as representatives of northern and southern civil society. In each beneficiary country, representatives of government and civil society are members of country-coordinating mechanisms, which develop and submit grant proposals to the Fund. The process is radical, yet imperfect. Strong and consistent leadership is required at the country level, and fair and transparent practices are critical to the grant making, implementation and reporting processes. However, the practice of funding interventions designed by beneficiaries is a departure from traditional development models in which donors often impose a blueprint for aid designed by foreign technical consultants. Optimistically, the Fund and its supporters aim that over five years, nearly 1.6 million people will receive much-needed AIDS drugs, making important strides in bridging the gap between those that need treatment and those that cannot obtain it. Moreover, the Fund is committed to devoting 60 per cent of its resources to Africa and two-thirds of its funding to support HIV/AIDS programmes.

At the time of the Global AIDS Fund's inception in 2002, UN Secretary-General, Kofi Annan, pushed for a $10 billion fund. If achieved, this would be a far-reaching improvement, since only an estimated $2.1 billion was going toward addressing the global pandemic. However, by April 2005, the Fund had only approved grants totaling $3.4 billion to 127 countries. Before its September 2005 replenishment meeting, less than $1 billion had been disbursed.[23] In 2005, both London and Washington failed to meet their pledges of $92 million and $435 million respectively. The reasons for this are complex. Tensions over the management of the Fund, US legislative restrictions and other issues have resulted in under-funding of the Fund. Other criticisms of the Fund have come from Africa. At their summit in Abuja in January 2005, the AU's heads of state noted that the Global AIDS Fund had failed to become the kind of partnership once envisaged. African leaders criticised the fact that the Fund's Expert Technical Review Panel had only three Africans among its 26 members.[24] Furthermore, the Fund has not addressed the structural challenges for delivering AIDS treatment and correcting some of the capacity challenges of Africa's health systems.

The UN High-level Panel Report and the UN Secretary-General's Response

The UN High-level Panel's report of December 2004 is not groundbreaking in terms of the debate on infectious diseases – and HIV/AIDS in particular – as a security threat. However, the report captures current thinking about AIDS and other existing and future diseases that could threaten states and societies. First, the Panel report articulates the emerging consensus that security, development, and human rights are linked. Once conceived as "distinct", these three issues are envisioned as existing on an overlapping continuum. As such, if international peace and security is linked to the global economy and the realisation of universal human rights, the health of people – even in remote places – has become more integral to overall global stability. Second, the Panel's report identifies the state as critical to ensuring collective security and speaks to the concern that HIV/AIDS may undermine state capacity. In its definition of the six clusters of threats, infectious diseases rest within a socio-economic framework as a new threat.

The overriding principle is framed in the High-level Panel report's synopsis: "Any event or process that leads to large-scale death or lessening of life chances and undermines states as the basic unit of the international system is a threat to international security".[25] HIV/AIDS

191

has reduced life expectancy among other indicators related to morbidity and mortality. Before UNAIDS chief Peter Piot's March 2006 remarks about life expectancy, small states and HIV/AIDS, Alex de Waal had noted in 2003 that reductions in life expectancy would translate into shorter life expectancy at adulthood. In the countries hardest hit by AIDS, life expectancy at birth is between 40 and 45 years. This means that when a person reaches adulthood, they can expect to live another 20 to 30 years.[26] In the context of the High-level report, HIV/AIDS – a health issue – has become a "security issue" worth discussing and addressing among military experts, diplomats and politicians. This new trend should not be underestimated: if governments feel pressured to focus more on threats such as disease and poverty, they may take more seriously the values of human freedom and dignity and relinquish their long-held preoccupation with "hard threats" relating to regime survival. If the trajectory begun by HIV/AIDS alters the grand idea of "security", there may be three modest, but positive long-term benefits. First, we may witness the emergence of Africa's ordinary people and vulnerable groups as political actors. Second, the focus on HIV/AIDS may increase awareness of, and commitment to, the social sector among international donors. Third, the impact on societies and an outraged citizenry could draw new attention to the provision of social welfare by African governments.

The High-level Panel's report does create a kind of *fait accompli* by positioning AIDS (and other infectious diseases) as a threat to the security of the state. As a contribution to the debate on policies to mitigate the impact of the pandemic, this is an entry-point for accelerating national action and mobilising a response that strengthens health infrastructures in order to prevent, treat and manage HIV/AIDS. Furthermore, because the High-level Panel, and the UN Secretary-General, Kofi Annan in his follow up report to the Millennium Summit of March 2005, frame AIDS as a threat to international peace and security, there is an implicit call for a global acceleration of the response in terms of security, development and HIV/AIDS interventions. The Panel's recommendation to the UN Security Council to revisit the issue of HIV/AIDS as a security threat is an example of this. The report's call for a major initiative to rebuild global public health capacities is another.

Finally, the UN Secretary-General's March 2005 report, *In Larger Freedom: Towards Development, Security and Human Rights for All* [27] calls for poor UN member states to recommit themselves to strengthening "good governance"; to combat corruption; to enable their private sectors; to maximise domestic resources, and to implement comprehensive national strategies to meet the Millennium Development targets of halving poverty by 2015. (See Legum in this volume). Wealthy UN member states are asked to commit to undertaking efforts to achieve the target of 0.7 per cent of gross national income for official development assistance (ODA) and to move towards 100 per cent debt cancellation. They are also requested to consider full funding for the Global Fund.[28]

These lofty but urgent goals articulated by the High-level Panel and the UN Secretary-General effectively require member states to take a hard look at their response to AIDS within the prism of international peace and security. For rich nations, this means taking seriously their commitments. Developing nations, for their part, are being forced to admit that their war against AIDS has been riddled with failure and that they must take urgent steps to address the pandemic. Whether or not the Panel's report and Kofi Annan's recommendations will result in developing countries addressing the issue of state capacity in the midst of AIDS, or if rich countries will turn their rhetoric about north–south partnerships to fighting disease and poverty into genuine action, remains to be seen. More importantly, both sides will have to act in concert if opportunities are not to be lost and responses are not to be ineffective.

Prospects for a Security Framework: Failures and Successes

At the heart of the High-level Panel's report is a call for strengthening institutions and mechanisms devoted to delivering development, "good governance", and ultimately, security. Many of these institutions – governments, regional organisations, and the UN and its agencies – are state-centric. The state being placed at the centre of the new security framework is therefore obvious and necessary. In many rich as well as poor countries, however, a slow response on the part of national governments has exacerbated the spread of HIV/AIDS domestically and internationally. The period since 1980 provides a useful assessment of how governments have managed HIV/AIDS. I will next assess the response of poor African and rich northern countries to the pandemic.

The State's Response: African Solutions?

African governments must mobilise resources, raise awareness and deliver treatment to address the HIV/AIDS pandemic.[29] In the early stages of the epidemic, most African leaders chose to ignore the epidemic. Historian John Iliffe writes that Zaire's Mobutu Sese Seko placed a four-year gag rule on his country's press on all matters relating to HIV. Kenya's Daniel Arap Moi wanted to quarantine all AIDS patients and accused the west of "hate speech" when it raised the issue of HIV/AIDS in Africa. Even the revered South African leader, Nelson Mandela, was reluctant to discuss HIV/AIDS publicly due to what he described as cultural issues. Iliffe explains that:

> For political leaders, moreover, HIV/AIDS was a profoundly distasteful subject to mention in public. It questioned their competence because they had no remedy, it threatened to raise demands for assistance that they could not afford to give, it distracted them from more pressing anxieties, it was potentially divisive, its victims had as yet no political voice, and it might damage their country's image.[30]

Yet in 2001, African governments pledged to commit 15 per cent of their national budgets to combat HIV/AIDS, tuberculosis and malaria through the Abuja Declaration and Plan of Action for HIV/AIDS, Malaria and Tuberculosis. For the most part, there has been a transformation from wilful ignorance to HIV/AIDS advocacy and mobilisation. The reasons for the sea change are as complex as the epidemic. First, by the early 1990s, the number of AIDS deaths confirmed that the epidemic had become generalised in national populations. Clearly, previous inaction had to become indefensible, a regret that several African leaders – including Nelson Mandela – have since expressed.[31] Contradicting this trend, Ugandan leader Yoweri Museveni – long heralded as a key driver of Uganda's response – first became alarmed by the epidemic when it became clear that many of his senior military officers were HIV-positive as early as September 1986. Museveni instructed *all* government officials to discuss HIV/AIDS at *all* public meetings.

Second, success is possible – Uganda and Senegal (and now Kenya and Zimbabwe) – are examples. Senegal was able to prevent HIV/AIDS from becoming a generalised epidemic and under president Abdou Diouf, who stepped down in 2000, the government stabilised the country's adult HIV infection rates at around one per cent. Admittedly, epidemiologists have noted that Senegal had good conditions for containment: a strong Islamic tradition, a sexually transmitted infection (STI) programme dating back to the 1970s, a nearly legal commercial sex worker industry which was easier to regulate, established acceptance of using condoms with casual partners and near-universal male circumcision. However, with Diouf's leadership, the country also quickly made an effort to control the blood supply, mobilise community leaders and activate civil society in the fight against HIV/AIDS.

Uganda, however, would not be so fortunate. In 1986, the country was emerging from years of civil war, with no health infrastructure to speak of, and its HIV epidemic was the worst in the world: the country had an average prevalence rate of 24 per cent in its capital of Kampala in 1987. Two key actors are largely responsible for the declining rates: government and civil society. As a matter of urgency, the government of Museveni established an AIDS control programme with a strict policy of openness; it mobilised local council leaders at the grassroots levels; established public education programmes; and lobbied aggressively with international actors such as the WHO to get as much help as possible. Most importantly, HIV/AIDS became an issue for community mobilisation. Information about the causes and consequences of HIV/AIDS spread from state-sponsored media actions to more informal campaigns and finally to personal contact through families. In this regard, people living with HIV/AIDS were critical to these efforts and formed grassroots movements such as the AIDS Support Organisation (TASO), with full encouragement from the government.

Though there has been some debate about the extent of Uganda's epidemic, UNAIDS has noted that Uganda's HIV prevalence had fallen to 4.1 per cent by 2003.[32] The country's success has become a point of pride for many African leaders, and given many others the moral courage to confront the pandemic head-on.

Additional declarations to act are buttressing the role of African governments. At the AU summit in Maputo, Mozambique in 2003, African leaders passed a second plan of action on Malaria, HIV/AIDS, Tuberculosis and Other Related Diseases.[33] The AU has also institutionalised AIDS

Watch Africa (AWA), an *ad hoc* coalition of African leaders, as part of the AU Commission's HIV/AIDS Strategic Plan for 2005–2007.[34] These steps reflect increased political will, but in terms of actual mobilisation of resources and implementation, not much has been done. The mid-term review on the implementation of the Abuja Declaration took place during a special AU summit in Abuja, Nigeria in May 2006. Thus far, only Botswana has met the 15 per cent health expenditure target. However, Gambia, Ghana, Tanzania, Uganda and Zimbabwe are making progress towards reaching this goal by devoting between 12 and 14.5 per cent of their national budgets to the health sector.[35] Largely, the response has been at country-level, and while this is important, regional efforts are key to the successful control of the pandemic. The Southern African Development Community (SADC) has also developed its own comprehensive strategy to address HIV/AIDS. Some of SADC's strategies are to promote a programme for the care of vulnerable children and orphans; to develop an initiative to regulate the distribution of antiretroviral therapy medicines; to strengthen networks of mid-wives and healthcare professionals; to support networks of people living with HIV/AIDS; and to educate southern African media outlets on HIV/AIDS issues.[36]

Under the rubric of the 2001 UN Declaration of Commitment on HIV/AIDS, member states, including African governments, agreed to time-bound, concrete targets for fighting HIV/AIDS. In 2003, UNAIDS reviewed progress made towards achieving these goals and identified critical challenges that explained why more resources had not been made available to the fight against AIDS. These were: first, insufficient financial resources; second, lack of human resources and technical capacity; third, HIV/AIDS stigma and discrimination; and fourth, weak monitoring and evaluation capacity. Even though there was increased financial commitment on the part of bilateral and multilateral donors, 50 per cent of African countries reported to UNAIDS that they had insufficient resources for increasing their HIV/AIDS prevention and treatment programmes.[37]

If the obstacles to fully mobilise an adequate response to HIV/AIDS go beyond receiving resources from external sources, this has not been captured in the assessment of their performance by African governments. African governments reported that they have been unable to deliver on their promises without really accentuating the hardships that the continent continues to face in securing sustainable financing and escaping the burden of its staggering external debt of $290 billion. Ironically, global as well as African civil society actors have been more vocal in this respect, making radical and important links between shortfalls in aid and inequities in the international economic infrastructure, and Africa's poor response to AIDS. Strong gestures and arguments from African governments supporting these protests have been rare and AU leaders have often failed to support the moral outrage of civil society actors.

The State's Response: Rich Countries

Western governments have played a visible role in addressing HIV/AIDS. The identification of HIV/AIDS as a security threat in fact emanates from America. In 2000, the US National Intelligence Council categorised AIDS as a global infectious disease with non-traditional security implications. Setting a precedent, the UN Security Council, under the US presidency of its UN ambassador, Richard Holbrooke, held a special session on HIV/AIDS as a security issue in January 2000. The Council adopted Resolution 1308 in July 2000 which identified HIV/AIDS as a threat to international peace and security. Subsequently, the UN General Assembly Special Session on HIV/AIDS Declaration of Commitment in 2001 included recommendations for HIV/AIDS interventions in the governance and security sectors. In July 2005, UNAIDS executive director, Peter Piot, briefed the Security Council on the progress made in implementing Resolution 1308. A 2003 report by the UNAIDS Office on AIDS, Security and Humanitarian Response, *On the Frontline*, was also revised and published in July 2005 to explain the UN's progress in mainstreaming HIV/AIDS into traditional security issues such as conflict management and international peacekeeping.[38]

Under the presidency of George W Bush, the US government increased funding to developing countries. Importantly, Bush engineered an emergency HIV/AIDS initiative for 14 African and Caribbean countries. Announced in January 2003, the US President's Emergency Plan for AIDS Relief (PEPFAR) aimed to deliver $15 billion over five years, thereby seeking to prevent seven million new HIV infections and provide treatment to two million people. America's AIDS plan has been recognised as extraordinarily ambitious on the part of a single donor, and helped to raise expectations of other rich countries. In 2004, the

US Congress allotted $2.4 billion for PEPFAR spending. Experts have taken on board the rising debate on the long-term challenges of HIV/ AIDS and have made three recommendations for PEPFAR: first, the initiative should integrate its support to HIV/AIDS programmes with strategies that strengthen public health systems; second, PEPFAR should convene a commission to consider options for financing antiretroviral therapy; and third, the programme should expand its support to societal issues such as the vulnerability of women and the role of militaries and peacekeepers.[39] Despite its clear commitment to the global fight against AIDS, controversy over the Bush initiative has arisen over its advocacy of abstinence and preferential support to faith-based initiatives.

Africa's development partners, however, have largely failed to do enough to fight HIV/AIDS. A glaring example is the outcome of the Group of Eight industrialised countries (G-8) summit in Gleneagles, Scotland in July 2005. Earlier in that year, British Prime Minister Tony Blair's Commission for Africa Report had called for an additional $25 billion in aid to Africa each year for the next three to five years. (See Gambari in this volume). Without significant increases in aid, it was argued, sub-Saharan Africa would fail to achieve any of the Millennium Development Goals. At Gleneagles, the G-8 countries agreed to increase aid to Africa from $25 billion to $50 billion by 2010. The G-8 also pledged to increase resources for universal access to AIDS treatment, again by 2010. In part, this pledge emanated from guilt: the G-8's Kaminski Africa Action Plan of 2002 had been scantily implemented and the Global Fund will still need about $18 billion in 2007 and $22 billion in 2008 to meet the demands of containing HIV/AIDS and the other pandemics affecting the developing world.[40]

However, according to the "Make Poverty History" movement, the G-8 promise of 2010 was too little, too late. Even if the wealthiest nations in the world are willing to increase aid to $50 billion, their record of accomplishment remains uneven. None of the G-8 countries – Britain, Canada, France, Germany, Italy, Japan, Russia and the US – have reached the 0.7 per cent of GNP for ODA set as far back as 1970. As Stephen Lewis, the UN's Special Envoy for HIV/AIDS in Africa noted in 2005:

> It is Official Development Assistance that will tell the tale for
> Africa. It is Official Development Assistance that goes to the social
> sectors, health and education in particular, giving governments

the chance, the opportunity, the hope of overcoming poverty and the burden of disease. There is no other source of funds that goes so directly to the sectors on which the most vulnerable citizens of Africa depend.[41]

How will the annual $50 billion aid target be reached? At Gleneagles, Paris and London said that they would meet their ODA target by 2012 and 2013 respectively. Canada, though the original advocate for the 0.7 per cent ODA target, failed to make any firm commitments at Gleneagles. Germany and Italy declared that they would only be guided by the health of their economies. Realistically, the expectations for these two countries are low. The second richest of the G-8 countries, Japan, currently devotes 0.18 per cent of its GNP to development assistance; doubling its aid will thus only add another $1.5 billion to the G-8's collective pool of resources. No one expects Russia, with its own massive domestic problems, to meet the target. Experts agree that if the $50 billion target is to be reached, the United States as the richest G-8 country, should be contributing a great deal more than the $3 billion it disburses a year. The US 2002 Millennium Challenge Account, which was expected to reach $5 billion a year, has proved to be feeble. By 2005, only about 15 per cent of the Millennium Challenge Account's funds had been allocated to four developing countries.

Finally, civil society and development experts have noted that over 60 per cent of the west's development assistance *never* reaches the people it claims to help. Too much foreign assistance pays for foreign consultants and services provided by the donor country, often at inflated prices. Moreover, much of current aid is linked to conditionalities such as privatisation of industries. Indeed, Jeffrey Sachs has noted that of the annual $3 billion spent in Africa, only about $1 billion actually supports poverty reduction.[42] If the G-8 countries continue to do business as usual, they will have to commit nearly $100 billion a year just to ensure that the promised $50 billion proves to be real aid. That is unlikely to happen. Inevitably, development assistance, as it is currently implemented, will not significantly contribute to solving Africa's human security crisis. [43]

A Common Vision: Closing the Capacity Gap

The UN High-level Panel's report noted that the response to the HIV/AIDS pandemic had been "shockingly late and shamefully ill-resourced" and advocated a major initiative to rebuild global public health capacities. In terms of aligning with African states, this recommendation mirrors emerging, nascent perspectives from African leaders. Although the follow-up implementation has been tepid since Abuja in 2001, African leaders are at this moment moving on a number of capacity issues. While not implicitly being about boosting state capacity, these moves indicate a burgeoning ownership of the health issue and its relevance to preventing, managing and eliminating the continent's pandemics.

The pandemic's broad interaction with all segments of society has highlighted the importance of addressing people-centred realities in Africa. Margaret Legum, in this volume, examines the impact of the Washington Consensus' structural adjustment policies (SAPs) on the social sector in developing countries. The legacy of these programmes has resulted in an appalling deficit in social capital. HIV/AIDS has taken advantage of Africa's weak healthcare systems, its moribund educational systems, and its fragile state institutions: with such poor capacity for addressing a major public health care crisis, it is no wonder that Africa's HIV/AIDS epidemic is so high. Moreover, in countries where political leadership was silent and refused to publicly address HIV/AIDS because of sexual taboos and wilful ignorance, the epidemic gained a huge advantage: the ten-year incubation period before HIV progresses to AIDS allowed further contamination.

Sub-Saharan Africa has only 1.3 per cent of the world's health workforce, although it bears 25 per cent of the world's disease burden. Roughly one million more health workers are needed to address this capacity gap. Current expenditure in most African countries is below $20 per capita per annum. This is half or less of the $35–40-minimum required to meet basic healthcare needs.[44] Constructive self-criticism has not prevailed: little is said about the lack of coordination between African ministries of health, finance, development and gender, and how this has crippled the effective management of resources. As late as 2005, an issue that heavily impacted the response to AIDS has finally been articulated and raised at the highest levels of African governments: national treasuries continue to cap resources for the health sector. Finally, governance has not been sufficiently articulated as an important element in combating AIDS. Governance deficits such as limits on political participation, and marginalisation of community-based initiatives, civil society organisations and the private sector continue to limit options for public–private partnerships that could help mobilise and popularise national HIV/AIDS programmes and generate grassroots community healthcare initiatives.

AU member states are beginning to think about how to keep the continent's health workers in Africa, instead of losing them to Europe and North America. The AU notes that Africa's health-care workforce "density is 0.8 per 1000 population, compared to a world average of 4.2, and then there are severe urban/rural imbalances".[45] Africa's health ministers have now agreed to meet on an annual basis to coordinate their advocacy initiatives. These pragmatic moves are in line with the recommendations of the High-level Panel and the UN Secretary-General's March 2005 report. More importantly, there has been a substantive policy shift when it comes to addressing HIV/AIDS: African governments now argue that real solutions must be implemented within a framework for closing the capacity gap between the continent's health crisis and the infrastructure needed for long-term success. If experts such as UNAIDS' executive director Peter Piot are correct, HIV/AIDS will continue to be a challenge for Africa until at least 2060. Efforts to develop long-term strategies now are therefore essential.

Concluding Thoughts: The Historical Legacy of AIDS and Security

For the first twenty years of the epidemic, HIV/AIDS was defined as a health crisis. The response from policymakers was largely driven by a medical approach, and little consideration was given to the long-term implications of HIV/AIDS for African states and societies. The MDGs will remain an ephemeral wish-list as long as African countries continue to struggle to educate millions of orphans, fill human resource capacity gaps and deliver expensive treatment to nearly a third of their working adults. Hopefully, this recognition will influence any future UN reform. In the meantime, African perspectives on HIV/AIDS and other social and development factors for security remain uneven and unclear. The High-level Panel report may increase attention to these issues if only because it strongly emphasises the need for governments to be accountable for the impact of the pandemic and warns that the toll of HIV/AIDS on societies could undermine the international system.

In the long-term, when historians look back to the beginning of the twenty-first century, they still may say: after slavery, colonialism, and the Cold War, Africa experienced an enemy so insidious that it radically influenced the trajectory of democratisation and development on the continent. Future African *griots* (story-tellers) might place the blame on the UN and African governments. Africa's future may be a distorted mosaic of inequality: small pockets of urban-dwelling elites who survived AIDS are the minority; angry and disenfranchised youths living in mega-city slums without clean water, food, work, shelter, or medicine form the majority; and a vast rural poor continue to eke out an increasingly difficult existence perhaps not materially worse than now, but certainly existentially worse than their impoverished and illiterate forefathers and foremothers half a century before. Africa must avoid this bleak future by acting urgently, with its international partners, to win the battle against HIV/AIDS.

Notes

[1] African Union and United Nations: Africa Launches Bold, Renewed Effort to Step Up HIV Prevention (Addis Ababa, Ethiopia, 12 April 2006).

[2] See the Joint United Nations Programme on HIV/AIDS (UNAIDS) and the World Health Organisation (WHO): AIDS Epidemic Update (Geneva: December 2005, available at: http://www.unaids.org/epi/2005/doc/report_pdf.asp, accessed 15 April 2006).

[3] See UNAIDS, UN Children's Fund (UNICEF) and United States Agency for International Development (USAID): *Children on the Brink 2004: A Joint Report of New Orphan Estimates and a Framework for Action* (New York: July 2004). Available at http://www.unicef.org/publications/files/cob_layout6-013.pdf (accessed 16 April 2006).

[4] UNAIDS/WHO, Epidemic Update, p.17.

[5] Piot, P (UNAIDS Executive Director): "Getting Ahead of AIDS: The Long-Term Agenda", Washington: Woodrow Wilson International Centre for Scholars, 9 March 2006.

[6] UN High-level Panel on Threats, Challenges and Change, A More Secure World: Our Shared Responsibility, Report of the Secretary-General, A/59/565, December 2004.

[7] See the Human Security Centre: Human Security Report 2005: War and Peace in the 21st Century (The Human Security Centre and the Liu Institute for Global Issues, Universities of British Columbia, London and Vancouver: Oxford University Press, 2005), p VIII; and AU: Draft Text of the Common African Defence and Security Policy (Addis Ababa, Ethiopia: 20–21 January 2004), adopted at the AU Heads of State and Government Summit, Addis Ababa, Ethiopia, 7– 9 July 2004, as cited in Cilliers, J: Human Security in Africa: A Conceptual Framework for Review (African Human Security Initiative, 2004). On structural violence see Scheper-Hughes, N: Death Without Weeping: The Violence of Everyday Life in Brazil (Berkeley: University of California Press, 1992) and Uvin, P: Aiding Violence: The Development Enterprise in Rwanda (West Hartford: Kumarian Press, 1998), pp.103–8.

[8] Human Security Centre: Human Security Report 2005, p.viii.

[9] For the debate on these issues five years ago, see the International Crisis Group (ICG): HIV/AIDS As A Security Issue (Brussels, Washington, DC: ICG, June 2001) and de Waal, A: "AIDS-related National Crises in Africa: Food Security, Governance and Development Partnerships" in IDS Bulletin Vol. 33, No. 4, 2002, pp. 120–26.

[10] The South African Military Health Services (SAMHS): The Comprehensive Plan for the Holistic Management of HIV and AIDS in the Department of Defence: 2005–2010 (Tshwane, 5 March 2005), p. 2. South African policymaking and activist communities distinguish between Human Immunodeficiency Virus (HIV) – the virus – and Acquired Immunodeficiency Syndrome (AIDS) – the condition that eventually ensues when HIV is left untreated. The South African military health services and other government programmes therefore do not use "HIV/AIDS" but "HIV" and "AIDS" in their documents.

[11] See the Centre for Conflict Resolution (CCR) reports, HIV/AIDS and Militaries in Southern Africa, Windhoek, Namibia, 9–10 February 2006 (available at: http://ccrweb.ccr.uct.ac.za) and HIV/AIDS and Human Security: An Agenda for Africa, Addis Ababa, Ethiopia, 9–10 September 2005, available at: http://ccrweb.ccr.uct.ac.za (accessed 16 April 2006).

[12] UNAIDS: AIDS and the Military (New York and Geneva: UNAIDS, May 1998; no longer available or in circulation) also cited in remarks made by the UNAIDS Executive Director, Dr Peter Piot, at UN General Assembly, High-level Meeting on HIV/AIDS, New York, 22 September 2003.

[13] Barnett, T & Prins, G: HIV/AIDS and Security: Fact, Fiction, and Evidence: A Report to UNAIDS (Geneva and London: UNAIDS and London School of Economics, March 2005).

[14] Barnett, T & Prins, G: HIV/AIDS and Security, p. 8.

[15] UN High-level Panel on Threats, Challenges and Change, A More Secure World: Our Shared Responsibility, Report of the Secretary-General, A/59/565, December 2004, Part Two, Para 8, p.79.

[16] Barnett, T & Prins, G: HIV/AIDS and Security, p.38.

[17] For example, see Fourie, P & Shonteich, M: "Africa's New Security Threat: HIV/AIDS and Human Security in Southern Africa" in African Security Review Vol 10, No4, 2001; Shell, R: "Halfway to the Holocaust: the Economic Demographic and Social Implication of the AIDS Pandemic to the Year 2010 in the Southern African Region" in African Renaissance, Konrad Adenauer Foundation Occasional Paper Series, 2002; and Shonteich, M: "HIV/AIDS and Security", Regional Governance and AIDS Forum, IDASA/UNDP HIV Development Project for Southern Africa, April 2–4 2003.

[18] Cohen, D: "Human Capital and the HIV Epidemic in sub-Saharan Africa" in International Labour Organisation Programme on HIV/AIDS and the World of Work (Geneva: ILO, June 2002); and UN Economic Commission for Africa, Commission on HIV/AIDS and Governance in Africa: Africa: The Socio-Economic Impact of HIV/AIDS (Addis Ababa: CHGA, 2004).

[19] The UN Development Programme (UNDP); the World Health Organisation (WHO); the International Labour Organisation (ILO); the UN Population Fund (UNFPA); the UN Children's Fund (UNICEF); the UN Economic, Social and Cultural Organisation (UNESCO); the UN Organisation for Drug Control (UNODC); the World Food Programme (WFP); and the UN High Commission for Refugees (UNHCR) are the core member agencies of UNAIDS. The World Bank has integrated HIV/AIDS into its support for national and sectoral planning, financial management and infrastructure development.

[20] UNAIDS Office of AIDS, Security and Humanitarian Response: Progress Report (unpublished paper, 2005) and UNAIDS: On the Front Line: A Review of Policies and Programmes to Address AIDS Among Peacekeepers and Uniformed Services (New York: July 2003).

[21] Iliffe, J: The African AIDS Epidemic: A History (Oxford: James Currey Limited), pp. 138–40.

[22] AU: *Abuja Declaration on HIV/AIDS, Tuberculosis and Other Related Infectious Diseases* (Abuja, Nigeria: 24–27 April 2001), OAU/SPS/Abuja 3.

[23] Ndinga-Muvumba, A: "Too Late to Make HIV/AIDS History" in *South African Labour Bulletin* Vol. 29, No. 4, August/September 2005.

[24] AU Commission: Consideration of an Interim Situational Report on HIV/AIDS, Tuberculosis, Malaria and Polio: Framework on Actions to Accelerate Health Improvements in Africa, 6th Ordinary Session of the Heads of States and Governments of the African Union, Abuja, Nigeria, January 2005.

[25] UN High-level Panel on Threats, Challenges and Change, A More Secure World: Our Shared Responsibility, Part Two, Synopsis, p. 25.

[26] De Waal, A: "How Will HIV/AIDS Transform African Governance?" in *African Affairs* 102 (2003), p. 5.

[27] *In Larger Freedom: Towards Development, Security, and Human Rights for All:* Report of the Secretary-General, A/59/2005, 21 March 2005.

[28] *In Larger Freedom*, Annex, para 5, p. 56.

[29] See CCR: HIV/AIDS and Human Security: An Agenda for Africa.

[30] Iliffe, J: The African AIDS Epidemic, pp. 66–67.

[31] Iliffe, J: The African AIDS Epidemic, pp. 66–67.

[32] See UNAIDS/WHO: AIDS Epidemic Update (Geneva, December 2004), p. 25.

[33] AU: *Maputo Declaration on Malaria, HIV/AIDS, Tuberculosis and Other Related Infectious Diseases*, 10–12 July 2003, Maputo, Mozambique, Assembly/AU/Decl.6.

[34] AU: *The AU Commission HIV/AIDS Strategic Plan 2005–2007*; and *AIDS Watch Africa (AWA) Strategic Plan* (Sirte, Libya: 28 June – 2 July 2005), EX.CL/194.

[35] AU: *Progress Report on the Implementation of the Plan of Action of the Abuja Declaration for Malaria, HIV/AIDS and Tuberculosis* (Gaborone, Botswana: 10–14 October 2005).

[36] See CCR: HIV/AIDS and Militaries in Southern Africa.

[37] UNAIDS: Implementation of the 2001 Declaration of the UN General Assembly Special Session (UNGASS) on HIV/AIDS (New York: UNAIDS, May 2003).

[38] See UNAIDS: On the Front Line.

[39] Council on Foreign Relations and Milbank Memorial Fund: Addressing the HIV/AIDS Pandemic: A US Global AIDS Strategy for the Long Term (New York: Council on Foreign Relations and Milbank Memorial Fund, 2004).

[40] Ndinga-Muvumba, A: "Too Late to Make HIV/AIDS History".

[41] Lewis, S: Race Against Time (Toronto: House of Anansi, 2005), p. 26.

[42] Sachs, J: The End of Poverty: Economic Possibilities for Our Time (New York: Penguin Press, 2005).

[43] Lewis, S: Race Against Time, pp. 28–31.

[44] AU Commission: *Consideration of an Interim Situational Report on HIV/AIDS.*

[45] AU Commission: *Consideration of an Interim Situational Report on HIV/AIDS,* p.7.

11

Tackling Security Threats: International Organised Crime

Peter Gastrow

INTERNATIONAL CONCERN OVER the rapid global increase in transnational organised crime, and the response from the United Nations (UN) General Assembly in adopting an international convention to counter it, predates the September 2001 attacks on the World Trade Centre in New York and the Pentagon in Washington DC.[1]

The UN Convention against Transnational Organised Crime – the Palermo Convention – was signed during December 2000 by 126 member states, including 31 from Africa. During the preceding two-year negotiation process, participation by African states tended to be patchy and uneven. Many countries experienced relative disadvantage to the richer and more powerful states. They could only afford small delegations and lacked the requisite support staff or expertise to negotiate effectively. Despite this, the process was not marked by controversies over multilateralism versus unilateralism or by attempts to coerce weaker states to toe the western line. The term "transnational organised crime" is not as weighted with political tension as the term "terrorism"; the Palermo Convention therefore enjoys wide support, as indicated by its many signatories. This explains why the UN High-level Panel report *A More Secure World: Our Shared Responsibility* and the follow-up report of the UN Secretary-General, *In Larger Freedom: Towards Development, Security and Human Rights for All*, contain only short sections on transnational organised crime and why little debate occurred about these recommendations.[2] In essence, both reports call upon member states to speed up the implementation of the Palermo Convention and other related international legal instruments.

It would be a pity if Africa does not respond to the recommendations on transnational organised crime outlined in the two reports, since such criminal activities have a debilitating effect on many African states. Sophisticated organised criminal networks impede development, undermine governance and criminal justice systems, and fuel civil conflicts on the continent. In many African countries, transnational organised crime poses a more fundamental threat to human security than terrorism. A considered response from African states to this subject is therefore critical.

This chapter will briefly outline the process culminating in the Palermo Convention. It will detail the development of transnational organised crime in Africa and contend that concerted action by African states as well as the international community is required to address this threat. Governments, the United Nations, and the international community must give the same priority to tackling transnational organised crime as it received before 11 September 2001. The chapter will examine current international measures to combat money laundering and identify the shortcomings of these efforts in Africa. In addition, attention will be given to the severe capacity problems experienced in many parts of Africa and the need for further international support initiatives to maximise the convention's impact. If under-resourced states are to be successful in implementing the large number of requirements they have to meet under the convention, enhanced coordination of these initiatives will be essential.

International Responses to the Growth of Transnational Organised Crime

The very concept of "transnational crime" is relatively new. The UN Crime Prevention and Criminal Justice Branch coined the term in 1975 in order to identify certain criminal phenomena transcending national borders, transgressing the laws of several states or having an impact on more than one country.[3] During the 1970s and 1980s, legislation on organised crime centred on confronting the domestic threat it posed. Increasingly, however, governments realised that they required legal assistance from other states in which organised criminal groups had links in order to prosecute criminal groups effectively. The number of bilateral legal assistance treaties increased sharply during the 1980s and calls grew for international measures to be developed on the narcotics trade and money laundering.

In many African countries, the unstable political and economic environment of the 1980s encouraged the expansion of organised criminal networks and contributed to the "internationalisation" of organised crime. While African states became increasingly aware of the cross-border activities of crime syndicates this did not immediately translate into legislative initiatives to counter organised crime. Economic development and political stability in many post-independence African countries had deteriorated substantially from the end of the 1970s. (See Legum in this volume). The 1980s were characterised by a decline in agricultural and industrial production, a reduction of per capita income, dwindling trade and growing debt.[4] As a result of the growing debt crisis faced by many states, there were often acute shortages of imported goods and this led to the proliferation of illicit smuggling. Black market activities grew in an effort to fill the gap. Many countries were forced to accept loans from the International Monetary Fund (IMF) and the World Bank based on the condition that they fundamentally restructure their economy. In exchange for loans, governments were required to adopt structural adjustment programmes (SAPs). For example, donors insisted that the number of civil servants be slashed, that state assets be privatised and that states should not regulate production and distribution. (See Legum in this volume).

African states were thus faced with the daunting challenge of both adapting from state-led to structural adjustment-led market economies, as well as moving from autocratic rule to multi-party democratic systems. With few exceptions, the SAPs generated devastating results for African countries. Not only were these policies largely ineffective on a macroeconomic level, there were elements in the political leadership who skilfully managed the reforms for their individual benefit. These elements were able to use the SAPs to indulge in "practices of accumulation" – or more bluntly corruption – by carving out profitable areas for their own personal business activities. Africa's political entrepreneurs combined public office with commercial ventures, inevitably advancing corruption and, in turn, organised crime. The corrupt practices of those in high office brought them into contact with "middlemen" – often from beyond their borders – and other entrepreneurs who were operating in the criminal markets. One of the symptoms of the dramatic transformations in many African states was therefore "the growing implication of African economic and political entrepreneurs (or European, Arab, Asian and Latin American operators who are based in Africa) in activities which may be considered illegal or criminal, according to western criteria which have tended to be adopted by the international system as a whole".[5]

By the early 1990s, it was clear that transnational organised crime had grown significantly, and that the range of crimes had broadened considerably beyond trafficking in narcotics. Globalisation and increasing economic interdependence had fuelled this phenomenon. The weakening of state authority in many parts of the world, including Africa, had reduced the risks facing transnational organised crime networks. These actors were able to exploit new opportunities to expand their markets. Transnational organised crime in Africa was increasingly driven by domestic criminal networks, as well as international criminal organisations that were innovative and cooperated internationally, but also competed with others when it was in their interest to do so.

Since 1990, the UN has played a more conspicuous role in tackling transnational organised crime. In December 1992, the General Assembly expressed its alarm at the "rapid growth and geographic extension of organised crime in its various forms, both nationally and internationally" and acknowledged "the need for global efforts commensurate with the magnitude of national and transnational crime".[6] In addition, the Assembly stressed that priority must be given "to the struggle against all activities of organised crime, including the illicit arms trade and traffic in narcotic drugs, cultural property theft, money laundering, the infiltration of legitimate business and the corruption of public officials".[7]

The US also began to take on a leading role in support of global action during the mid-1990s. In US President Bill Clinton's 50th anniversary speech to the UN in October 1995, he gave prominence to the threat posed by organised crime. Subsequently, Clinton issued Presidential Directive 42, declaring organised crime to be a threat to global security, and mobilising the US government to fight against it. African leaders also called for international action to counter organised crime at a meeting in Dakar, Senegal in 1997, advancing calls for negotiations over a UN convention.

Following a two-year negotiation process, the Palermo Convention was signed in December 2000. The desire of African states to support the Convention was evident in their signing of the document. Then events on 11 September 2001 unfolded. America's "war on terrorism" was propelled to the top of the global security agenda, leaving transnational organised crime and the Palermo Convention lower down the international priority list. (See Baregu in this volume). The convention eventually came into force in September 2003. By April 2004, 102 states had signed the convention, but some of the most prominent players during the negotiating process had not yet acceded to it. These included Britain, Germany, Pakistan, the US, Japan, India and Italy. If fresh initiatives to speed up the implementation of Palermo are to succeed, then the full commitment of influential countries will be essential.

The Extent of Organised Crime in Africa

Any generalisations about the extent and impact of organised crime in Africa ought to be treated with caution. With 53 states and a population of over 800 million, Africa's diverse economic, political and social environments need to be carefully considered. In addition, there is a dearth of reliable crime data, as crime statistics are available for only about half of all African countries and this data often originates from multiple sources, covering different periods. Perceptions of the extent of organised crime in Africa are often shaped by anecdotal information and by media reports that refer to specific cases of arrests or seizures.

Statements by police officers and politicians frequently express alarm at the growth of transnational organised crime and at how this trend is undermining economies and criminal justice systems in African countries. The former National Commissioner of Police in Botswana, Norman Moloboge, recently lamented: "It is evident that transnational organised crime is wreaking havoc in almost all our countries nowadays".[8] Steve Tshwete, South Africa's former Minister of Safety and Security, pointed to the potentially disastrous consequences of transnational organised crime for "good governance" and the economy, and stressed that greater political will was required to "confront the phenomenon head-on with all the might and ruthlessness that can be summoned".[9]

The United Nations Office on Drugs and Crime (UNODC) currently produces a global organised crime index, which compares organised crime levels in different regions of the world. In light of the unreliable data on organised crime in Africa and elsewhere, this chart should be read as one based on the available – albeit inadequate – information on organised crime. It nevertheless provides an indication of the high levels of organised crime in sub-Saharan Africa and should thus be of serious concern to governments on the continent as well as to the international community.

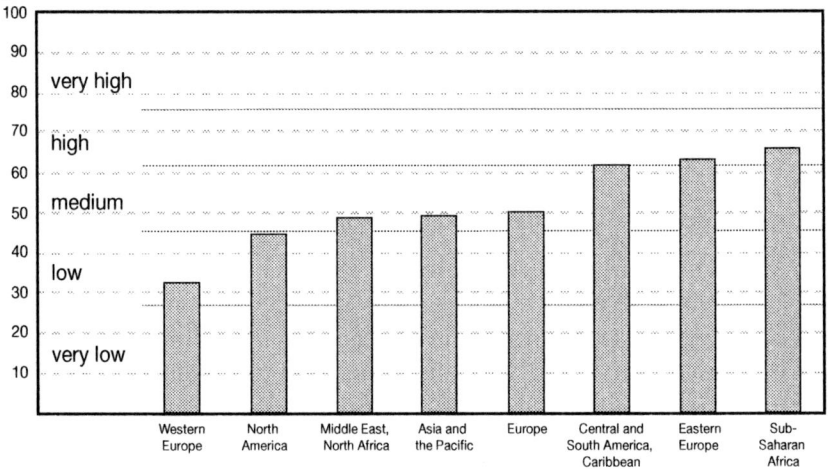

Figure 11.1 UNODC organised crime index by region[10]

There can be no doubt about the serious threat posed by transnational organised crime in Africa, particularly to poor countries. Weak and under-resourced states tend to encourage the penetration of state and business structures by organised criminal groups. They do so at a lower risk than in better-resourced countries. Sophisticated criminal networks have the capacity to buy political access and influence at the highest levels of government. Weak states in which such developments remain unchecked can become caught up in a cycle in which organised crime creates the conditions for its own growth, gradually weakening the ability of the already weak state to combat crime. Under such circumstances, the risk of states themselves becoming criminalised is real. To reverse such situations requires extraordinary interventions.

Civil wars and conflicts on the continent have further exacerbated the situation since they have created "free-for-all" zones, leaving local and international criminal groups and corporations free to plunder valuable natural resources with impunity in countries such as the Democratic Republic of the Congo (DRC), Liberia and Sierra Leone. Organised criminal groups that entrench themselves during periods of conflict tend to subvert the establishment of new institutions and economic growth in the post-conflict phase. For already poverty-stricken citizens in post-conflict societies, the activities of organised criminal groups tend to perpetuate humanitarian crises, frustrate development assistance and undermine legitimate economic activity. Outside Africa, events in Kosovo revealed that the growth of organised crime could prove a major obstacle to economic development as well as to the establishment of new national institutions such as police, customs and the judiciary.

Recommendations of the UN High-level Panel Report

Collective security

The recommendations of the High-level Panel on *Threats, Challenges and Change* are premised on the acceptance by the international community of the concept of "collective security". The report explains that "depending on wealth, geography and power, we perceive different threats as most pressing. But the truth is we cannot afford to choose. Collective security today depends on accepting that the threats which each region of the world perceives as most urgent are in fact equally so for all".[11] If this reasoning is to be properly applied, then those threats deemed most urgent by African countries ought to be accepted by the rest of the world as equally urgent, and the international community should respond to them accordingly.

Despite its flaws, the notion of "collective security" constitutes a progression from state-centric "security". Collective security advances the concept of security into a realm where development and the safety of citizens receive greater priority. The UN Commission on Human Security defines human security as "protecting the vital core of all human lives in ways that enhance human freedoms and human fulfilment".[12] This broad definition marks a shift in the understanding of security, which is best exemplified in Kofi Annan's Millennium Development Goals (MDGs) of 2000 and the expressed desire of achieving "freedom from fear" and "freedom from want". These are regarded as vital freedoms, fundamental to both human existence and development.

"Collective security" is therefore a concept that Africa should embrace. If the UN adopts it, the interpretation and implementation of collective security will present major challenges. Active participation by African states in the debates shaping interpretation of the new concept is required if a more holistic notion of collective security is to become the accepted international norm. The High-level Panel report further notes that "to be credible and sustainable a collective security system must be effective, efficient and equitable" and that "the credibility of any system of collective security also depends on how well it promotes security for all its members, without regard to the nature of would-be beneficiaries, their location, resources or relationship to Great Powers".[13] The report acknowledges that "too often the United Nations and its member states have discriminated in responding to threats to international security".[14] This type of discrimination is bound to continue unless a more active role is played by African states in defining what is "equitable". We need to ensure that the UN does not just assert that a threat to one is a threat to all, but that the world body acts accordingly to promote this ideal.[15]

Most African governments regard poverty, underdevelopment and disease as the most urgent threats to human security on our continent. (See Chinery-Hesse in this volume). Transnational organised crime and corruption are significant contributors to underdevelopment and poverty. African governments as well as the international community therefore ought to recognise organised crime as a greater and unprecedented threat to weak states.

Implementing the Palermo Convention

Transnational organised crime poses a global threat and is not peculiar to Africa. However, such crime is particularly rampant in weak states, many of them in Africa, due to both the scarce resources to address it and the lack of capacity to implement the Palermo Convention. This was recognised in Article 30 of the convention, which deals with "implementation of the convention through economic development and technical assistance".[16]

Among other recommendations, this article calls on states to: enhance international cooperation, taking into account the negative effects of organised crime on sustainable development; enhance financial and material assistance to support the efforts of developing countries to fight transnational organised crime effectively and to help them implement this convention successfully; and provide technical assistance to developing countries and countries with economies in transition, to assist them in meeting their needs for the implementation of this convention. To facilitate such assistance, Article 30 of the convention created a designated account through which funding to support developing countries could be channelled.[17]

However, the incentives offered to poorer countries during the Palermo negotiating process seemed to dwindle once the convention had been finalised. While efforts have been made by the UNODC, the Commonwealth Secretariat in London, and some donors to provide technical assistance for developing countries, broader support for the effective implementation of the convention has been absent. The High-level Panel report correctly found that: "States and international organisations have reacted too slowly to the threat of organised crime and corruption. Statements about the seriousness of the threat have rarely been matched by action".[18] The degree to which the US "war on terror" has diverted resources intended to support the implementation of the Palermo Convention is hard to determine. Also difficult to establish is whether African governments have exhibited sufficient political will to implement the convention. By April 2005, 31 African states had ratified or acceded to the convention.[19]

The successful implementation of the Palermo Convention is a prerequisite for effective international action against transnational organised crime in Africa. The High-level Panel report understandably proposes that "member states that have not signed, ratified or resourced these Conventions and Protocols should do so, and all member states should support the United Nations Office on Drugs and Crime in its work in this area".[20] This recommendation should be supported and acted upon by African governments, as well as those countries such as Britain and the US that have the resources and the capacity to contribute significantly towards the efficacy of the convention, but have not yet ratified it.

Money laundering

After detailing the immensity of funds laundered by criminals, the High-level Panel report recommended "a comprehensive international convention on money laundering that addresses these issues needs to be negotiated, and endorsed by the General Assembly".[21] This recommendation elicited considerable debate over the practicality of implementing yet another international convention.

Many developing countries appear to support this recommendation, since the current international regulatory system against money laundering is pursued by intergovernmental organisations driven by industrialised countries. As a result, poorer nations have little say in these organisations and receive minimal understanding for the domestic circumstances with which they have to contend. Regulatory steps aimed at curbing money laundering that prove effective in the strong and sophisticated financial sectors of rich countries might not always be appropriate in poorer countries where the informal or "shadow economy" is often larger than the formal economy.

Article Seven of the Palermo Convention requires states to establish a comprehensive domestic regulatory and supervisory regime to deter and detect all forms of money laundering for banks, non-bank financial institutions and other bodies susceptible to money laundering. International standards have been set to determine how best to achieve this objective. These have been devised by the Financial Action Task Force Against Money Laundering (FATF). This body, founded at the Group of Seven (G-7) industrialised countries' summit in 1989, initially consisted of member states, the European Union (EU) Commission, and eight other countries. Membership currently stands at 31 countries and 2 regional organisations.[22] South Africa has recently been accepted as the only African member and China has observer status on the taskforce. To qualify for membership of the FATF a country must, among other factors, "be strategically important".

Since its inception, the FATF has formulated nine "special recommendations" aimed at "setting standards for national money laundering and countering terrorist financing programmes" and "evaluating the degree to which countries have implemented measures that meet those standards".[23] These recommendations are applicable to all countries. Considerable pressure is being exerted on governments to implement these recommendations, but many poor countries have found it difficult to implement them and are concerned about the consequences of non-compliance. In some African countries, less than ten per cent of the working population use bank accounts to deposit money.[24] There is growing concern that stringent international requirements could further discourage the use of banking institutions in African countries, thereby weakening their already small financial sectors.

These concerns have led to some developing countries calling for a more equitable international approach to money laundering in which their interests are also taken into account. The High-level Panel report's recommendation that a comprehensive convention on money laundering "be endorsed by the General Assembly" reflects a desire to make such a new approach truly multilateral.

Those who are sceptical about a possible new UN convention on money laundering have cited practical and resource problems as grounds for not supporting such an initiative. Most developing countries are finding it difficult to keep pace with the implementation requirements of existing UN conventions. Many are lagging behind not only with the implementation of the Palermo Convention, but also with some of the conventions relating to terrorism. In addition, another UN Convention against Corruption was finalised in 2005 and awaits implementation.

Further, the FATF recommendations on money laundering and the financing of terrorism have not been effectively implemented in many parts of the world. Against this background, the argument that adequate space and international support should be provided to implement existing conventions properly before commencing with new initiatives does have validity. African countries are likely to hold different positions on this, partly because of the diverse economies on the continent and their uneven capacities to implement international conventions. The fifteen ministers from African countries who were mandated by the African Union (AU) to consider the High-level Panel report and to formulate recommendations for an African common position – the Ezulwini Consensus – in Swaziland in February 2005, deliberated the issue of money laundering. In their draft recommendations, they fell short of calling for a comprehensive new convention against money laundering and, under the heading "Transnational Organised Crime", merely recommended that "special attention be given to issues such as money laundering, and fiscal paradises, as well as modern slavery and all forms of human exploitation".[25] The only other draft recommendation beneath the above heading calls on AU member states to ratify and accede to the UN Protocol on human trafficking.

"Special attention" implies that attempts to combat money laundering should be dealt with in a more coordinated way, and that African governments should take initiatives in this regard. African countries can contend that they should have greater input into the decisions of the FATF on money laundering. This in turn would require greater debate in Africa, which has been largely absent until now. South Africa – the only African member of the FATF – is its chair in 2006 and this may present an opportunity for African countries to place their concerns and demands on the FATF agenda in a more effective way.

State capacity-building

The final recommendation of the High-level Panel to combat organised crime more effectively calls on the UN to "establish a robust capacity-building mechanism for rule-of-law assistance".[26] The Panel invites regional organisations and multinational institutions to assist with these efforts actively. Very few people would object to this recommendation in principle, but its ambiguity does not lend much to the promise for effective action. From an African perspective, it is in the areas of capacity-building and the provision of financial and technical support to achieve it, that the greatest need exists and, at the same time, that most promises by international organisations have failed to materialise. "Rule-of-law assistance" in essence denotes assistance that would enable countries to establish effective criminal justice systems in which the rule-of-law prevails. This, in turn, involves a properly financed, trained, and professional police service; a resourced and skilled prosecution service capable of prosecuting according to domestic and international laws; a judiciary that is independent and non-corruptible; and a well-functioning prison or correctional service structure.

Weak criminal justice systems are currently the major impediment to the implementation of international legal instruments that could combat organised crime in Africa. Pledges to provide assistance to poorer states to strengthen their criminal justice systems are common but seldom realised. Nevertheless, recent UN Conventions that are dependent on effective criminal justice systems for their implementation also contain elaborate provisions for UN member states to assist developing countries. For example, Article 30 of the Palermo Convention calls for the implementation of the convention through economic development and technical assistance, including the provision of a designated UNODC account through which to channel financial contributions. Article 60 of the UN Convention against Corruption requires state actors to contribute financially to the efforts of poorer countries to apply the convention through the provision of technical assistance programmes and projects. The Article also calls on governments to make voluntary contributions to the UNODC to promote the implementation of the convention.

Similarly, the UN's Counter Terrorism Committee has sought to channel technical assistance to member states in areas such as border control, extradition, mutual legal assistance, and asset forfeiture – all factors that are directly relevant to combating transnational organised crime. The UNODC Secretariat in Vienna, Austria, has also implemented separate programmes to provide technical assistance to member states on issues relating to training, legislative drafting, extradition and mutual legal assistance. The different UNODC programmes provide such technical assistance through separate initiatives for each of the conventions on terrorism, organised crime and corruption. FATF, the IMF and the World Bank have also provided technical and other assistance to countries to promote the effective implementation of the FATF recommendations on money laundering and the financing of terrorism. In addition, bilateral projects between rich and poor countries have sought to provide assistance through the funding of projects and intergovernmental organisations such as the Commonwealth Secretariat.

Against this background, and the many other international commitments and initiatives, the recommendation by the High-level Panel for the establishment of "a robust capacity-building mechanism for rule-of-law assistance" will not progress significantly unless it becomes directly linked to an effort for greater coordination of international initiatives. Emphasis ought to be on increased coordination in providing technical and development assistance to strengthen criminal justice systems, and not just on the establishment of yet another fund.

Concluding Thoughts

The High-level Panel report contains a range of recommendations for UN reform, some of them critical to the future development of the organisation. It is understandable that strategic issues raised in the report – for example the composition of the UN Security Council – attracted the most intense debate and controversy. (See Adebajo as well as Jonah in this volume). However, for millions of Africans, tangible improvements relating to development, security and human rights and the enhancement of human security on the continent, remain the central issues. Transnational organised crime is only one contributor to fear and deprivation but it is one that can be addressed, provided the necessary political will and international support is forthcoming. In conclusion, I will highlight four key steps that the United Nations could adopt to further this objective.

First, vigilance will be required by African states to ensure that the concept of "collective security" is applied equitably and without discrimination. Africa should be central to debates on "collective security" and on shaping the interpretation of what is "equitable". Second, there appears to be unanimity that the UN Convention against Transnational Organised Crime should be implemented more effectively. If African states can show greater political will, they will have a basis from which to insist that the technical and development assistance committed to this area be met by rich countries and international organisations.

Third, the recognition that special measures are needed to counter money laundering on the continent is beyond doubt. However, African governments need to develop a more coherent approach towards the factors that these measures should incorporate and how to forge alliances with countries in other regions that face similar challenges. A new UN convention against money laundering is just one of a number of avenues available to counter this problem, and at this stage, may not be the most effective one. Finally, the UN can play a vital role in streamlining the many designated accounts, technical assistance programmes, initiatives by international organisations and bilateral support programmes to counter transnational crime. Through effective global coordination, a more coherent system that can be properly monitored must be developed. The present diffuse approach is not producing the required results and continues to tax the capacity of poorly-resourced states to respond adequately to the scourge of international organised crime.

Notes

[1] The Convention was adopted by General Assembly Resolution 55/25(A/RES/55/25) 15 November 2000.

[2] United Nations: *A More Secure World: Our Shared Responsibility,* Report of the United Nations Secretary-General's High-level Panel on Threats, Challenges and Change. (United Nations Department of Public Information DPI/2367, December 2004) and *In Larger Freedom: Towards Development, Security and Human Rights For All,* Report of the UN Secretary-General, Follow-up to the outcome of the Millennium Summit. 21 March 2005, A/59/2005.

[3] Mueller, G O W: "Transnational Crime: Definitions and Concepts" in *Transnational Organised Crime,* 4, (Autumn/Winter 1998), (London: Frank Cass & Co, 1998), p. 13.

[4] Freund, B: *The Making of Contemporary Africa: The Development of African Society since 1800.* Second Edition (London: Macmillan Press, 1998), p. 253.

[5] Bayart, J-F, Ellis, S & Hibou, B: "The Criminalisation of the State in Africa" in *African Issues,* (1999), p. 8.

[6] UN General Assembly Resolution 47/87 on doc A/RES/47/49 of 16 December 1992 at http://www.un.org/documents/ga/res/47/a47r087.htm (accessed 12 February 2006).

[7] UN General Assembly resolution A/RES/47/87 of 16 December 1992.

[8] Commissioner Norman Moleboge, National Commissioner of the Botswana Police, in a paper presented to the Regional Strategic Programme Framework Conference on Drugs and Crime Prevention Priorities in Southern Africa, organised by the UNODC, Johannesburg, 5 August 2002.

[9] Tshwete, S: "Organised Crime in Southern Africa: Assessing Legislation" (ISS Monograph No 56, ISS, Pretoria, June 2001), p. 9: "Organised crime is a problem in South Africa and in its SADC neighbours, just as it is a problem in most countries of the world. The government is well aware of the fact that the consequences could be disastrous for good governance and the economy in the absence of the political will to confront the phenomenon head-on with all the might and ruthlessness that can be summoned".

[10] Dr. Ugi Zvekic, Regional UNODC Office for Southern Africa, Pretoria. Presentation made at the Alliance for Crime Prevention Conference in Cape Town, January 2004.

[11] *A More Secure World: Our Shared Responsibility,* paragraph 79.

[12] Ogata, S. & Cels, J: "Human Security: Protecting and Empowering the People" in *Global Governance* 9 (2003), p. 274.

[13] *A More Secure World: Our Shared Responsibility,* Article 31 and para. 40.

[14] *A More Secure World: Our Shared Responsibility,* para. 41.

[15] *A More Secure World: Our Shared Responsibility,* para. 43.

[16] http://www.unodc.org/pdf/crime/a_res_55/res5525e.pdf (accessed 30 December 2005).

[17] Article 30 (2) (c): "To that end, States Parties shall endeavour to make adequate and regular voluntary contributions to an account specifically designated for that purpose in a United Nations funding mechanism."

[18] *A More Secure World: Our Shared Responsibility,* para. 167.

[19] UNODC website: http://www.unodc.org/unodc/en/crime_cicp_signatures_convention.html, (accessed 30 December 2005). Countries that had ratified or acceded to the Convention by 30 April 2005 were: Algeria, Benin, Botswana, Burkina Faso, Central African Republic, Djibouti, Egypt, Equatorial Guinea, Gabon, Gambia, Guinea, Kenya, Lesotho, Liberia, Libyan Arab Jamahiriya, Malawi, Mali, Mauritius, Morocco, Namibia, Niger, Nigeria, Rwanda, Senegal, Seychelles, South Africa, Sudan, Togo, Tunisia, Uganda and Zambia.

[20] *A More Secure World: Our Shared Responsibility,* para. 172.

[21] *A More Secure World: Our Shared Responsibility,* para. 174.

[22] www.fatf-gafi.org. Current members are: Argentina, Australia, Austria, Belgium, Brazil, Canada, Denmark, European Commission, Finland, France, Germany, Greece, Gulf Co-operation Council, Hong Kong (China), Iceland, Ireland, Italy, Japan, Luxembourg, Mexico, Kingdom of the Netherlands, New Zealand, Norway, Portugal, Russian Federation, Singapore, South Africa, Spain, Sweden, Switzerland, Turkey, United Kingdom and United States.

[23] http://www.fatfgafi.org/document/28/0,2340,en_32250379_32236930_33658140_1_1_1_1,00.html and
http://www.fatf-gafi.org/document/9/0,2340,en_32250379_32236920_34032073_1_1_1_1,00.html (accessed 30 December 2005).

[24] Kasumuni, L: "Only six per cent of Tanzanians use banks", IPP Media, 24 March 2004 at http://ippmedia.com/ipp/guardia/2004/03/24/7686.html (accessed 23 June 2004). An estimated four per cent of Malawians use banks for depository purposes according to interviews amongst bankers and leaders in the financial sector conducted by Institute for Security Studies (South Africa) researcher Annette Huebschle.

[25] Paragraph 12 (A) (v) of the "Draft Recommendations of the Ministerial Committee of Fifteen on the Report of the High-level Panel on the Reform of the United Nations System".

[26] *A More Secure World: Our Shared Responsibility*, para. 177.

Section Four

©Obed Zilwa/Trace Images

African Actors and Responses

12

South Africa, the UN, and Human Rights

Kader Asmal

ON 10 MAY 2004 AN extraordinary event occurred in South Africa. On the tenth anniversary of his inauguration as the first president of a democratic South Africa, Nelson Mandela addressed a joint sitting of the country's parliament. Although he described himself as a "pensioner" retired from political life, Madiba (his clan name) was clearly still engaged with the urgent problems of politics, both locally and globally. His pointed observations about recent international events were featured in media accounts of his speech. Mandela noted: "We watch as two of the leading democracies, two leading nations of the free world [the US and Britain], get involved in a war that the United Nations did not sanction; we look on with horror as reports surface of terrible abuses against the dignity of human beings held captive by invading forces in their own country".[1]

The violence unleashed in 2003 by the US in Afghanistan and Iraq showed the devastating effects of the exercise of unilateral power. According to Mandela, this defiance of the United Nations and abuse of human dignity was not an anomaly. He perceived a larger pattern emerging in global politics. In these recent events, Mandela declared, "We see how the powerful countries, all of them so-called democracies, manipulate multilateral bodies to the great disadvantage and suffering of the poorer developing nations".[2]

Although the media expressed surprise at these critical comments, finding these remarks particularly "newsworthy", Mandela was undertaking a strategic analysis that he has consistently advanced. On an earlier occasion, he observed, "Mankind as a whole is today standing on the threshold of great events – events that at times seem to threaten its very existence".[3] Madiba spoke these words at a meeting of the African National Congress (ANC) in 1951 at which he addressed the major themes of war and peace, and conflict and its resolution in the global arena.

In this analysis of global threats, Mandela identified military forces, headed by "the ruling circles in America", that were "prepared to go to war in defence of colonialism, imperialism, and their profits" but he also identified the psychological dynamics in which global forces were "determined to perpetuate a permanent atmosphere of crisis and fear in the world". Assuming that frightened people cannot think clearly, those forces were attempting, he observed, "to create conditions under which common men [and women] might be inveigled into supporting the building of more and more atomic bombs, bacteriological weapons, and other instruments of mass destruction". Although ordinary people had become targets of this military and psychological violence, they also had the resources, as Mandela recognised, to build peace by "rising from being the object of history to becoming the subject of history", through becoming "conscious creators of their own history".[4]

Over half a century later, I believe we must adopt the same strategic analysis. First, assessments of conflicts must be multidimensional. Although armed struggles might be an element, other dimensions of conflict include psychological, social and economic dynamics. All of these factors feature in the "structural causes" of conflict, crisis and violence. We have sought to develop a multidimensional analysis of military force, one driven by a commitment to human rights, not only as a matter of theory but also as a method for practical intervention. In South Africa, at the level of strategy, this has contributed to demilitarising the country and humanising its military in the post-apartheid era.

Second, although we know that people can be disempowered by conflict, they can also provide the resources for becoming conscious agents in creating their own destiny in situations of conflict. Ordinary people, as Nelson Mandela insisted, can be peacebuilders. Within South Africa, there have been pioneering efforts to design and implement programmes in peace education and conflict resolution for children, youth, teachers and parents. These projects have made important contributions – contributions to both peace and education – by providing students with resources for conflict mediation and providing schools with a model for educational transformation. Structures have also been created in government to monitor South Africa's involvement in international conflicts to ensure that basic human rights principles are observed.

South Africa, of course, is part of a globalising world. The unilateral actions by powerful states, which Mandela identified, created a crisis in the international order, undermining the efficacy of international institutions. Over ten years ago, the German philosopher, Jurgen Habermas, anticipated the defining geopolitical opposition of our times: the confrontation between states committed to multilateral cooperation and states embarking on unilateral agendas. According to Habermas:

> The politically decisive distinction exists between those who take the UN's jurisdiction seriously and, therefore, want to permit participation only in operations under UN command, as opposed to those who want to procure a broader political and military room for action for individual nations or union of nations.[5]

Human Rights

Efforts to reinforce human rights instruments and to revitalise the multilateral institutions of the United Nations could certainly benefit Africa as well as the rest of the world. (See Scanlon in this volume). We are all familiar with the conventional genealogy of human rights, from the American Declaration of Independence of 1776, through the French Rights of Man of 1789, to the post-war European attempt to reconstitute itself through the Universal Declaration of Human Rights of 1948. In this tradition, rights are grounded in the human person because every human is "created in the image of God" (in the American formula), or endowed with "the sacred demands of natural law" (in the French formula), or is an inviolable "representative of humankind" (in the formulation of the United Nations).[6] Even critical accounts, such as the critique by Neil Stammers, who places the emergence of human rights in struggles over political and economic power, nevertheless attributes the origin of rights to the West.[7]

This genealogy has led to a backlash. Some scholars have criticised the western bias underpinning the concept of human rights, concluding that "to argue that human rights has a standing which is universal in character is to contradict historical reality."[8] Others, taking the critique further, have proposed that the discourse of human rights has provided an ideological cover for western interests as a weapon in the "armoury of imperialist ideology" or as a seductive illusion "at the service of the economic and geopolitical interests of the hegemonic capitalist states".[9]

It is historically inaccurate, however, to assume that both the idea of human rights and the ideals it espouses were exclusively a product of the West. Human rights are not solely or essentially the property of the West. The notion of human rights arises wherever people are oppressed and struggle for liberation. "Wherever oppression occurs," as Ugandan scholar, Mahmood Mamdani, has observed, "there must come into being a conception of rights".[10] Therefore, human rights cannot be the privileged property of the West.

If the West is not the origin of human rights, it is also not the future of these rights. Over the second half of the twentieth century, all advances in the theory and practice of human rights were produced outside of the West, as the scope of human rights was extended from the "selective" liberal definition of human rights as political rights in western countries to include socio-economic, cultural, environmental, women's and children's rights, and other extensions of the "liberal" principle of basic, inalienable rights.

In South Africa, the African National Congress has a long human rights tradition.[11] In 1943 the first comprehensive formulation of human rights – *Africans' Claims in South Africa* – anticipated the UN's Universal Declaration of Human Rights of 1948 by five years and set the framework for the Women's Charter (1954), the Freedom Charter (1955), and other landmarks in the ANC human rights tradition. In the third section of *Africans' Claims in South Africa*, the ANC leadership formulated the first comprehensive Bill of Rights for South Africa. In the text of this "Bill of Rights: Full Citizen Rights and Demands" the ANC called for rights to full citizenship; to land; to industrial participation and fair labour practices; to trade; to education; to public health services; and to freedom from any form of discrimination. This Bill of Rights stands as one of the most significant landmarks in the quest to restore the human dignity of black South Africans and is distinguished by its inclusive and expansive vision of human rights. By linking political and socio-economic rights, the ANC's Bill of Rights in 1943 anticipated the evolution of international human rights from "first generation" political rights to "second generation" social and economic rights.

As the heart and soul of *Africans' Claims in South Africa*, the ANC's Bill of Rights of 1943 refutes any claim that the very idea of human rights was inherited from Europe or North America. Here is an indigenous African document, far ahead of developments in the rest of the world, which worked out basic human rights in the face of their denial in racist South Africa.

Sovereignty

South Africans do not need to be convinced of the value of legitimate international instruments and institutions. For those of us who worked in the liberation movement in the struggle against apartheid, we were already accustomed to operating from a global perspective, in stark contrast to the unilateral, isolationist posture adopted by the apartheid regime. We relied on the international support of a global anti-apartheid movement that drew together the United Nations, human rights bodies, and a host of other transnational agencies in mobilising opposition to oppression. However, we also developed a critical analysis of sovereignty to deconstruct the legitimacy of the apartheid state and to create space for liberation movements that were dispersed across many nations. The current efforts to revitalise multilateral institutions will require a rethinking of what is meant by "sovereignty" in international law, international relations and international institutions.

The system of states inherited from the Westphalia Treaty of 1648, implicitly operates with a definition of state sovereignty – in the classic formulation by the sociologist Max Weber – as the "organised exercise of legitimate violence over a territory".[12] These three features of the modern state – demarcated territory, monopoly on the use of force and political legitimacy – no longer seem adequate to protect the "sovereignty" of smaller states in the global order. Globalisation, however defined, has subtly but substantially eroded state sovereignty in many areas such as currency regulation, trade relations and migration.

In this globalising world, is it possible to redefine state sovereignty, not as the organised exercise of legitimate force, but as the "organised exercise of the public good"? Here I invoke the phrase "public good" to refer to a value that can be enjoyed by everyone and cannot be denied to anyone.

These defining features of a public good, which economists identify in more technical terms as non-rivalrous value and non-excludable value, should be central to our understanding of state sovereignty. In this rendering, sovereignty is the state's capacity to protect and extend the shared, inclusive values inherent in public goods. (See Mwanasali as well as Deng in this volume).

For thinking about human rights, the notion of the public good is essential. It goes to the heart of the matter. As Immanuel Kant recognised, "everything has either a price or a dignity. If it has a price, something else can be put in its place as an equivalent; if it is exalted above all price and so admits of no equivalent, then it has a dignity."[13] Human dignity – individually and collectively – cannot be determined by the pricing mechanisms of the market.

All of this might seem idealistic. It might seem like a good idea, perhaps, but not realistic. As Habermas has observed, in the reality of politics, including the reality of international politics, "ideas will prostrate themselves before interests every time".[14] Nevertheless, I believe that this reformulation of sovereignty, in keeping with the idea promoted by the United Nations of "sovereignty as responsibility", will be crucial for revitalising multilateral institutions. (See Mwanasali in this volume). The public good, even in a globalising world, is in everyone's interest.

The National Question

In simple outline, I would like to suggest our struggle for human rights in Africa has gone through three phases: national, transnational and global.

First, in the anti-colonial nationalist phase, South Africans struggled for human rights by advancing what Martiniquan scholar, Frantz Fanon, called "national consciousness". As an intellectual of the African diaspora, moving from the Caribbean to Algeria, Fanon emphasised national liberation as a liberation of consciousness. By developing an anti-colonial national consciousness, Fanon proposed, "Individual experience, because it is national and because it is a link in the chain of national existence, ceases to be individual, limited and shrunken and is enabled to open out into the truth of the nation and the world".[15]

According to Fanon, this was not the "volkish", ethnic or inward-looking nationalism experienced in both Nazi Germany and apartheid South Africa. Instead, for Fanon, anti-colonial nationalism was the door to internationalism. National consciousness in Fanon's sense "which is not nationalism, is the only thing that will give us an international dimension". According to Fanon,

> the building of a nation is of necessity accompanied by the discovery and encouragement of universalising values. Far from keeping aloof from other nations, therefore, it is national liberation which leads the nation to play its part on the stage of history. It is at the heart of national consciousness that international consciousness lives and grows.[16]

Second, in the transnational phase, even within liberated, post-colonial nations, many of us have not experienced the liberating "international consciousness" that Fanon promised. Instead, the "nation", however constructed, has set intractable limits on our horizons. In this regard, another leading intellectual of the African diaspora, Malcolm X, in the United States, saw the need to transform the liberation struggle in his country from petitioning for civil rights to demanding human rights. Malcolm X argued: "We need to expand the civil rights struggle to a higher level – to the level of human rights".[17]

These universal rights, however, were not a "gift" from the West. They arose out of the denial of humanity and human rights in colonial situations. Since they were not secured by any nation, human rights could only emerge as a transnational project in the African diaspora. Of course, conquest and colonisation, slavery and apartheid, were already international. As Paul Gilroy has observed, "The modern world-system responsible for the expansion of Europe and consequent dispersal of black slave labourers throughout Europe and the new world was from its inception an international operation". Descendants of slavery, according to Gilroy, necessarily "exhibit the tendency to transcend a narrowly national focus". Accordingly, he rejects the organising principle of "national units" on the grounds that "the African diaspora's consciousness of itself has long been defined in and against constricting national boundaries."[18]

Third, in the current global phase of our struggle for human rights, we have had to consolidate our gains and also look to the future. Africans can consolidate what they have accomplished by remaining true to the basic principles of a non-racial pan-Africanism. Here I invoke the words of my teacher, Chief Albert Luthuli, president of the ANC from 1952 until his death in 1967, to recall these principles: "Our interest in freedom is not confined to ourselves only" Luthuli said in his ANC presidential address of 1953. "We are interested in the liberation of all oppressed people in the whole of Africa and in the world as a whole".[19] Clearly, Luthuli's vision of freedom in South Africa was advanced in solidarity with the struggle for freedom throughout Africa and the larger world. Looking to the future, the Nobel Peace Laureate affirmed the principle of non-racialism, which was clearly identified in concrete terms in the ANC's Freedom Charter of 1955 and eventually enshrined in the South African Constitution of 1996. Others have picked up this vision. Caribbean scholar Horace Campbell, for example, in setting out his vision of a pan-Africanism in the twenty-first century, has advocated a de-racialised and non-sexist version of African unity.[20] In a globalising world, this non-racial, non-sexist understanding of the African diaspora holds out hope for a new internationalism that reconnects what was dispersed by colonialism, slavery and apartheid.

Today, for many people, globalisation is a source of resentment. This is not because the global movement of money, technology and people has made the world a global village, but because these forces have been widening the gap between rich and poor in a world which is becoming increasingly polarised; politically, culturally and economically. How could this source of despair become a repository of hope? If the notion of human rights has a future, it must be in harnessing global forces to a politics of hope. Advancing a powerful critique, while never giving up hope, India's Nobel Laureate, Amartya Sen, has argued that we must "ask questions not only about the economics and politics of globalisation, but also about the values and ethics that shape our conception of the global world."[21]

When I chaired the World Commission on Dams between 1998 and 2001, we worked out an approach to decision-making in development projects that I called "globalisation from below".[22] Within a human rights framework, this approach considered the rights and risks of global investors, but insisted on highlighting the human rights, as well as the considerable risks, of people who were most directly affected by projects. As we brought peasants, workers, women's groups and representatives of indigenous people into the debate, we saw the tremendous potential of grassroots globalisation for advancing human rights in transnational negotiations. In many other areas, I believe the future of human rights will also depend upon this new "globalisation from below".[23]

Globalisation from below is producing new forms of social activism across national borders. Mexican political analyst, Jorge Castañeda, has identified these new initiatives as "longitudinal nationalism", which is advanced by social actors from various nations who work together to challenge policies in one or more states.[24] Unlike the old nationalisms which tended to represent narrow national interests, this "longitudinal nationalism" seeks to advance what I have been calling the "public good" that is ultimately in everyone's interest.

We might want to say that public good is just another language for human rights. But it is a language that directly engages the global economy as an alternative to the commodification of all values. As such, our commitment to the public good goes to the heart of Amartya Sen's call to clarify "the values and ethics that shape our conception of the global world".[25] In the future of human rights, revitalising our conception of the public good – as a basis for national sovereignty, democratic governance and economic development – holds the promise of transforming our despair into hope in a globalising world. We will find the future of human rights in the midst of the hardest cases. As a transformative agent, human rights will be deployed at their best every time we engage the sources of our despair as avenues for revitalising hope. All of this, of course, requires great courage and imagination. We can only seek to seize this moment for the public good.

Concluding Thoughts

The very idea of human rights – adapting Kant's formulation – takes dignity as an end in itself, beyond any price. Two hundred years ago, following the slave revolt in Haiti which established the first independent African republic of modern times, the French named their price. They exacted reparations from Haiti for loss of property – that is, for their loss of value from the slaves they regarded as their human property – by structuring a schedule of compensation that Haitians only finished paying in 1947. As this arrangement suggests, for most of the past two centuries, international law has been governed by price rather than by dignity.

The recently deposed Haitian president, Jean-Bertrand Aristide, has been maligned in the US and other quarters as a tyrant, a despot, and a violator of human rights. But the flashpoint that led to Aristide's forced removal from office and from his country in 2004 followed almost immediately on his attempt to recover the money that Haitians had paid the French government in reparations for slavery. Basically, he submitted a bill. Allowing for inflation, he determined that Haitians had paid the government of France an amount equivalent to $21 billion. He wanted the money back.[26]

In recent years, trans-Atlantic campaigns for reparations, linking Africans and African-Americans, have been advanced, trying to calculate the price of such massive damage to human dignity in the international trade and exploitation of human beings as slaves. Here was a case, however, in which the price had already been calculated. We know the amount set by the French; we know the amount paid by the Haitians. By such a pricing mechanism, the French could pay reparations for the unjust payments that had been extracted from Haiti.

But this would have set a precedent for reparations. It would have encouraged new calculations of the monetary damages that should accrue for the suffering, exploitation and dehumanisation of slaves and their heirs in the Americas. If we can put a price on France's loss of human property, then we can also put a price on Haiti's loss of human dignity, so long as that pricing is understood as an act of human solidarity and not as another attempt to reduce human dignity to market pricing. After all, only those who have never had their dignity reduced to a price would think that a price should not be paid for violating human dignity.

As far as interests are concerned, Lord Palmerston, England's "gunboat" secretary of state for foreign affairs, reminded everyone in the early nineteenth century that England did not have permanent allies but permanent interests. In one of his most perceptive insights, South Africa's President Thabo Mbeki recently noted that states in the global south can not exercise their interests individually due to their relative lack of power, while larger states could do so. Therefore, it was necessary that African countries in particular should act in concert so that collective self-interest can generate pressure to achieve common objectives. This was borne out in the multilateral trade negotiations under the Doha round which started in 2002 at the World Trade Organisation (WTO) in Geneva and continues today.

Our work in revitalising multilateral institutions will require rethinking what we mean by human rights and "sovereignty" in international relations and international institutions. There exist a number of organisations – for example, the African Union (AU), the Economic Community of West African States (ECOWAS), the Intergovernmental Authority on Development (IGAD) the Economic Community of Central African States (ECCAS) and the Southern African Development Community (SADC) – who are potential partners with the UN in taking effective collective measures for the prevention and removal of threats to peace in Africa. By exploring African resources and strategies for revitalising multilateral institutions such as the UN, we must look to Africa not as the problem but as a crucial partner in the work at hand.

First, the composition of the UN Security Council needs to be changed. This process has been stalled. It needs to be revived. (See Jonah in this volume). Permanent membership for at least one African state would go a long way towards enhancing cooperation between the UN, the AU, and relevant regional economic communities in taking effective measures to prevent or remove threats to peace and security on the continent. (See Adebajo in this volume). The power differential which determined the identity of the five permanent members of the Security Council – the United States, Britain, France, Russia and China – has changed completely. The reform of the Bretton Woods institutions – the World Bank and the International Monetary Fund (IMF) – can also not be postponed indefinitely.

Second, the AU formulated a Common African Defence Policy in February 2004 that is remarkably thorough. The goals and objectives extend from defence cooperation to mutual trust, from conflict prevention to post-conflict reconstruction, from humanitarian assistance to environmental protection. This policy, entrusted to the AU's 15-member Peace and Security Council (PSC), contains a comprehensive plan for peace. The obvious problem with this plan, of course, is the high cost of implementation. When I was South Africa's Minister of Education between 1999 and 2004 I adopted the slogan, "If you think education is expensive, try ignorance". In this situation we could say "If you think peacekeeping, peacemaking and peacebuilding are expensive, try to measure the costs of conflict". Nevertheless, these African initiatives will need to be effectively funded. They will need to be thoroughly integrated into the New Partnership for Africa's Development (NEPAD), they must be supported by donor agencies and they must be a priority for the UN.

Third, while recognising the need for international support, we must continue to focus on formulating African solutions to African problems. Regional economic communities such as ECOWAS, SADC and IGAD, with their history of conflict resolution, also have a history of dealing with peacemaking and peacebuilding in their various regions. The creation of this new security architecture in Africa is providing an extremely valuable opportunity to reflect on what might be learned from this wealth of experience.

Fourth, in a world divided between public institutions and the private sector, many commentators look to "civil society" as an antidote to allegedly corrupt public institutions and inevitably competitive private interests. Often we are told that "civil society" is weak or ineffective, or even absent in Africa. Such denials of African civil society fail to understand the vitality of the social networks informed by trust, which enable people to work together to achieve common goals. Such networks empower people to survive conflicts. They also allow people to recover from conflicts. In the work of preventing and removing threats to peace on the continent, we have a lot to learn from the vitality of social networks in Africa. Recently, it has become fashionable to refer to these networks as "social capital": the resources available to people who are included in social networks based on trust. In Africa, we might be poverty-stricken, but we are rich in the "social capital" of mutual regard, recognition and support under difficult, and often impossible, conditions of deprivation. Otherwise, to put it bluntly, we would not survive. Our social networks might not fit a classic western, liberal interpretation of civil society; that does not mean that civil society is absent in Africa. It means that we need to reconceptualise what is meant by the term "civil society". How then do we enable and energise existing social networks, based on trust, in which people might work together to prevent conflicts, resolve conflicts, and recover from conflicts? (See Murithi in this volume).

Finally, what many political analysts such as the American, Joseph Nye, call "soft power", the fine arts of diplomacy, negotiation and building trust, has become increasingly difficult to promote in our world. In our current geopolitical terrain, we are confronted with the brutal coercion of unilateral force and the subtle coercion of globalising co-optation. In these exchanges, "soft power" only seems weak. Our experience in South Africa, however, has taught us the "soft power" of recognising our diversity, negotiating through our differences, and imagining a common ground as the source of our strength. I have no intention of being prescriptive. I have no illusion that the resolution of our conflict in South Africa provides a model for the region, for Africa, or for the world. Nevertheless, if we are looking for lessons, grounded in experience, we should not forget that, in our lifetimes, we have witnessed the transformation of one of the most intractable conflicts in the world, in South Africa.

Recalling the words of Nelson Mandela – himself a prophet of "soft power" – we must affirm the "solidarity of peace-loving nations". Our objective on the continent is therefore to redefine "solidarity" so that it means establishing vital links and real networks between the United Nations, the African Union, regional economic communities, African states, civil society and other social agents. It is not enough merely to want peace. We must make peace, keep peace, and build peace through new initiatives in African solidarity and African networks for peace.

Notes

[1] Address by Nelson Mandela during a joint sitting of Parliament to mark ten years of democracy in South Africa, 10 May 2004, Cape Town available at http://www.anc.org.za/ancdocs/history/mandela/2004/nm0510.html (accessed 7 February 2006).

[2] See, for example, Quinn, A: "Mandela, in farewell speech, slams Iraq war" at http://www.aegis.com/news/re/2004/RE040520.html (accessed 9 November 2005).

[3] Mandela, N: *In His Own Words: From Freedom to the Future: Tributes and Speeches* (London and Johannesburg: Little Brown and Jonathan Ball, 2003).

[4] Mandela, N: *In His Own Words: From Freedom to the Future: Tributes and Speeches.*

[5] Habermas, J: *The Past as the Future* (Cambridge: Polity, 1994), p. 144.

[6] Arendt, H: *The Origins of Totalitarianism* (New edition) (New York: Harcourt Brace Jovanovich, 1966), pp. 299–300.

[7] Stammers, N: "Human Rights and Power," in *Political Studies* 16 (1993), pp. 70–82.

[8] Pollis, A & Schwab, P: *Human Rights: Cultural and Ideological Perspectives* (New York: Praeger, 1979), p. 4.

[9] Shivji, I G: *The Concept of Human Rights in Africa* (London: Codesria, 1989), 3; de Sousa Santos, Boaventura: "Toward a Multi-Cultural Conception of Rights" in *Zeitschrift fur Rechts-Soziologie* (1997), p. 1.

[10] Mamdani, M: "The Social Basis of Constitutionalism in Africa" in the *Journal of Modern African Studies* 28,3 (1990), p. 228.

[11] See Asmal, K, Chidester, D & Lubisi, C (eds.): *Legacy of Freedom: The ANC's Human Rights Tradition:* Africans' Claims in South Africa, *the* Freedom Charter, *the* Women's Charter *and other Human Rights Landmarks of the African National Congress* (Johannesburg: Jonathan Ball, 2005).

[12] Weber, M: "Politics as a Vocation" in Gerth, H H & Wright Mills, C (eds. and trans.): *From Max Weber: Essays in Sociology* (New York: Basic Books, 1958), p. 78.

[13] Kant, I: *Groundwork of the Metaphysical of Morals*, trans. Paton, H J (New York: Harper, 1964), p. 102.

[14] Habermas, J: *The Past as the Future*, pp. 9–10.

[15] Fanon, F: "The Pitfalls of National Consciousness", *The Wretched of the Earth* (New York: Grove Press, 1963).

[16] Fanon, F: "Reciprocal Bases of National Culture and the Fight for Freedom" in *The Wretched of the Earth* (New York: Grove Press, 1963), p. 248.

[17] Malcolm X: "The Ballot or the Bullet?" in Breitman, G (ed.): *Malcolm X Speaks: Selected Speeches and Statements* (New York: Grove Press, 1965), pp. 34–35.

[18] Gilroy, P: *There Ain't No Black in the Union Jack* (London: Hutchinson, 1987).

[19] Luthuli, A: "Presidential Address to the 42nd Annual Conference of the African National Congress", Queenstown, 18–20 December 1953 at http://www.anc.org.za/ancdocs/history/lutuli/lutuli1.html#ITEM2 (accessed 28 May 2004).

[20] Campbell, H: "Pan Africanism in the Twenty-First Century," in Abdul-Raheem, T (ed.): *Pan Africanism: Politics, Economy and Social Change in the Twenty-First Century* (New York: New York University Press, 1996).

[21] Sen, A: "It's Right to Rebel," *YaleGlobal* (19 November 2002) at http://yaleglobal.yale.edu/article.print?id=444 (accessed 20 June 2004).

[22] Asmal, K: "Chair's Preface: Globalisation from Below" in *World Commission on Dams, Dams and Development: A New Framework for Decision-Making* (London and Sterling, VA: Earthscan, 2000).

[23] Asmal, K: "Environment and Sustainability: Looking to the Future" in *The Partnership Principle: New Forms of Governance in the 21st Century* (London: Archetype Publishers, 2004), pp. 184–94.

[24] Castañeda, J: *Utopia Unarmed: The Latin Left after the Cold War* (New York: Vintage, 1994), p. 308.

[25] Sen, A: "It's Right to Rebel," *YaleGlobal* (19 November 2002).

[26] Hallward, P: "Option Zero in Haiti" in *New Left Review* 27 (May–June 2004).

13

Towards a Symbiotic Partnership: The UN Peacebuilding Commission and the Evolving AU/ NEPAD Post-conflict Reconstruction Framework

Tim Murithi

> Our record of success in mediating and implementing peace
> agreements is sadly blemished by some devastating failures.
> Indeed, several of the most violent and tragic episodes of the 1990s
> occurred after the negotiation of peace agreements... If we are
> going to prevent conflict we must ensure that peace agreements
> are implemented in a sustained and sustainable manner.
>
> *(Kofi Annan, In Larger Freedom, March 2005)*

POST-CONFLICT RECONSTRUCTION processes depend principally on the commitment and efforts of the primary actors in a dispute. There is, however, a role for external actors such as civil society and intergovernmental organisations. The United Nations (UN) Peacebuilding Commission was established in September 2005 with the express mandate of assisting countries in post-conflict transitions to consolidate their peacebuilding processes. The African Union (AU) and its flagship programme, the New Partnership for Africa's Development (NEPAD), has also enumerated a framework to enhance the capacity and efficacy of African countries to promote peace and to consolidate reconstruction. (See Mwanasali in this volume). As things stand, there is still no formal relationship between the Peacebuilding Commission and the AU/NEPAD framework for post-conflict peacebuilding and reconstruction. Currently, there are no formal relationships between the Peacebuilding Commission and other regional bodies. This chapter will make the case for greater collaboration between the UN Peacebuilding Commission and the AU/NEPAD framework. In particular, we will argue that the Peacebuilding Commission and the AU and NEPAD need to develop a *symbiotic partnership* predicated on complementarity. Such a relationship is necessary to avoid the duplication or replication of functions and to strategically target the disbursement of mobilised resources.

This chapter will briefly outline the challenges of post-conflict peacebuilding and reconstruction. It will then briefly enumerate what is meant by the promotion of a symbiotic partnership. This will be followed by an assessment of the emergence of the UN and AU frameworks for post-conflict reconstruction, before identifying ways in which a symbiotic partnership can be forged between the UN and the AU.

The Challenge of Post-conflict Reconstruction

The conflicts that have plagued parts of post-colonial Africa have brought about the collapse of social and economic structures and generated political tension. Infrastructure has been damaged and education and health services have suffered, not to mention the environmental damage that has been caused by conflict. Socio-economic development has also been severely retarded as a result of the carnage and destruction caused by conflict. The effects of conflicts in terms of refugee flows into neighbouring countries and the emergence of internally displaced persons (IDPs) has demonstrated that no African country is an island unto itself. (See Deng in this volume). Refugee camps in the Mano River Union region of Guinea, Liberia and Sierra Leone have served as a source of instability for countries in the region. It is estimated that there are close to three million refugees in Central Africa alone. The Refugee–Warriors in the Democratic Republic of the Congo (DRC) from the Rwandan genocide of 1994 remain a source of concern for all the key actors in the Great Lakes region. 200 000 refugees have spilled into Chad as a result of the violent conflict in Sudan's Darfur region, creating tension along the border. These situations illustrate the need for effective post-conflict reconstruction processes and the institutions to back them up. IDPs and refugees make it difficult for host communities and displaced communities to settle down and initiate development. Therefore, a central pillar of post-conflict reconstruction is the incorporation of IDPs and refugees into the host community, or the repatriation of refugees – after consideration of the possible risks – back to their country of origin.

By post-conflict reconstruction, we are referring to the medium to long-term process of rebuilding war-affected communities.[1] This includes the process of rebuilding the political, security, social and economic dimensions of a society emerging from conflict. It also includes addressing the root causes of the conflict and promoting social and economic justice as well as putting in place political structures of governance and the rule of law in order to consolidate peacebuilding, reconciliation and development efforts. Local populations in war-affected regions generally tend to be the most damaged by the scourge of violence. Women and children are often faced with tremendous social upheaval. Reconstruction therefore needs to proceed with the active participation of these sectors of society. An effective strategy for promoting post-conflict reconstruction necessarily has to take into account all of these elements. Such a strategy must promote measures and propose the establishment of institutions that will strengthen and consolidate peace in order to avoid a relapse into conflict. As the UN High-level Panel report of December 2004 noted, half of all countries emerging from conflict in the post-Cold War era relapsed into conflict within five years as a result of inadequate post-conflict peacebuilding.[2]

Toward Symbiosis in Peacebuilding and Post-conflict Reconstruction

One of the problems facing peacebuilding and post-conflict reconstruction processes is the proliferation of external actors. These actors engage with post-conflict reconstruction processes for various reasons. While there are those who are genuinely interested in improving the welfare of the target populations, there are others who may seek to engage with post-conflict reconstruction processes in order to secure their own economic or political interests. Non-governmental and intergovernmental organisations primarily fall into the former category. However, there are instances where these organisations can harbour ulterior motives for engaging in a post-conflict reconstruction process.

External actors come with self-ascribed mandates to assist with peacebuilding processes. As a result, there can often be a proliferation of external actors in any given post-conflict situation. The process of rebuilding the political, security, social and economic dimensions of a war-affected community requires several different programmes functioning simultaneously. However, if multiple actors are conducting their affairs without any sense of coordination, then a duplication of functions can occur. This can lead to a waste of human and financial resources. Even though the efforts of external actors are well intentioned, they can ultimately undermine the very objective that they are trying to advance. One solution is to ensure that there is a greater degree of coordination based on an understanding of the needs of the local target population. This means that external actors and organisations have to establish a level of symbiosis in their peacebuilding and post-conflict reconstruction efforts.

Symbiosis refers to a relationship between two organisms or organisations that is mutually enhancing and complementary. A symbiotic relationship therefore benefits both organisms and organisations. With reference to peacebuilding, a symbiotic organisation operating in tandem with another seeks to promote a partnership in order to achieve the ultimate objective: post-conflict reconstruction. Inter-organisational symbiosis in post-conflict reconstruction essentially means promoting a complementarity of functions and avoiding the duplication or replication of activities.

Three strategies for symbiosis in post-conflict reconstruction include: first, articulating more explicitly a commitment to partnership with other post-conflict reconstruction actors in the policies and mandates of their organisations; second, since policy does not always translate into practice, institutional structures need to be established to ensure that this interface actually takes place; finally, once these official structures exist, it is important to ensure that they actually work together on the ground.

The key objective of establishing a symbiotic partnership between two organisations would be to promote a complementarity of functions. Such a partnership would also seek to identify areas in which there is an unnecessary duplication of functions. The next section will examine the emergence of the UN and AU frameworks for post-conflict reconstruction prior to assessing how these organisations can enhance their strategies for promoting symbiosis in post-conflict reconstruction efforts in Africa.

The UN Peacebuilding Commission's Post-conflict Reconstruction Mandate

The UN Charter of 1945 makes provision for the promotion of peace, notably through Article 33 which states that "parties to any dispute, the continuance of which is likely to endanger the maintenance of international peace and security, shall, first of all, seek a solution by negotiation, enquiry, mediation, conciliation, arbitration, judicial settlement, resort to regional agencies or arrangements, or other peaceful means".[3] However the UN, for the 60 years of its existence, has had more conflict resolution failures than successes – particularly during the Cold War – and has not lived up to its ambitious mandate of maintaining international peace and security.

The first post-Cold War effort to reform the UN in order to effectively address the issue of building peace was undertaken by former UN Secretary-General, Boutros Boutros-Ghali. In *An Agenda for Peace*, published in 1992, Boutros-Ghali set out an international strategy for conflict prevention, peacemaking, peacekeeping, and post-conflict peacebuilding.[4] Post-conflict reconstruction has therefore been part of the lexicon of rebuilding war-affected communities for more than a decade. The end of the Cold War also increased incidences of intra-state conflict, which complicated post-conflict reconstruction efforts. The support that had previously been provided by the superpowers during this era of ideological polarity was gradually withdrawn from both governments and armed rebels. This meant that internal disputes were left to degenerate into even more pronounced violence in war-affected countries. In Africa, major challenges were faced in rebuilding war torn countries such as Somalia and Angola. The role of the UN in assisting to promote peace was prominent in the case of Mozambique between 1992 and 1994. In the twenty-first century, Africa is still plagued by the persistence of post-conflict challenges. The United Nations has maintained an engagement with Africa and is currently involved in post-conflict reconstruction efforts across the continent in southern Sudan, Sierra Leone, Liberia, the Central African Republic (CAR) and Guinea-Bissau.

UN Secretary-General, Kofi Annan, in a March 2005 report, *In Larger Freedom: Towards Development, Security and Human Rights for All*,[5] recommended that UN member states establish a Peacebuilding Commission to fill the institutional gaps that exist with regards to assisting countries make the transition from war to lasting peace. Annan noted that the UN's record in implementing and monitoring peace agreements has been tainted by some devastating failures, for example Angola in 1993, Rwanda in 1994, Bosnia in 1995 and East Timor in 1999. Since, as earlier noted, about half of all countries that emerge from war lapse back into violence within five years, an integral part of addressing the "scourge of war" must involve establishing an institutional framework to ensure that peace agreements are carefully implemented and post-conflict peacebuilding is properly consolidated.

It was after Annan's 2005 report that debates about the creation of the UN Peacebuilding Commission increased. This culminated, in September 2005, in the UN World Summit and the 60th session of the General Assembly at which the recommendations of the report were reviewed. The General Assembly adopted an *Outcome Document*[6] at the close of the meeting, which the UN Secretary-General described as "a once-in-a-generation opportunity"[7] to forge a global consensus on development, security, human rights and reform. On 20 December 2005, the UN Security Council and its General Assembly concluded their negotiations on the operationalisation of the recommendation of the World Summit and adopted joint resolutions establishing the UN Peacebuilding Commission.[8]

Birth and Function of the UN Peacebuilding Commission

Paragraph 97 of the *Outcome Document* recognised "the need for a coordinated, coherent and integrated approach to post-conflict peacebuilding and reconciliation."[9] The document also identified the importance of "achieving sustainable peace and recognising the need for a dedicated institutional mechanism to address the special needs of countries emerging from conflict towards recovery".[10] On this basis, the General Assembly decided "to establish a Peacebuilding Commission as an inter-governmental advisory body".[11] The established Peacebuilding Commission backed by a Peace Support Office and "a multi-year standing Peacebuilding Fund" marks a new level of strategic commitment to enhancing and sustaining peace after conflict.

As noted earlier, the Peacebuilding Commission intends to "bring together all relevant actors to advise on and propose integrated strategies for post-conflict peacebuilding and recovery".[12] The core work of the

Commission will be its country-specific activities. It will strive to ensure that the international community supports national authorities, but the focus will have to be on country-based realities. The Peacebuilding Commission has committed itself to ensuring that national priorities are supported by the necessary mobilisation of resources. Predictable and reliable funding will need to be identified for short-term early recovery activities as well as financial investment for development over the medium- to longer-term period of recovery. The Peacebuilding Fund is therefore tasked with ensuring the provision of these resources.

The Peacebuilding Commission has been endowed with a monitoring and review function. At regular intervals, the Commission will meet to review the progress towards medium-term recovery goals, particularly with regards to developing public institutions and laying the foundations for economic recovery. The role of the new body will be to alert the international community if progress is not being made so as to avoid a relapse into violent conflict. The Commission, through effective post-conflict peacebuilding and reconstruction, will also in effect have a preventive role in terms of preventing violence from recurring.[13] During the debates leading up to the creation of the Peacebuilding Commission, several countries from the global south did not want to provide the Commission with a conflict prevention or preventive diplomacy role.[14] This was due to fears of an infringement on their sovereignty by more powerful states in the rich north. The Peacebuilding Commission will therefore focus more on post-conflict peacebuilding than on conflict prevention.

More concretely, the Peacebuilding Commission will have an organisational committee for a specific country which will include representatives from the country under consideration; countries in the region engaged in the post-conflict process; other countries that are involved in relief efforts and/or political dialogue; as well as relevant regional and sub-regional organisations; the major financial, troop and civilian police contributors involved in the recovery effort; the senior United Nations representative in the field and other relevant United Nations representatives; and regional and international financial institutions such as the African Development Bank (ADB), the World Bank and the International Monetary Fund (IMF).[15]

In order to support this work, the Peacebuilding Commission is assisted by a Peacebuilding Support Office staffed by qualified experts in the field of peacebuilding. The Peacebuilding Support Office will prepare the substantive inputs for meetings of the Peacebuilding Commission through analysis and information gathering. The office will also contribute to the planning process for peacebuilding operations by working with the relevant lead departments in the UN, the international community and civil society. The office will further conduct an analysis of best practices and develop policy guidance as appropriate.

The need to address global security challenges through global responses requires the recognition that African concerns are the world's concerns. The "responsibility to protect" doctrine needs now to become mainstreamed into international politics.[16] (See Mwanasali in this volume). However, military interventions should be consistent with the purpose and principles of the UN Charter. In particular, they should comply with the provisions of Article 51 of the UN Charter which authorises the use of force only in cases of legitimate self-defence. The UN is not capable of solving all the problems faced by Africa. It is therefore important to identify what the UN can realistically do for Africa. Challenges such as the humanitarian catastrophe in Sudan's Darfur region have proved to be particularly resistant to decisive UN action due to the interests of powerful countries behind the scenes, notably China's oil interests. The UN is nevertheless conducting peace operations in Sudan, Côte d'Ivoire, the Democratic Republic of the Congo, Burundi, Liberia, Ethiopia/ Eritrea and Western Sahara. The UN also has a political office for Somalia. Historically, the UN in Mozambique, Angola and Rwanda has conducted peace operations with mixed results. Commentators have subsequently argued that local solutions to peacekeeping and peacebuilding are preferable because these actors often have a better understanding of the region they are working in. In the absence of robust local peace operations, there is still a need to strengthen the role of the UN in keeping Africa's peace and promoting economic development and democratic consolidation efforts on the continent. The UN must also play a role in consolidating post-conflict reconstruction efforts through the effective monitoring and policing of the illicit trade of natural resources and small arms, as well as curtailing the activities of mercenaries in war-affected regions. Finally, the world body should continue to play an important role in assisting refugees and internally displaced persons.

Structure and Membership of the Peacebuilding Commission

The permanent Organisational Committee of the Peacebuilding Commission will include 31 members and its decision making process will be based on consensus. The UN Security Council will be represented by seven members, including its permanent five members: the United States, Russia, Britain, France and China and two selected by the Council; while the UN's Economic and Social Council (ECOSOC) will be represented by seven members. The membership will also include the top five contributors of funds to the UN and the top five contributors of peacekeeping troops.[17] In March 2006, Denmark and Tanzania were selected by the UN Security Council as the two additional members to complement the five permanent members.[18]

There is a strong case for African membership of the Peacebuilding Commission. South Africa, Nigeria, Senegal, Ghana and Kenya are Africa's leading troop contributors in ongoing peacekeeping operations. These countries have distinguished themselves in the field of peacekeeping. They can thus bring a substantial amount of institutional memory to the work of the Peacebuilding Commission.

In terms of the staff complement within the Peacebuilding Commission and the Peacebuilding Support Office, there should be a representation weighted towards individuals from countries affected by war. In particular, there should be significant African representation since the Peacebuilding Commission is seeking to play a vital role in promoting a more secure future for Africa.

The successful creation and operationalisation of the Peacebuilding Commission has significant implications for Africa. This is an unprecedented framework which, if it succeeds in its objectives, can reduce and ultimately stop the loss of human life due to the recurrence of conflicts on the continent. Africa is plagued with a number of post-conflict situations that need to be urgently addressed. If the Peacebuilding Commission becomes politicised, then the opportunity for it to function in the short- to medium-term will be severely hampered. If given the necessary backing, a pragmatic Peacebuilding Commission that is appropriately funded can, as Kofi Annan noted, go a long way "to improve our success rate in building peace in war-torn countries."[19] The challenge, as with all other cases of institution building, will be to convert rhetoric into reality. Effective partnerships between the Peacebuilding

Commission and other intergovernmental organisations must be urgently established. In particular, the efficacy of the Peacebuilding Commission will depend on the degree to which it can create symbiotic partnerships with other international organisations such as the African Union, a subject to which we now turn our attention.

The African Union and NEPAD Post-conflict Reconstruction Framework

The African Union has the primary responsibility for peace and security on the continent, according to its Constitutive Act of 2000 signed by 53 African countries. NEPAD's role is to support post-conflict reconstruction and the mobilisation of resources for the AU Peace Fund. In theory, the AU and its NEPAD programme are supposed to be working closely together and coordinating their efforts. In practice, the communication lines between the AU Secretariat in Addis Ababa, Ethiopia, and the NEPAD Secretariat in Midrand, South Africa, are not as clear as they should be, despite NEPAD becoming a specialised agency of the AU in 2006.

The African Union has recognised that, in order to achieve its goals of sustainable peace and development, there is a need to adopt a comprehensive strategy for post-conflict reconstruction.[20] In this regard, the AU and NEPAD have developed an African Post-conflict Reconstruction Policy Framework through a broad consultative process that included partnering with civil society organisations in April 2005.[21] This Policy Framework emphasises the link that exists between the peace, security, humanitarian and development dimensions of post-conflict reconstruction and peacebuilding. Previously, in March 2002, the NEPAD Heads of State and Government Implementation Committee (HSGIC) had met in Abuja, Nigeria, to map out the objectives of the AU and NEPAD with regards to post-conflict reconstruction. The HSGIC requested the NEPAD Subcommittee on Peace and Security to "support efforts at developing early warning systems… [and] support post-conflict reconstruction and development… including the rehabilitation of national infrastructure, the population, as well as refugees and internally displaced persons".[22]

NEPAD's Implementation Committee also emphasised the importance of focusing on disarmament and demobilisation programmes based on ending the illicit trade of small arms. The leaders further stressed the promotion of democracy, human rights and the upholding of the rule of law as the basis for Africa's post-conflict reconstruction strategy. The intention behind the creation of the African Post-conflict Reconstruction Policy Framework was to articulate a policy that would coordinate and guide the AU Commission, the NEPAD Secretariat, regional economic communities (RECs) such as the Economic Community of West African States (ECOWAS), the Intergovernmental Authority on Development (IGAD), the Southern African Development Community (SADC), the Economic Community of Central African States (ECASS) and the Arab Maghreb Union (AMU), civil society, the private sector and other internal and external partners, in the process of rebuilding war-affected communities. This is based on the premise that each country should adopt a post-conflict reconstruction strategy that responds to its own particular context.

Aspects of the AU Post-conflict Reconstruction Policy Framework

Key aspects of the AU Policy Framework include the attempt to put in place the pillars of a post-conflict reconstruction system that recognises the importance of an appropriate response to complex emergencies, to social and political transition following conflict, and to long-term development. Therefore, according to the Policy Framework, a post-conflict reconstruction system has at least five dimensions: security; political transition, governance and participation; socio-economic development; human rights, justice and reconciliation; and, coordination, management and resource mobilisation. In order to maximise the chances of establishing an effective post-conflict reconstruction process, there must be an acknowledgement of the importance of ensuring that there is a degree of complementarity and mutual reinforcement between these five dimensions. Policy planning therefore has to proceed on the basis of establishing coherence among the strategies that are adopted for each of the five areas.

The AU policy framework also acknowledges that each conflict situation is context-specific. As such, the post-conflict reconstruction strategy adopted must correspond to the specificities of each situation. Post-conflict reconstruction systems and strategies therefore have to be relatively flexible in responding to changing situations. For example, making the transition from a complex emergency situation in Sierra

Leone may require different strategies to deal with peacebuilding given the particular nature of the conflict which involved the massive looting of state resources in particular, diamonds and timber. The people of Sierra Leone would need to feel reassured by any post-conflict reconstruction process that the injustices of the past are addressed through the process. This means that social and political transitions after conflict must reflect this need. The institutions and mechanisms put in place to consolidate post-conflict reconstruction also have to emerge from these considerations. The Special Court for Sierra Leone was established in 2000, and operationalised in 2002, to deal with the atrocities committed by the leaders of the various armed movements during the decade-long war. The Lomé Peace Agreement established the Sierra Leone Truth and Reconciliation Commission in 1999, to address the human rights abuses and violations of international humanitarian law. Both of these bodies have contributed towards dealing with the difficult post-conflict situation that Sierra Leone's citizens are confronting. This does not mean, however, that such institutions can be transplanted to deal with the post-conflict process for example, in Burundi, which had, and to a certain extent still has, qualitatively different challenges. Essentially, the AU's Policy Framework provides an overall strategy from which individual country programmes can develop their own context-specific plans and strategies.

Another aspect of the AU Policy Framework includes recognition that there is a natural relationship between peace, security and development. In this context, the Policy Framework proposes the need to address the false dichotomy that is often advocated between political stability and economic efficiency. In reality, this is a false dichotomy because one presupposes and reinforces the other: one cannot have economic efficiency without political stability, nor can one have the effective management of economies without political order and the rule of law.

The AU Policy Framework also identifies "the lack of sufficient local ownership and participation" in post-conflict reconstruction.[23] Externally driven post-conflict reconstruction processes cannot be sustained if they are not owned by the people they are targeting. When the international community – in the form of the UN, bilateral actors and international civil society – come into a post-conflict reconstruction process, they immediately distort the economies of the war-affected regions in which they are operating. It is therefore vital for strategies to be adopted that emphasise transferring the management of all affairs directly to the local citizenry in the shortest time possible. In order to ensure this, there needs to be greater collaboration between the AU, NEPAD and regional economic communities as well as external actors to outline an exit strategy and timetable for external actors when a mission is being planned. This is vital in order for war-affected communities to become self-reliant and self-sufficient in the shortest time possible.[24]

The AU/NEPAD Policy Framework has proposed the establishment of a joint Post-conflict Reconstruction Unit to undertake the day-to-day task of coordinating and implementing this work. The Unit would also undertake advocacy and develop post-conflict reconstruction programmes in partnership with civil society, RECs and other intergovernmental organisations. The Policy Framework has further identified the need for resource mobilisation. It also emphasises the need for a more strategic targeting of sections of society that are in greatest need: child soldiers, IDPs, refugees, women, victims of sexual violence and persons afflicted with HIV/AIDS. In order to focus efforts to raise funds, an AU Peace Fund has been established to channel resources into post-conflict reconstruction.

Recent Developments on the AU's Post-conflict Reconstruction Agenda

The AU in collaboration with the South African-based NGO, SaferAfrica, convened a meeting in September 2005 in Durban, South Africa, which brought together representatives of the AU's 15-member Peace and Security Council and other AU member states' permanent representatives.[25] The objective of the meeting was to reflect on post-conflict reconstruction and development efforts in Africa.[26] The meeting discussed the experiences and lessons learned by various organisations working in the field of post-conflict reconstruction and development. Durban also identified the key actors and the institutional set-up and coordination that will be required to generate broad agreement on the criteria for an AU framework for post-conflict reconstruction and development. The meeting further suggested that, in order to ensure the necessary resources for successful post-conflict recovery, an AU-managed African Development Fund could be established to act as a catalyst for accessing and targeting resources for the continent's peacebuilding needs.

An effective AU post-conflict strategy must also focus on disarmament, demobilisation and reintegration (DDR) of ex-combatants with a view to ensuring that demobilised fighters have access to rehabilitation programmes that enable them to acquire new skills and to facilitate their transition back into society after conflicts. Security sector reform (SSR) is also vital for ensuring that national defence and police forces re-orient their activities towards building sustainable peace in their respective countries. The Durban meeting noted that national institutions need to be rebuilt to ensure the consolidation of democratic governance, the rule of law and the protection of the human rights of citizens in transitional societies. In order to guarantee the sustainability of these institutions, education and training must be provided to establish professionalism and integrity in these efforts.

Concluding Thoughts: Towards a Symbiotic Partnership

In order to enhance the symbiotic partnership between the UN and the AU, there is a need to forge formal links between the UN Peacebuilding Commission and the AU/NEPAD framework. One way in which this could be done is through a Memorandum of Understanding (MoU). The MoU would outline the specific areas in which inter-organisational collaboration can yield the greatest impact with regards to peacebuilding efforts in Africa. An MoU on the specific issue of post-conflict reconstruction would emphasise the importance of establishing a symbiotic partnership to deal with the multiple challenges that war-affected societies face.

The creation of the UN Peacebuilding Commission and the articulation of the AU/NEPAD Policy Framework suggest that the opportunity now exists for the consolidation of post-conflict reconstruction systems. These systems will include a network of institutions, mechanisms and processes that can guide, plan, monitor and evaluate post-conflict reconstruction efforts in Africa. The challenge as always is one of transforming these policies into coherent and practical strategies on the ground. This will require a greater degree of partnership between the institutions of the UN and those of the AU.

The UN Peacebuilding Commission will be critical for Africa. There is still the prevailing danger that if the Commission becomes politicised and used to serve the parochial interests of powerful countries, then it may be stillborn. The continent is plagued with a number of post-conflict situations, which urgently need to be addressed. If the Peacebuilding Commission becomes politicised, then the opportunity for it to function in the short to medium-term will be severely hampered. If given the necessary backing, however, a pragmatic Peacebuilding Commission that is appropriately funded could go a long way to "improve our success rate in building peace in war torn countries."[27] Even though the AU Policy Framework exists, it is unclear whether the organisation will be able to mobilise the resources and build the capacity to undertake peacebuilding effectively. This is why it is necessary to establish a symbiotic relationship with external actors like the UN and the World Bank, which have far more resources and experience in this critical area. To succeed, this relationship must be based on a complementarity of functions. In order to overcome some of the limitations currently affecting post-conflict reconstruction efforts in Africa, a symbiotic relationship between the UN and the AU must avoid the duplication or replication of functions. There is no question of whether the UN Peacebuilding Commission and the African Union should collaborate. The only question is how deep the partnership between the two organisations should be in order to improve and enhance post-conflict reconstruction efforts in Africa.

Notes

[1] See Lund, M: "A Toolbox for Responding to Conflict and Building Peace" in Reychler, L & Paffenholz, T (eds.): *Peacebuilding: A Field Guide* (Boulder, Colorado: Lynne Rienner, 2001); and Wallensteen, P: *Understanding Conflict Resolution: War, Peace and the Global System* (Thousand Oaks, California: Sage Publications, 2002).

[2] High-level Panel on Threats, Challenges and Change, *A More Secure World: Our Shared Responsibility*, New York: United Nations, 2004.

[3] United Nations, *Charter of the United Nations*, 24 October 1945, Article 33.

[4] Boutros-Ghali, B: *An Agenda for Peace: Preventive Diplomacy, Peacemaking and Peacekeeping*, (New York: United Nations, 1992).

[5] Annan, K: *In Larger Freedom: Towards Development, Security and Human Rights for All*, UN document A/59/2005, 21 March 2005.

[6] United Nations General Assembly: *Outcome Document*, 14 September 2005.

[7] Centre for Conflict Resolution: *A More Secure Continent: African Perspectives on the High-level Panel Report* (Cape Town: Centre for Conflict Resolution, April 2005).

[8] United Nations General Assembly: *The Peacebuilding Commission*, A/60/L.40, New York: United Nations, 20 December 2005.

[9] UN: *Outcome Document*, para. 97.

[10] UN: *Outcome Document*, para. 97.

[11] UN: *Outcome Document*, para. 97.

[12] UN: *Outcome Document*, para. 97.

[13] Guicherd, C: "Picking up the Pieces: What to Expect from the Peacebuilding Commission" in *Friedrich Ebert Stiftung: Briefing Papers*. Report of conference organised by the Friedrich Ebert Foundation (FES) in cooperation with the German Federal Ministry of Economic Cooperation and Development (BMZ), 6 December 2005, p. 3.

[14] African Union: *The Common African Position on the Proposed Reform of the United Nations: The Ezulwini Consensus*, Seventh Extraordinary Session of the Executive Council, Ext/EC.CL/2 (VII), Addis Ababa: African Union, 7–8 March 2005.

[15] UN: *Outcome Document,* para. 100.

[16] International Commission on Intervention and State Sovereignty: *The Responsibility to Protect*, (Ottawa: International Development Research Centre, 2001); Deng, F et al: *Sovereignty as Responsibility: Conflict Management in Africa* (Washington, DC: The Brookings Institution, 1996); and Weiss, T & Hubert, D: *The Responsibility to Protect: Research, Bibliography and Background* (Ottawa: International Development Research Centre, 2001).

[17] Stetten, J. & Steinhilber, J: "UN Peacebuilding Commission" in *Friedrich Ebert Stiftung: Dialogue on Globalisation* (New York: FES, 11 January 2006), p. 2.

[18] See *Progress Report on UN Reform*, available at www.reformtheun.org (accessed 21 March 2006).

[19] Annan, K: UN Secretary-General Address to the World Summit, 14 September 2005.

[20] Centre for Conflict Resolution and the Centre for Policy Studies: *The AU/NEPAD and Africa's Evolving Governance and Security Architecture* (Johannesburg, 11–12 December 2004). (Available at http//ccrweb.ccr.uct.ac.za).

[21] New Partnership for Africa's Development: *African Post-conflict Reconstruction Policy Framework* (Midrand: NEPAD Secretariat, June 2005).

[22] New Partnership for Africa's Development: *African Post-conflict Reconstruction Policy Framework*.

[23] New Partnership for Africa's Development: *African Post-conflict Reconstruction Policy Framework*.

[24] Samii, C: *Developing Peace Partnerships in Africa: Report from the 35th Annual Vienna Peacemaking and Peacekeeping Seminar* (New York: International Peace Academy, 2005).

[25] African Union: *Report of Proceedings: The 4th Brainstorming Retreat of the Peace and Security Council*

and other AU Member States' Permanent Representatives to the African Union (AU) on Post-conflict Reconstruction and Development in Africa (Durban: 4–5 September 2005).

[26] SaferAfrica: *Pax Africa* Vol.2, No.2, June–September 2005, p. 1.

[27] Annan, K: UN Secretary-General Address to the World Summit, 14 September 2005.

14

Terrorism and Counter-terrorism: Dialogue or Confrontation?

Mwesiga Baregu

PERHAPS ONE OF THE two most controversial and yet urgent challenges facing the international community today is that of international terrorism and counter-terrorism.[1] The other pressing concern is the deepening indebtedness, impoverishment and marginalisation of the majority of the world's societies and peoples. The two challenges are interrelated with reciprocal effects. Hardly a day passes without some political development or violent incident related either to terrorist acts or to counter-terrorist responses, particularly since the terrorist bombing of the twin towers of the World Trade Centre in New York and the Pentagon in Washington DC on 11 September 2001. Simultaneously, hardly a day passes without thousands of children and other vulnerable groups dying from hunger, abject poverty or preventable diseases. The main argument in this chapter is that the two processes are interlinked and probably arise from the same phenomenon: globalisation.

Although terrorism has existed in a variety of forms for centuries, current concerns and responses to the phenomenon emanate from what has popularly come to be known as the 9/11 tragedy. It is this event that has focused global attention on international terrorism and sparked controversy over the definition, manifestations and implications of terrorism, and what can or should be done about it. In the last few years, numerous debates have sought to build some consensus on how to define terrorism and what the most appropriate responses to it are.

However, there has been little success from these efforts so far, and there is still no coherent international consensus on the "nature of the beast" and how to contain it.

In the meantime, since the "war on terror" was declared by America on Al-Qaeda in 2001, we have witnessed the invasion of Afghanistan in 2001 and Iraq in 2003, and could see further incursions spread into Iran and Syria. This campaign has been led by the Anglo-American alliance under the principle of "act now, obtain United Nations consensus later". This is particularly apparent in Iraq's case during which the "coalition forces" invaded the country despite the UN Security Council having denied them authorisation. This was carried out under the pretext that the world was facing a "clear and present danger" from Saddam Hussein's government's possession of Weapons of Mass Destruction (WMDs). The disregard of the UN's opinion not only made the war an illegal contravention of the UN Charter, it also established a dangerous precedent in the international system. The failure to find WMDs in Iraq and the removal of the government of Saddam Hussein from power under the unconvincing explanation of the need for "regime change" further served to weaken the UN system. The emergent Iraqi resistance against foreign occupation, and the widely reported inhumane treatment of prisoners of war in Abu Ghraib prison by "coalition forces", as well as the killing of innocent civilians – dismissed as "collateral damage" – have exacerbated the situation by alienating more Iraqis and creating new sympathisers with terrorist causes around the world.

The continued instability in Iraq and Afghanistan suggests that this unilateralist approach is not effective in the fight against terrorism. Some analysts contend that these methods encourage terrorism in the long run, particularly if they are viewed as a result of "reaping the whirlwind" or the blow-back of American foreign policy. Apart from the fact that this approach disallows accusations against US foreign policy, it also diverts world attention away from Washington's foreign policy errors and seems to legitimise them. A military approach to such a complex problem is bound to achieve undesirable consequences. According to some analysts, the many innocent casualties of military retaliation "will, of course, create more desperate and embittered childless parents and parentless children, and so recruit more maddened people to terrorists' cause".[2] Counter-terrorism itself thus progressively resembles terrorism.

Approaches to addressing the occurrence of terrorism and counter-terrorism are as many and diverse as the multiple definitions of the problem. The contention of this chapter is that the way one defines a problem determines how one approaches its solution. In the case of terrorism, there are at least two broad definitions that can be identified. The first is the behavioural approach. This definition focuses on events such as 9/11 and identifies them as anomalous to the international system and views the perpetrators as political radicals or religious fanatics. According to this definition Islamic fundamentalism has been placed at the centre of the war against terror, thus potentially targeting all Muslims, alienating and ultimately enraging them.[3] The other definition is a structural one. This approach focuses on historical processes and relations of power in the international system rather than on isolated events and the behaviour of individuals. In this scheme, terrorist incidents are endogenous to the international system and such incidents are merely symptoms of a deeper malaise in the system.[4]

While the US and its allies have largely espoused a confrontational approach, weaker states have tended to advocate dialogue or, at least, a combination of peaceful and forceful methods. This has polarised debate in the international community and continues to block concerted action to address the issue of terrorism. These developments are central to understanding the current failure to combat international terrorism despite the fact that a number of poorer countries, including some African countries like Tanzania and Morocco, have adopted counter-terrorism legislation mainly at the behest of Washington.

The solution to any problem can only be as good as the diagnosis which carefully identifies the root causes of the problem. Logically, this means that thorough analysis and explanation of a condition must precede the prognosis and prescription. Otherwise, the danger of addressing the symptoms while the disease gets worse are very real and the costs become correspondingly high. In the case of responding to the latest wave of terrorism, however, it seems that it is precisely this mistake that America and some of its allies have made. Unfortunately – though perhaps understandably in reacting to the events of 9/11 – more emphasis was placed on responses rather than on the causes of the problem in order to come up with a long-term solution to it. It was assumed that America in particular, and the west in general, were under attack, when in reality it was the legacy and actions of US foreign policy that was being confronted. A less generous interpretation would suggest that speculation over the extent of international terrorism deliberately distorted the facts to serve imperialist objectives. The reality is that the events of 9/11, while atrocious, were ostensibly symbolic actions aimed at drawing attention to certain deep-seated grievances. While rapid reactions can be populist in the short-term, in the long run they can be counter-productive to preventing terrorism and achieving peacebuilding goals, which must remain at the core of the UN's agenda. Indeed, if not properly handled, short-term measures may exacerbate the problem rather than alleviate or solve it in the long run.

The issue of the definition of the problem of terrorism is not made easier by the 2004 report of the UN Secretary-General Kofi Annan's High-level Panel on *Threats, Challenges and Change*. This report notes that the UN's ability to formulate a comprehensive strategy to confront terrorism "has been constrained by the inability of member states to agree on an anti-terrorism convention including the definition of terrorism".[5]

Constraints on Choices for Action

Perceiving terrorism as behavioural rather than structural bears significant implications for the course of actions adopted, as well as their efficacy. A number of elements define and structure the policy space in which choices are made. Seven key factors are significant in making these choices.

First, international terrorism is a global problem arising from global processes; it can thus only be effectively addressed through multilateral cooperation. The current global challenge is the choice between the evolution of an international system where the rule of law protects the interests of all equally, or a global jungle in which a Darwinian survival of the fittest becomes the norm. Such acts as the Anglo-American attack on Iraq without UN authorisation will surely result in copy-cat impunity by terrorist groups. The 9/11 incidents should have been viewed as an opportunity to re-envisage the future rather than unleash a Christian "crusade" on infidels – Bush's initial language in the days after 9/11.

Second, there must be clear resolve and commitment from all countries to cooperate. This can only be obtained through mutual respect between states and the upholding of the UN Charter of 1945, which calls for sovereign equality and non-aggression between states. The violation of the national sovereignty of weaker states by the powerful will precipitate the rise of ultra-nationalism. Peaceful methods of persuasion rather than the use of coercion and confrontation should be employed internationally.

Third, in order to obtain such commitment, there must be a genuinely negotiated international consensus not only on the nature of terrorism but also on its root causes in the contemporary world. An imposition of a uniform approach to legislation aimed at countering terrorism – which has been the practice since 9/11 – is bound to fail. In order to be effective, such legislation must emanate primarily from domestic popular engagement and consent as well as from international consensus.

Fourth, international structural exploitation, inequalities, indignities, deprivations and all forms of injustice are currently more obvious due to modern communication. This lies at the root of dissent and protests leading to the growth of aggression and violent acts based on frustration or desperation.

Fifth, international terrorism is in essence a moral, political and intellectual challenge rather than a military challenge. Wholesale and unmeasured military responses may therefore create the illusion of temporary respite but are, in the long run, counter-productive. These actions often serve to aggravate the very conditions that breed terrorism in the first place.

Sixth, terrorism can take a multiplicity of forms, including the growing occurrence of suicide missions. These actions are therefore difficult to predict – and hence prevent – with any measure of certainty. This is compounded by the difficulty of predicting where, when, and how terrorist acts are likely to occur. Simply stated: one country acting as global policeman cannot anticipate all incidents, nor can it be everywhere at all times.

Finally, no country or group of countries has the capacity to address the problem of terrorism effectively and independently in the long term. The contributions of all countries are imperative to success. However, all countries must see themselves as stakeholders in the process, and inclusion in the global system must be the overarching strategic goal.

Africa and the War on Terror

Following the bombings of American embassies in Dar es Salaam, Tanzania and Nairobi, Kenya in 1998, African countries – under the leadership of the Organisation of African Union (OAU) – responded by launching a collective initiative to combat terrorism on the continent. The 1999 Algiers Convention against terrorism has since been ratified by almost all African countries which have also, at the behest of the US, adopted national counter-terrorism legislation in their own countries. Most African states have also signed many of the 12 major international conventions and protocols against terrorism.[6] The 2002 attacks on an Israeli-owned hotel and an El-Al passenger aircraft in Mombasa, Kenya, have led to the intensification of American counter-terrorism activities in East Africa and the Horn of Africa.

In the wake of 9/11, there appeared to be two strategic options facing Africa. First, Africa is likely to receive less development assistance from the US, which is currently more preoccupied with its own security interests. This suggests a shift back to the Cold War policy of "benign neglect" towards most of Africa. Second, due to Africa's weak states and fragile economies, the continent may invite all kinds of opportunistic anti-American terrorist groups. Africa receives particular attention from the US due to the large Muslim population of over 308 million on the continent, particularly in countries such as Somalia, Nigeria and in west Africa's Sahel region. US naval forces are patrolling Africa's east coast under the Combined Joint Task Force – Horn of Africa (CJTF–HOA). An American army base, with 900 troops, has also been established at Camp Lemonier in Djibouti since 2002, which is well placed for a number of strategic interests. It therefore appears that rather than a policy of benign neglect, US policy in Africa involves deeper engagement and more systemic interventions.[7]

In April 2004, at the East African Counter-terrorism Initiative Conference, William Pope, Deputy Coordinator for Counter-terrorism at the US State Department noted:

> Sadly, the continent of Africa is vulnerable to the threat of international terrorism and is of particular importance in the global effort to counter the terrorist threat... Although we are concerned about attacks anywhere in Africa, we consider East Africa and the Horn – Djibouti, Somalia, Sudan, Uganda, Ethiopia, Kenya and Tanzania – to be at particular risk.[8]

What then are the implications of resurgent American unilateralism for Africa? Before 9/11, there was considerable euphoria and enthusiasm about the possibilities of an African Renaissance, led particularly by South African president, Thabo Mbeki. Some even referred to the new millennium as "an African century".[9] Efforts to translate these aspirations into concrete plans of action have culminated in the much-vaunted New Partnership for Africa's Development (NEPAD)[10] of 2001, which was expected to increase vastly the external resources flowing into Africa. (See Gambari in this volume). Since the US, under President George W Bush, will be largely preoccupied with its own national security, "homeland security" and the economic security of American people, resources could mainly be available to African governments if they assist with these counter-terrorism goals. African countries might thus in future have to define their national priorities in terms of US threat perceptions and defence priorities by committing to a number of conditions.[11]

First, in the area of governance, we are likely to witness intensified interference in the internal affairs of African countries, including direct external efforts to monitor terrorism within specific countries.[12] The concept of juridical sovereignty – particularly as it applies to African countries – could be blatantly abandoned in favour of realist (power) sovereignty. This process will partly be reinforced by the weakness or virtual non-existence of states in some countries. Somalia is a classic example of such "failed states". Some analysts have contended that the principle of sovereignty, which underlies the UN Charter, should be abandoned altogether in such cases.[13]

Second, African governments could, in future, be forced to demonstrate that their defence policies are designed and organised in ways that enhance America's national security objectives. Resources may be increased in this area, with African armies progressively becoming appendages of the US defence establishment. In 2003, Bush announced the creation of a $100 million East African Counter-terrorism Initiative (EACTI).[14] This involves military training for border and coastal security; control of the movement of goods and people across borders; aviation security capacity-building; terrorist financing prevention; and police training – all directed not at the internal security of the citizens of east Africa, but at protecting the security of American citizens. Indeed, this initiative is likely to intensify internal insecurity by lowering the threshold of excessive repressive force against legitimate democratic protest, as was witnessed at the University of Dar es Salaam in April 2004. In this incident, the police met a peaceful protest by university students over a law that abolished grants in favour of student loans with repressive violence, largely because the protest route went past the American Embassy.

Third, African countries will be required to cooperate fully with the United States in ensuring the protection of its homeland and people, even if it means exposing their own countries and people to all manner of danger. This could conceivably include renewed efforts in biological warfare research, opening up countries to American intelligence organisations, attuning intelligence data to systems feeding American systems, and being subjected to all kinds of surveillance. Activities such as terrorist tracking and drug trafficking to the US could eventually come directly under country branches of US security agencies including the Central Intelligence Agency (CIA) and the Federal Bureau of Investigation (FBI).

Finally, as for economic policy, African governments could come under even closer direction by the US. All economic activity could become focused on feeding America's military–industrial complex. Thus, we are likely to see increased activity in extractive industry – particularly oil – rather than manufacturing industry, and intensified control of African markets by multinational companies. Yet the economic aspirations articulated by the American-supported NEPAD are that the challenge is for the people and governments of Africa to understand that development is a process of empowerment and self-reliance. Hence, it is asserted that Africans must not be wards of benevolent guardians, but instead be the architects of their own sustained upliftment. That is unlikely to be realised under NEPAD in its current form.

It will be important to watch the extent to which African governments will be able to respond to American demands to remove terrorist elements from their midst. Since this is dependent on state capacity, most African governments will be found wanting in this regard. This situation is likely to be exacerbated by deepening conditions of poverty and deprivation which may encourage discontent and lead to "terrorist" forms of political activism. Thus, George W Bush's State of the Union message to Americans in January 2002 would seem pertinent to most African countries:

> My hope is that all nations will heed our call, and eliminate the terrorist parasites that threaten their countries and ours. Many

countries are acting forcefully... But some governments will be
timid in the face of terror. And make no mistake: if they do not
act, America will act.[15]

Given America's reluctance to engage in a meaningful international
dialogue in the search for a consensual definition of terrorism – one
of the failures of the UN reform efforts at the General Assembly in
September 2005 – as well as the fact that both the US and Israel have
refused to sign the UN General Assembly Resolution 42/159 of 1987
against terrorism, we are entering an extremely volatile era in which
Washington has arrogated to itself the right to intervene in any country, as
it may wish, without necessary recourse to the UN Security Council.[16]

Regional vs International Intervention

The issue of international intervention has taken on more significance
since the US war on terror was launched in 2001. Critical questions centre
on when it is legitimate to intervene, under what circumstances, by whom,
with what authority, by what means, with what mandate and with what
"exit strategy". With the recent US-led interventions in Kosovo (1999)
and Iraq (2003), the question of authority takes on particular significance.
The 2001 report of the International Commission on Intervention and
State Sovereignty (ICISS) emphasises the role of the UN Security Council
in sanctioning any "humanitarian interventions".[17] The report stated that
"there is no better or more appropriate body than the Security Council
to authorise military intervention for human protection purposes".[18]
Only when the Security Council rejects a proposal or fails to deal with it
in a reasonable time are alternative options recommended by the ICISS.
Action by regional or sub-regional organisations under Chapter VIII of
the UN Charter is deemed to be a measure of last resort. Even when
such regional action is undertaken, subsequent authorisation must still be
sought from the Security Council. Thus, the ICISS report has a clear bias
towards centralisation through the UN. (See Mwanasali in this volume).

In this chapter, there are two key arguments regarding the position
and role of regional arrangements in peacekeeping. At the conceptual
level, the ICISS report somewhat contradicts former UN Secretary-
General Boutros Boutros-Ghali's 1992 report *An Agenda for Peace*, which
argued that:

> Under the Charter, the Security Council has and will continue to have primary responsibility for maintaining international peace and security, but regional action as a matter of decentralisation, delegation and cooperation with the United Nations efforts could not only lighten the burden of the Council but also contribute to a deeper sense of participation, consensus and democratisation in international affairs.[19]

While this agenda seeks to amplify the role of regional arrangements in peacekeeping operations, the ICISS report confines this role to a peripheral one. In relation to African conflicts, the Security Council is in a quandary. On the one hand, the UN – owing to material and political constraints – is unable to undertake timely and effective steps to prevent or contain conflicts. This is demonstrated by its total failure to act during the Rwandan genocide in 1994 (See Anyidoho in this volume), and the recent procrastination in deploying a force in eastern Democratic Republic of the Congo (DRC). On the other hand, the Security Council has failed to promote regional arrangements, and even sought to obstruct some regional initiatives.

This dovetails with the emerging and pervasive "lead nation" and "coalition of the willing" doctrines that we have seen at work during conflicts in Kosovo and Iraq. These are not a result of consensus at the UN. Rather, these doctrines are being unilaterally imposed by the powerful and influential members of the UN against the will of the majority of states, and sometimes without the full authorisation of the Security Council. These actions are thus steadily undermining and eroding the authority and legitimacy of the UN as a whole. It should be noted that the same countries that undertake these unilateral actions have been arguing against the establishment of effective UN-supported regional mechanisms. This situation arouses "skepticism among many non-western and developing countries – that the West seeks *carte blanche* to do what it wants – as well as among western states – that too many countries seek to hide behind the protection of sovereignty".[20]

There are many arguments in favour of regional peacekeeping arrangements, but the fundamental justification derives from Chapter VIII of the UN Charter which states, *inter alia*, that the Security Council should encourage associations or agencies that promote peace at the regional level. The importance of strengthening regional capacity to maintain peace in the region is based on four critical factors. First, African governments have a better understanding of regional issues and can respond quicker to crises. This is particularly relevant in the post-Cold War era as peacekeeping concerns in Africa are low on western agendas. Second, African states have a vested interest in stable regional peace since conflicts tend to flow over their boundaries; spilling refugees, rebels and arms across borders. Third, regional operations may prevent or at least attenuate post-colonial "sphere of influence" struggles that have featured and currently play a major part in the Rwanda and Congo conflicts. Finally, regional peacekeeping efforts are more likely to lead to durable regional peace and security arrangements between countries.

Concluding Thoughts: What Can the UN Do?

Considerations of these regional concerns should guide the choices of the United Nations as it contemplates the various options for peacebuilding and peacekeeping in Africa. What can not be overstated is that the UN must take charge of initiatives and strive to embrace and articulate a clear long-term vision of global peace and security, based on the protection of state sovereignty. The challenge for the UN therefore is to listen to, and respond to, behavioural concerns over terrorism as it makes its way towards the structuralist vision of a free, fair and just world. To achieve this, the UN should adopt the following six measures.

First, the UN must explicitly embrace the "structural" definition of terrorism that seeks to go beyond the policing and combative approach adopted by the United States and its allies. This approach is clearly exacerbating the problem by swelling the ranks of potential terrorists. The use of violence must be considered as the very last resort and, when it occurs, this must be strictly done within the established rules and procedures spelt out under Chapter VII of the UN Charter. This will help to restore the fledgling legitimacy of the UN system as a whole.

Second, in order to allay American fears about Africa becoming a breeding ground and refuge of terrorists, concerted efforts must be made to stem the tide of state failure and the erosion of sovereignty on the continent. This means that the UN must invest not only in governance capacity-building, but also in enabling African states to address basic socio-economic problems such as the provision of education and health. Poverty, alienation and dehumanising conditions must be recognised as the root causes of desperation and aggression leading to terrorism.

Third, the UN must strive to depolarise the international system by reiterating the common dangers faced by the world community, including weapons of mass destruction. However, the UN must urge powerful western countries to yield to genuine internationalism in diplomacy and pursue multilateralism in international disarmament efforts. Unilateralism, global domination and the subversion of fundamental UN norms such as the sovereignty of states are a recipe for global catastrophe. If new norms and values are to emerge, they must result from a negotiated multilateral process rather than an imposed unilateral one.

Fourth, the UN should quickly redirect its efforts to the goals of its enfeebled Economic and Social Council in order to bridge the growing gap between rich and poor states and to fulfil the objectives of the Millennium Development Goals of halving poverty by 2015. (See Legum in this volume). The truism that a hungry man is an angry man could not be more appropriate in a world where fast electronic communication delivers obscene opulence to television screens of the sick and starving in an instant.

Fifth, the UN General Assembly must recapture its authority, which was lost during the east–west rivalry of the Cold War. Civil society must also move closer to the centre of formal UN activities. A more visibly democratic and inclusive UN system will promote democracy more credibly among its member states, and particularly among smaller and weaker states in Africa which are more likely to become new breeding grounds for terrorism.

Finally, the UN Security Council must be reformed to reflect post-Cold War security concerns. (See Adebajo as well as Jonah in this volume). The Security Council must also move to legitimise and lend credence to international criminal legal institutions such as the Hague-based International Criminal Court in such matters as international terrorism and war crimes.

Notes

1 See International Peace Academy (IPA): *Responding to Terrorism: What Role for the United Nations?* (New York: IPA, 2002).

2 Johnson, C: "Blowback" in *The Nation*, 15 October 2001.

3 For this kind of concern in Africa see Lyman, P & Morrison, S: "The Terrorist Threat in Africa" in *Foreign Affairs* 84, 1 (2004).

4 See Baregu, M: "Beyond September 11: Structural Causes and Behavioral Consequences of International Terrorism" in IPA *Responding to Terrorism: What Role for the United Nations?* (New York: IPA, 2002), p. 40.

5 UN: *A More Secure World: Our Shared Responsibility. Report of the Secretary-General's High-level Panel on Threats, Challenges and Change* Department of Public Information DPI/2367 (2004).

6 US Department of State: Patterns of Global Terrorism – 2003. Available at www.globalsecurity.org/security

7 Lobe, J: "U.S. Military 'Footprint' Extends to Africa" available at www.OneWorld.net 9 (accessed May 2003). For concrete policy proposals along these lines see Lyman and Morrison, "The Terrorist Threat in Africa".

8 Pope, W: "Opening Remarks" at the East African Counter-terrorism Initiative Conference, Kampala, Uganda, April 21 2004 at www.state.gov

9 Presidents Mbeki of South Africa, Obasanjo of Nigeria, Wade of Senegal and Bouteflika of Algeria are associated with this initiative and were all invited to the G-8 Kananaskis Summit, July 2002. NEPAD seems to have been designed to supplant the Sirte initiative led by Libya proposing a more transformative and self-reliant approach to the renewed African Union.

10 The President of Gambia Yahya Jammeh recently cynically translated it as "knee pad" – to cushion the knees of begging heads of state who are likely to kneel for a long time to come. See http://www.fingaz.co.zw/fingaz/2003/October/October23/1575.shtml (accessed 20 March 2006).

11 That is the clear message from the G-8 Kananaskis, Canada Summit in July 2002. Apart from stressing that future support to Africa would crucially depend on the G-8's respective priorities and procedures they only pledged $6 billion out of $64 billion expected under NEPAD. Oxfam described the offer as "repackaged peanuts". See Talbot, C. "G8 rejects Africa Aid Plea". World Socialist Web Site, 3 July, 2002.

12 Established under UN Security Council Resolution 1373 (2001), the Counter-terrorism Committee (CTC) under the chairmanship of Britain is charged with the responsibility of ensuring that members of the UN report regularly on the steps taken to combat terrorism in their countries. A recent parliamentary debate on the Counter-terrorism Act in Tanzania (passed on 5 November 2002) was quite acrimonious, raising questions about the lack of popular discussion, the abridgement of fundamental rights, the repressiveness of the legislation and the surrender of sovereignty.

13 See Brzezinski, Z: *The Grand Chessboard: American Supremacy and its Geostrategic Imperatives* (New York: Basic Books, 1997); Cooper, R: "The Post-Modern State" in Leonard M (ed.): *Re-ordering the World: the Long-term implications of September 11th* (London: Foreign Policy Centre, 2002); Mallaby, S: "The Reluctant Imperialist: Failed States and the Case for American Empire" in *Foreign Affairs* (April 2002). While Brzezinski and Mallaby argue in favour of global US hegemony, Cooper proposes some kind of condominium solution entailing a redivision of the world among European powers reminiscent of the nineteenth century.

14 Pope, J: "Opening Remarks" of the East African Counter-terrorism Initiative Conference, Kampala, Uganda, April 21, 2004.

15 US State of the Union Address of George W Bush, 29 January 2002.

16 See http://www.un.org/documents/ga/res/42/a42r159.htm (accessed 12 April 2006). Under

such conditions, simply invoking UN Security Council Resolution 1373 (2001), which was understandably passed in the heat of the moment and in good faith, is not enough. A process of consensus building must accompany the CTC's monitoring role. This does not appear in the CTCs "Achievements in its first 12 months". See "The Counter-Terrorism Committee brochure".

[17] See *The Responsibility to Protect,* Report of the International Commission on Intervention and State Sovereignty. (Ottawa: International Development Research Council, 2001) available at www.iciss.ca/pdf/Commission-Report.pdf (accessed 25 March 2006).

[18] See *The Responsibility to Protect.*

[19] Boutros-Ghali, B: *An Agenda for Peace,* second edition, (A/50/60-S/1995/1), (New York: UN Department of Public Information, 1995), para. 64.

[20] Pugwash Meeting No. 265. Joint meeting of the Pugwash study group on "Intervention, Sovereignty and International security and the International Commission on Intervention and State Sovereignty", Pugwash, Nova Scotia: 20–21 July 2001.

Conclusion

Helen Scanlon

> Our continent, more than any other, suffers from the fact that the multilateral system is not living up to its potential… The world will not enjoy development without security, nor security without development and will not enjoy either without respect for human rights… The better the United Nations works, the more all people will benefit, within and beyond Africa.
>
> *Kofi Annan, 4 July 2005*

While the "event" of UN (United Nations) reform in 2005 is effectively dead – culminating in a number of watered down proposals to redesign the world body – the reform drive as a process should not be lost. As this volume of essays has clearly indicated, the push to place development as intrinsic to peace and security on the agenda of an institution created 60 years ago has achieved increasing resonance in the recent reform debates. For the African continent this momentum should not be lost.

In September 2005 UN Secretary-General Kofi Annan noted that the UN summit would "be an event of decisive importance. The decisions to be taken at the meeting may determine the whole future of the United Nations. Even more important, they will offer us our best – perhaps our only – chance to ensure a safer, more just and more prosperous world in the new century".[1] What made 2005 critical for the UN to achieve change was the coalescence of three factors – first, an acceptance of the need for change as a result of the erosion of multilateralism created by the 2003 invasion of Iraq; second, the design of a detailed agenda for change

275

through the High-level Panel report and the UN Secretary-General Kofi Annan's subsequent report *In Larger Freedom*; and third, the opportunity for change offered by the world body's 60th anniversary.[2] Nonetheless, many UN member states did not consider that the United Nations had "come to a fork in the road" as Annan contended.[3] As a result, over 100 member states insisted that more time was necessary to fully consider recommendations for reform of the world body.

As we have seen, despite the overall failure to achieve acceptance of the 101 High-level Panel proposals for UN reform, member states did accept a few diluted proposals to create new institutions to strengthen the UN, which potentially have great relevance for Africa – the Peacebuilding Commission to assist countries' transitions from war to peace; the Human Rights Council to stem the impunity of human rights violators; and the promotion of the idea of a "responsibility to protect" to allow for intervention in cases of genocide.

Perhaps more importantly, the impetus created by the reform "event" resulted in the February 2005 Ezulwini Consensus by members of the African Union (AU) and, as such, for the first time since the UN's creation, the formulation of a coherent African perspective on the needs of the continent in relation to the world body. This is of particular significance considering that Africa has the largest continental representation in the UN (over a quarter of its membership) as well as being host to the highest number of peacekeeping and humanitarian initiatives deployed by the world body. The reform drive has also allowed African actors to assess fully what the key peace and security concerns that face the continent are, as it enters the twenty-first century.

Africa's Stake in UN Reform

Africa's stake in the UN reform process was most apparent in three key areas: first, peacekeeping, humanitarian intervention and peacebuilding on the continent where half of UN peacekeeping missions in the world are currently deployed; second, the need for sustainable development in a world where trade and aid are skewed to favour rich and powerful countries; and finally, the necessity to address human security challenges such as HIV/AIDS in a body where the traditional security challenges such as international terrorism are prioritised.

Among the successes of the High-level Panel on *Threats, Challenges and Change* and Annan's report *In Larger Freedom* was the proposal of ways through which the UN would be able to face the challenges of the twenty-first century – that collective action was preferable to unilateralism and that global security should be perceived as a shared responsibility. Through both of these reports, the concept of peace and security was broadened to include human security concerns, and in so doing it was acknowledged that development and security are inextricably linked.

The recent squabbles over UN reform revealed once again that reform initiatives within the world body will continue to founder as long as individual or groups of member states only support those measures that they themselves benefit from. These events also revealed the danger posed by the divisions created by African governments upholding parochial self-interest at the expense of promoting a unified continental perspective. These divisions amplify the already apparent inequality posed by dominant powers within the world body that currently often fails to safeguard the interests of small and medium-sized states. Further, the effective functioning of an African approach requires greater utilisation of the UN Secretariat and the promotion of more Africans to senior positions within the organ.

Some of the weaknesses of the recent reform drive include the failure to emphasise the need for policy coherence over international assistance; the lack of a clear definition of the mandate of the Peacebuilding Commission; and ambiguity over the source of resources necessary to successfully implement a comprehensive development and humanitarian strategy for Africa. The relationship between the New Partnership for Africa's Development (NEPAD) and the British-led Commission for Africa needs to be further developed in order to enact some of the key recommendations of the Commission and to galvanise more international support for sustained growth and poverty reduction on the continent.

Sovereignty as Responsibility

Twelve years after the Rwandan genocide, the crisis in Sudan's Darfur region has provoked questions over international intervention on the continent. With increased demand for peace operations worldwide, the UN's peacekeeping efforts in countries such as Mozambique, Sierra Leone, Liberia, Côte d'Ivoire and Congo have demonstrated the significance of external actors to the future of peacekeeping missions in Africa. In recent years, attention has focused on the ability of the United Nations and African organisations to respond to crises and to manage peacekeeping operations effectively. The AU and regional organisations are developing more capacity to tackle regional peace and security challenges, but the situation in Sudan's Darfur region has illustrated that this relationship is still a fledgling one.

The failure of the international community to intervene in the 1994 Rwandan genocide provided many lessons for the AU's ongoing mission in Sudan. The AU's intervention as peacekeeper in Darfur has revealed the limitations in the organisation's current peace and security structures both at its headquarters in Addis Ababa, Ethiopia and on the ground. While the AU's deployment of a force in the region shows a crucial recommitment to the protection of citizens across borders, logistical problems as well as the lack of political will to challenge the government in Khartoum, makes the situation stark. Nonetheless, this has again revealed the reticence of the international community to intervene effectively in conflict situations in Africa and highlights the need to strengthen continental capacity in such scenarios.

Recent conflicts on the continent have led to the acceptance that the intervention of local actors is preferable and the advantage of such initiatives is that they draw on local knowledge. The responsibility falls on national governments to provide security and to create the necessary conditions for economic recovery. The role of the international community – whether the AU or the UN – is to advise and support national efforts and to contribute to the mobilisation of sustainable and predictable resources to help societies recover from the scourge of violent conflicts.

The current challenge posed by internal displacement further places emphasis on the need to develop ways to respond effectively to prevent the displacement of populations, as well as to protect and assist those already displaced. The need for governments – with the support of the international community – to create conditions for peace, security, stability and the general welfare of its people is of central concern to the continent. To assist this development, the creation of the Human Rights Council holds great promise for the improvement of the capacity of the UN to promote and protect human rights. The lessons learnt from South Africa's post-apartheid human rights tradition have established a precedent for African states, which is being reinforced by a new human rights infrastructure on the continent. The expectation that the creation of the UN Human Rights Council generates is that it will make it harder for governments to continue to deny their obligation to protect and promote human rights. As a result, the new Human Rights Council could make a significant contribution to bolstering and supporting Africa's evolving human rights architecture.

Africa's Development and Human Security Challenges

Concerted action to help overcome current obstacles to Africa's development is required by Africa and its international partners. The need to cultivate a fairer international trading and financial system is vital for the continent, as is the need to further question the Washington Consensus and the current economic milieu. Scarce resources should go towards promoting the continent's health and education structures instead of being used to service unpayable debts.

Africa is currently foundering in its ability to meet the Millennium Development Goals' aim of halving poverty by 2015. The 2006 annual World Bank–International Monetary Fund Global Monitoring Report on the MDGs found that sub-Saharan Africa is lagging behind on almost all the human development aspects of the MDGs. For example, the poverty rate on the continent is 44 per cent, somewhat lower than the 2001 level of 46.4 per cent, but nonetheless projected to remain above 38 per cent by 2015. Further, the rate of school enrolment of girls in sub-Saharan Africa is still more than 15 per cent lower than that for boys.

The security dimension of HIV/AIDS has become increasingly apparent in the twenty-first century, especially on a continent where the pandemic is the leading killer of adults. This has implications for both national and continental security. The goals articulated by the High-level Panel and the UN Secretary-General's *In Larger Freedom* report require the continued acknowledgment of the threat posed by HIV/AIDS to international peace and security. While there has been an element of progress in the fight against AIDS on the continent, Africa still needs to act immediately – with its international partners – to curb the spread of HIV/AIDS. Rich member states must take seriously their commitments to achieve the target of 0.7 per cent of gross national income for official development assistance and to provide full funding for the Global AIDS

Fund. African governments, on the other hand, must acknowledge that strategies to combat HIV/AIDS on the continent have proved ineffective, and that urgent measures are needed to combat the pandemic effectively.

Transnational organised crime has been a further contributor to fear and deprivation in Africa but is a threat that, with the necessary political will and international support, can be addressed. The present diffuse approach to the issue is not producing the required results and continues to tax the capacity of poorly resourced states to respond effectively to the scourge of international organised crime. If African states can show commitment, then there is a sound basis to demand the necessary technical and development assistance from rich countries and international organisations. The UN still has a vital role to play in supporting programmes to counter transnational crime, and to help develop, through effective global coordination, a more coherent system that can be properly monitored.

African Actors and Responses

Peacekeeping and peacebuilding initiatives in Africa need to become more predictable, less fragmented, more closely aligned to individual country needs and targeted to local circumstances. The newly created Peacebuilding Commission can potentially assist this by improving UN post-conflict planning; ensuring financing in the period between the end of hostilities; the establishment of democratic structures and effective bureaucracies; and improving coordination of UN bodies and other key regional and global actors. While some scepticism exists over the mobilisation of sufficient resources required for post-conflict reconstruction efforts in Africa, the creation of the Commission is nonetheless of vital interest to the continent.

Concerns over the impoverishment and marginalisation of the majority of the world's societies have increasingly been sidelined by concerns over international terrorism. Nonetheless for the majority of Africans, improvements relating to development, security and human rights and the enhancement of human security on the continent remain the central issues. The two processes, however, are linked, and equal concern needs to be paid to development as vital to the future of global peace and security.

The event of UN reform may be over, but Africa can still play an important role in the future of the world body and can assist in ensuring that the UN adapts to meet the challenges of a changing world. Africa should be central to all debates on "collective security" and on shaping the interpretation of what is "equitable". In Africa, peace and development must go hand in hand if the "responsibility to protect" is to make a difference. The onus is now on individual African countries, the United Nations and the international community at large, to assist peace and development efforts on the continent. African voices raised during the formulation of any future reform initiatives are imperative, as any new model for global governance will affect the lives of Africa's 800 million people. Thus, the articulation of African concerns, which have now been voiced, should continue in order to ensure a more secure continent in the twenty-first century. We hope that this book of rich essays by a pan-African team of scholars and practitioners can contribute to these efforts.

Notes

[1] Report of the UN Secretary-General, Kofi Annan (A/59/545).

[2] See G. Evans "UN Reform: Why It Matters for Africa", Address to Africa Policy Forum, President of the International Crisis Group and Member of the Secretary-General's High-level Panel on *Threats, Challenges and Change*, Addis Ababa, 26 August 2005.

[3] Kofi Annan, *Address to the UN General Assembly*, 23 September 2003.

Selected Reading

Adebajo, A & Landsberg, C: *The Millennium Declaration Goals: Meeting Africa's Special Needs* (Columbia University, New York: Unpublished Paper, 30 September 2004).

Adebajo, A: "From Congo to Congo: United Nations Peacekeeping in Africa after the Cold War," in Taylor, I and Williams, P (eds), *Africa in International Politics: External Involvement on the Continent* (London: Routledge, 2004).

Adelman, H & Suhrke, A (eds.): *The Path of a Genocide: The Rwanda Crisis from Uganda to Zaire* (New Brunswick and London: Transaction Publishers, 1999).

African Union & United Nations: *Africa Launches Bold, Renewed Effort to Step Up HIV Prevention* (Addis Ababa, Ethiopia: 12 April 2006).

African Union: *Abuja Declaration on HIV/AIDS, Tuberculosis and other Related Infectious Diseases* (Abuja, Nigeria: OAU/SPS/Abuja 3, 24–27 April 2001).

African Union: *Draft Recommendations at the Ministerial Committee of Fifteen on the Report of the High-level Panel on the Reform of the UN System.* (Mbabane, Swaziland: CTTE/15/Min/ReformUN/Draft/Recomm [I], 20–22 February 2005).

African Union: *Report of Proceedings: The 4th Brainstorming Retreat of the Peace and Security Council and other AU Member States: Permanent*

Representatives to the African Union (AU) on Post-conflict Reconstruction and Development in Africa (Durban, South Africa: 4–5 September 2005).

African Union: *Report of the Chairperson of the Commission on the Situation in Darfur* (PSC/PR/2[XLV], 12 January 2006).

African Union: *Statement of Commitment to Peace and Security in Africa issued by the Heads of State and Government of Member States of the Peace and Security Council of the African Union* (Addis Ababa: 25 May 2004).

African Union: *The Common African Position on the Proposed Reform of the United Nations: 'The Ezulwini Consensus'*, 7th extraordinary session of the Executive Council of the African Union, Addis Ababa, 7–8 March 2005. (Ext/EX.CL/2(VII).

Alson, P: *The United Nations and Human Rights: A Critical Appraisal* (Oxford: Clarendon Press, 1992).

Anyidoho, H K: *Guns Over Kigali* (Accra: Woeli Publishing Services, 1997).

Arendt, H: *The Origins of Totalitarianism* (New York: Harcourt Brace Jovanovich, 1966).

Asmal, K, Chidester, D. & Lubisi, C (eds.): *Legacy of Freedom: the ANC's Human Rights Tradition: Africans' Claims in South Africa, the Freedom Charter, the Women's Charter and other Human Rights Landmarks of the African National Congress* (Johannesburg: Jonathan Ball, 2005).

Asmal, K: "Environment and Sustainability: Looking to the Future" in *The Partnership Principle: New Forms of Governance in the 21st Century* (London: Archetype Publishers, 2004).

Bailey, S & Daws, S: *The United Nations: A Concise Political Guide* (Basingstoke: Macmillan Press, 1995).

Barnett, T & Prins, G: *HIV/AIDS and Security: Fact, Fiction and Evidence: A Report to UNAIDS* (Geneva and London: UNAIDS and London School of Economics, March 2005).

Bayart, J, Ellis, S & Hibou, B: "The Criminalisation of the State in Africa" in *African Issues* (1999).

Bond, P (ed.): *Fanon's Warning: A Civil Society Reader on the New Partnership for Africa's Development*, Second Edition (Trenton and Asmara: Africa World Press, 2005).

Boutros-Ghali, B: *An Agenda For Peace* (New York: United Nations, 1992).

Boyd, A: *Fifteen Men on a Powder Keg: A History of the UN Security Council* (London: Methuen, 1971).

Campbell, H: "Pan Africanism in the Twenty-First Century" in Raheem, A (ed.): *Pan Africanism: Politics, Economy and Social Change in the Twenty-First Century* (New York: New York University Press, 1996).

Centre for Conflict Resolution: *A More Secure Continent: African Perspectives on the UN High-level Panel Report, A More Secure World: Our Shared Responsibility* (Cape Town: CCR Seminar Report, May 2005).

Centre For Conflict Resolution: *Building an African Union for the 21st Century: Relations with the RECS, NEPAD and Civil Society* (Cape Town: CCR Seminar Report, August 2005).

Centre for Conflict Resolution: *HIV/AIDS and Human Security: An Agenda for Africa* (Addis Ababa: CCR Seminar Report, September 2005).

Centre for Conflict Resolution: *HIV/AIDS and Militaries in Southern Africa* (Windhoek: CCR Seminar Report, February 2006).

Centre for Conflict Resolution: *The New Partnership for Africa's Security: The United Nations, Regional Organisations and Future Security Threats in Africa* (Cape Town: CCR Seminar Report, October 2004).

Centre for Conflict Resolution: *Women and Peacebuilding in Africa* (Cape Town: CCR Seminar Report, October 2005).

Cohen, R & Deng, F (eds.): *The Forsaken People: Case Studies of the Internally Displaced* (Washington, DC: Brookings Institution Press, 1998).

Cohen, R & Deng, F: *Masses in Flight: The Global Crisis of Internal Displacement* (Washington: Brookings, 1998).

Commission for Africa: *Our Common Interest: Report of the Commission for Africa* (London: Penguin Books, 2005).

De Waal, A: "AIDS-related National Crises in Africa: Food Security, Governance and Development Partnerships" in *IDS Bulletin*, 33, 4 (2002).

De Waal, A: "How will HIV/AIDS Transform African Governance?" in *African Affairs*, 102 (2003).

Deng, F & Lyons, T (eds): *African Reckoning: A Quest for Good Governance* (Washington, DC: Brookings, 1998).

Deng, F et al.: *Sovereignty as Responsibility: Conflict Management in Africa* (Washington: Brookings, 1996).

Deng, F: "Negotiating a Hidden Agenda: Sudan's Conflict of Identities" in Zartman, W (ed.): *Elusive Peace: Negotiating an End to Civil Wars* (Washington, DC: Brookings, 1995).

Donnelly, P: *Universal Human Rights in Theory and Practice* (Ithaca and London: Cornell University Press, 2003).

Elbe, S: *Strategic Implications of HIV/AIDS* (Oxford: Oxford University Press, 2003)

Evans, G: "When is it Right To Fight?" in *Survival* 46, 3 (Autumn 2004).

Fleshman, M.: "Human Rights Move up on Africa's Agenda: New African Court to Promote Rule of Law, End Impunity for Rights Violators" in *Africa Renewal*, 18, 2 (July 2004).

Flint, J & de Waal, A: *Darfur: A Short History of a Long War (African Arguments)* (London: Zed Books, 2006).

Fourie, P & Shonteich, M: "Africa's New Security Threat: HIV/AIDS and Human Security in southern Africa" in *African Security Review* 10, 4 (2001).

Franck, T: "A Holistic Approach to Building Peace" in Otunnu, O & Doyle, M (eds.): *Peacemaking and Peacekeeping for the New Century* (Lanham, New York, Boulder and Oxford: Rowman & Littlefield Publishers Inc., 1998).

Freund, B: *The Making of Contemporary Africa: The Development of African Society since 1800, Second Edition* (London: Macmillan Press, 1998).

Gambari, I: "The United Nations" in Baregu, M & Landsberg, C (eds.): *From Cape to Congo: Southern Africa's Evolving Security Challenges* (Boulder and London: Lynne Rienner, 2003).

Habermas, J: *The Past as the Future* (Cambridge: Polity, 1994).

Heinbecker, P & Goff, P (eds.): *Irrelevant or Indispensable? The United Nations in the Twenty-First Century* (Ontario: Wilfred Laurier University Press, 2005).

Human Rights Watch: *Protectors or Pretenders? Government Human Rights Commissions in Africa* (New York, Brussels, London, Washington: HRW, 2001).

Iliffe, J: *The African AIDS Epidemic: A History* (Oxford: James Currey Ltd, 2005).

International Commission on Intervention and State Sovereignty: *The Responsibility to Protect, Report of the International Commission on Intervention and State Sovereignty* (Ottawa: International Development Research Centre, 2001).

International Peace Academy/Centre on International Cooperation: *Refashioning the Dialogue: Regional Perspectives on the Brahimi Report on UN Peace Operations* (Johannesburg, Buenos Aires, Singapore and London: Regional Meetings, February–March 2001).

Jonah, J: "An Independent International Civil Service" in Ask, S & Mark-Jungkvist, A: *The Adventure of Peace: Dag Hammarskold and the Future of the UN* (New York: Palgrave Macmillan, 2005).

Jonah, J: "The United Nations" in Adebajo, A & Rashid, I (eds.): *West Africa's Security Challenges: Building Peace in A Troubled Region* (Boulder and London: Lynne Rienner, 2004).

Kälin, W: *Recent Commentaries about the Nature and Application of the Guiding Principles on Internal Displacement* (Washington, DC: The Brookings-CUNY Project on Internal Displacement, 2002).

Kanninen, T: *Leadership and Reform: The Secretary-General and the Financial Crisis of the Late 1980s* (The Hague and Boston, MA: Kluwer Law International, 1995).

Landsberg, C: "From African Renaissance to NEPAD... and back to the Renaissance" in *Journal of African Elections* 1,2 (September 2002).

Lewis, S: *Race Against Time* (Toronto: House of Anansi, 2005).

Mahbubani, K: "The Permanent and Elected Council Members" in Malone, D (ed.): *The UN Security Council: From the Cold War to the 21st Century* (Boulder and London: Lynne Rienner, 2004).

March, J & Olsen, J: *Rediscovering Institutions: The Organisational Basis of Politics* (New York: Free Press, 1989).

Mazrui, A: *Cultural Forces in World Politics* (London: James Currey, 1990).

Mazrui, A: *On Heroes and Uhuru-Worship* (London: Longman, 1967).

Mazrui, A: *Towards a Pax Africana* (Chicago: University of Chicago Press, 1967).

Mwanasali, M: "'From Non-interference to Non-indifference': Emerging Doctrine in Conflict Prevention in Africa" in Akokpari, J, Murithi, T & Ndinga-Muvumba, A: *Building an African Union For the Twenty First Century* (forthcoming).

Ndinga-Muvumba, A: "Too Late to Make HIV/AIDS History" in *South African Labour Bulletin* 29, 4 (August/September 2005).

Organisation of African Unity: *The International Panel of Eminent Persons to Investigate the 1994 Genocide in Rwanda and the Surrounding Events* (July 2000).

Pollis, A & Schwab, P: *Human Rights: Cultural and Ideological Perspectives* (New York: Praeger, 1979).

Prunier, G: *Darfur: The Ambiguous Genocide* (Ithaca: Cornell University Press, 2005).

Prunier, G: *The Rwandan Crisis: History of a Genocide* (New York: Columbia University Press, 1995).

Roberts, A & Kingsbury, B (eds.): *United Nations, Divided World: The UN's Role in International Relations* (Oxford: Oxford University Press, 1993).

Sachs, J et al.: *Investing in Development: A Practical Plan to Achieve the Millennium Development Goals* (Washington, DC: Communications Development Inc, 2005).

Sachs, J: "The Millennium Project: From Words to Action" in Heinbecker, P & Goff, P (eds.): *Irrelevant or Indispensable? The United Nations in the 21st Century* (Ontario: Wilfrid Laurier University Press, 2005).

Sachs, J: *The End of Poverty: Economic Possibilities for Our Time* (New York: Penguin Press, 2005).

Shivji, I: *The Concept of Human Rights in Africa* (London: Codesria, 1989).

Sorbo, G & Vale, P (eds.): *Out of Conflict: From War to Peace in Africa* (Uppsala: Nordiska Afrikainstitutet, 1997).

South African Military Health Services: *The Comprehensive Plan for the Holistic Management of HIV and AIDS in the Department of Defence: 2005–2010* (Pretoria: SAMHS, 5 March 2005).

Stammers, N: "Human Rights and Power," in *Political Studies* 16 (1993).

United Nations Conference on Trade and Development: *Economic Development in Africa: Debt Sustainability: Oasis or Mirage?* (New York and Geneva: United Nations, 2004).

United Nations: *A More Secure World: Our Shared Responsibility, Report of the United Nations Secretary-General's High-level Panel on Threats, Challenges and Change.* (United Nations Department of Public Information: DPI/2367, December 2004).

United Nations: *In Larger Freedom: Towards Development, Security and Human Rights For All, Report of the UN Secretary-General; follow-up to the outcome of the Millennium Summit.* (UN: A/59/2005, 21 March 2005).

United Nations: *Report of the Panel on United Nations Peace Operations* S/2000/809 (Brahimi Report, 21 August 2000).

United Nations: *We the Peoples: Civil Society, the United Nations and Global Governance: Report of the Panel of Eminent Persons on United Nations–Civil Society Relations* A/58/817 (Cardoso Report, June 2004).

Wallensteen, P: *Understanding Conflict Resolution: War, Peace and the Global System* (Thousand Oaks, California: Sage Publications, 2002).

Weiss, T & Hubert, D: *The Responsibility to Protect: Research, Bibliography and Background* (Ottawa: International Development Research Centre, 2001).

World Bank: *Post-conflict Reconstruction: The Role of the World Bank* (Washington, DC: The World Bank, 1998).

Zacarias A: *The United Nations and International Peacekeeping* (London: IB Tauris & Co., 1996).

Zartman, W: *Collapsed States: The Disintegration and Restoration of Legitimate Authority* (Washington: Lynne Rienner, 1995).

Zeleza, T & McConnaughay, PJ (eds.): *Human Rights, the Rule of Law, and Development in Africa* (Philadelphia: University of Pennsylvania Press, 2004).

Index

A

Abuja Declaration 38; 190; 194; 196
Adebajo, Adekeye 8
  see also Chapter 1
Adventist Development Relief Agency
  158-59
Afghanistan 40; 227; 262
Africa
  aligning HIV/AIDS and security 182-202
  and war on terror 265-69
  extent of organised crime in 211-13
  stake in UN Reform 276-77
African Development Bank (ADB) 249
African diaspora 232-34
African National Congress (ANC) 228; 230
  Bill of Rights, 1943 231
  Freedom Charter, 1955 235
African Renaissance 267
Africans' Claims in South Africa 230-31
African Standby Force (ASF) 8; 23; 147; 160
Africa Peer Review Mechanism (APRM)
  29-32; 75
Africa Programme 3
aid 32-34
AIDS
  see HIV/AIDS
AIDS Support Organisation, The (TASO) 195
AIDS Watch Africa (AWA) 195-96
Algeria 22; 24; 26-27; 30; 61; 90; 93; 232
Alliance of Eritrean National Forces (AENF)
  39
Amnesty International 142
A More Secure World: Our Shared Responsibility
  2; 20; 59; 184; 207

An Agenda for Peace 28; 247; 269
Angola 29; 37; 41; 53; 67; 76; 247-48; 250
Annan, Kofi 2; 4-7; 19-21; 23; 28; 38; 46;
  48; 51; 54; 57-58; 69; 71; 75; 77; 79-80; 84;
  89; 91; 99; 100-101; 103; 120; 131; 135-36;
  142-43; 148; 152; 155; 160-61; 176-78; 184;
  188; 190; 192-93; 214; 243; 247; 251; 264
Anyidoho, Gen Henry 6; 11
  see also Chapter 8
Arab Maghreb Union (AMU) 8; 23; 46; 253
Aristide, Pres Jean-Bertrand 235-36
Arusha Peace Agreement of 1993 24; 148-52
Asmal, Kader 6; 13
  see also Chapter 12
AU (African Union) 3
  and NEPAD frameworks for post-conflict
  peacebuilding and reconstruction 252-56
  AU/NEPAD Policy Framework 243-44;
  255-56
  establishment of 75
  perspective on 'responsibility to protect' 92-94
AU African Development Fund 255
AU Constitutive Act of 2000 28; 89-90;
  92-95; 97-99; 107; 141; 252
AU Darfur Integrated Task Force (DITF)
  155; 157
AU Mission in Sudan (AMIS) 95-98; 107;
  149; 155-56; 158; 160-61
AU Peace and Security Council (PSC)
  10; 31; 51; 94-98; 100; 149; 237; 255
  Protocol 95; 97-99
AU Peace Fund 252; 255

AU Post-conflict Reconstruction Policy Framework 253
AU Mission in Sudan (AMIS) 149

B

Baregu, Mwesiga 13
see also Chapter 14
Barre, Siad 33
Belgium 134; 153
Botswana 38; 184; 196; 211
Bouteflika, Pres Abdelaziz 24; 93
Boutros-Ghali, Boutros 27-28; 68; 116; 121; 149; 153; 247; 269
An Agenda for Peace 28; 247; 269
Brahimi, Lakhder 22; 61
Brahimi report 5; 22-23; 61
Brazil 25; 27; 34; 64-65
Bretton Woods institutions 33; 60; 65; 103; 174; 237
Britain 4; 6; 19; 25; 35; 63-64; 135; 151; 198; 211; 215; 227; 237; 251
Brookings–SAIS Project on Internal Displacement 121-22
Burundi 22; 24; 27; 67; 76; 250; 254

C

Canada 25; 155; 161; 198-99
Central African Republic (CAR) 5; 21; 29; 60; 77; 247
Central Intelligence Agency (CIA) 39; 268
Centre for Conflict Resolution (CCR) 3
China 6; 19; 25; 34; 58; 64; 70-71; 135; 137; 151; 216; 237; 250-51
Chinery-Hesse, Mary 2; 6; 8
see also Chapter 2
collective action
and crisis prevention 94-98
collective security 213-14
UN High-level Panel Report recommendations on 213-14
Combined Joint Task Force-Horn of Africa (CJTF-HOA) 39; 266
Commission of Africa
report of 82-84
Comoros 32
Conference on Security, Stability, Development and Cooperation in Africa (CSSDCA) 126

conflict prevention
recommendation of the High-level Panel report 78
Consortium of Humanitarian Agencies (CHA) 122
Cote d'Ivoire 24; 27; 32; 250; 277
counter-terrorism
and terrorism 261-72

D

Darfur, Sudan 11; 23; 41; 67; 76; 107; 277-78
collective action and crisis prevention 94-98
conflict in 10; 142; 147-51; 155-62; 244; 250
human rights abuses 136
debt 19; 176-177; 179-180; 209
Africa's 2-3; 33; 35; 172-73; 197
American 173
ratios 177
reduction 176
relief measures 2; 6; 12; 30; 80; 82; 101; 193
repayments 76; 172; 175; 180
service payments 81; 279
servicing capacity restoration 170
sustainable 177
write-off for Africa 36; 84
Déby, Idriss 32
De Klerk, F W 27
democratic governance 29-32
Democratic Republic of Congo (DRC) 4; 41; 244; 270
forcible disarmament of *Interahamwe* 99
Lusaka accord of 1999 24
natural resources plundering in 213
prevalence of HIV/AIDS, army 37
Refugee–Warriors in, from 1994 Rwandan genocide 244
UN deploy force in eastern 270
UN peace operations 250
Deng, Francis 6; 10-11; 28
see also Chapter 6
Doe, Samuel 33
Doha trade round 34; 80; 177; 179; 236
drug trafficking 50; 268

E

East African Counter-terrorism Initiative (EACTI) 267
ECOWAS Cease-fire Monitoring Group (ECOMOG) 23-24; 67; 100

Economic Community of Central
African States (ECCAS) 8; 23; 46; 237; 253
Economic Community of West African
States (ECOWAS) 8; 23-24; 46; 100;
238; 243; 253
Economic and Social Council
(ECOSOC) 3; 29; 54; 79; 103-104;
107; 133; 138-39; 143; 251
reform of 59-60
Egypt 26-27; 30; 64
Equatorial Guinea 76
European Union (EU) 34; 75; 155
EU Commission 216
Ezulwini Consensus 3; 25; 40; 64; 82; 99;
110; 138; 217; 276

F
Federal Bureau of Investigation (FBI) 268
Financial Action Task Force Against
Money Laundering (FATF) 216
France 1; 6; 19; 25; 36; 63-64; 95; 134;
150-51; 153-54; 198; 236-37; 251

G
G-8 (Group of Eight Industrialised Countries)
23; 34-35; 75; 83-84; 198-99
G-20+ (Group of 20+) 34
G-77 (Group of 77) 6; 58-59; 70-71; 137
Gambari, Ibrahim 6; 22; 26
see also Chapter 4
Gastrow, Peter 12
see also Chapter 11
Geldof, Bob 34-36
gendarmerie 150
Used for Rwanda's security force
gender 54; 105; 128; 141; 171; 186; 189; 200
Germany 1; 25; 63-66; 198-99; 211; 232
Ghana 4
APRM missions visits 30
civilian police deployed in Darfur 160
forces deployed in Kigali 151; 153-54
health expenditure 196
human rights commissions established in 142
peacekeeping operations, support for 251
soldiers in Rwanda 154
Global AIDS Fund 37; 190-91; 279
global apartheid
ending of 32-34
Global Fund to Fight AIDS, Tuberculosis

and Malaria (GFATM) 184; 188
globalisation 13; 105; 210; 231; 261
Gross Domestic Product (GDP) 173
Gross National Product (GNP) 2
for Official Development Assistance 59; 198
Japan 199
Guinea 244
Guinea-Bissau 5; 21; 32; 60; 247

H
Heavily Indebted Poor Countries (HIPC) 33
High-Level Panel
*Report of the High-level Panel on Threats,
Challenges and Change* 77-82
HIV/AIDS 3-5; 12; 49; 80; 101; 183-202
aligning HIV/AIDS and security 183-202
as security threat 20; 36-38; 183-184
defence forces, peacekeeping and 185-88
global response to 78; 189
human security and 185-86
impact, possible 186
prevention 38; 186
securitisation of 185-88
UN and Africa 183-202
*HIV/AIDS and Security: Fact, Fiction and
Evidence* 187
Humanitarian Ceasefire Agreement
(HCFA) 96; 151; 157
signing of, 8 Apr 2004 149
human rights
South Africa, the UN and 227-39
Human Rights Council 3
human rights initiatives, global 132-37
Human Rights Watch 133-34; 142

I
India 25; 27; 34; 64-65; 211
*In Larger Freedom: Towards Development,
Security and Human Rights for All* 4; 7;
20; 23; 29; 38; 59; 69; 75-76; 81; 99;
101; 131-32; 135-36; 176; 192; 207;
243; 247; 276-77; 279
Inter-Agency Standing Committee (IASC)
118; 120
Interahamwe 99; 153
Used for militia in eastern DRC
Intergovernmental Authority on Development
(IGAD) 8; 23; 46; 76; 119; 237; 253

internal displacement
  see also Internally Displaced Persons
    (IDPs)
  crisis of 112-15
  international challenge 111-28
Internally Displaced Persons (IDPs)
  113-14; 116-17; 119-24; 128; 150; 155;
  159; 244; 255
International Commission on Intervention and
    State Sovereignty (ICISS) 10; 28; 94; 269
  report 269-70
International Committee of the Red
    Cross (ICRC) 118; 158
International Criminal Court (ICC) 158; 272
International Development Association
    (IDA) 33
International Labour Organisation (ILO) 2; 45
International Monetary Fund (IMF) 1;
    33; 41; 60; 103; 167; 169-70; 172; 178;
    209; 219; 237; 249
  loans for Africa 171-72
International Organisation for Migration
    (IOM) 118
international organised crime
  see organised crime
International Peace Academy (IPA) 156
international terrorism 13; 20-21; 38-39;
    261; 263-66; 272; 276; 280
Italy 25; 153; 198-99; 211

J

Janjaweed 98; 158
  Used for Arab militia
Japan 25; 60; 63-66; 179; 198-99; 211
Joint UN Programme on HIV/AIDS
    (UNAIDS) 37; 183-84; 187-90; 195-97
Jonah, James 6; 9
  see also Chapter 3
Justice and Equality Movement (JEM) 149

K

Kabbah, Pres Ahmed 65
Kagame, Maj-Gen Paul 148; 151
Kenya 4; 26; 64
  American support for autocratic
    government in 39
  APRM missions visits 30
  bombing of US embassy in, 1998 50; 265
  combating HIV/AIDS 194

  forces deployed in Darfur 157
  HIV infection rate in 183
  peacekeeping operations, support for 251
  terrorist attack on El-Al aircraft in Mombasa
    266

L

Lagos Plan of Action (LPA) 32
Latin America 58; 63; 134; 139; 210
Legum, Margaret 12; 200
  see also Chapter 8
Lesotho 184
Liberia 5; 10; 21-22; 24; 26; 29; 33; 41; 53; 60;
    66-67; 100; 213; 244; 247; 250; 277
Live8 campaign 34-36
Luthuli, Chief Albert 233-34

M

Mandela, Pres Nelson 27; 35; 194;
    227-29; 239
Manuel, Trevor 60
Mauritius 4; 30
Mazrui, Ali 1
Mbeki, Pres Thabo 27; 236; 267
Médecins Sans Frontières (MSF) 159
Millennium Declaration 30; 34; 80; 101
  report on 75
  UN High-level Panel and 20-21
Millennium Development Goals (MDGs)
    3; 7; 9; 20-21; 34; 54; 59; 76-77; 80; 105; 174;
    176; 198; 214; 272; 279; 289
money laundering 216-18
Moussa, Amre 2; 45
Mozambique 23-24; 29-30; 76; 195; 247;
    250; 277
Mubarak, Hosni 27
Mugabe, Robert 31; 93
  see also Zimbabwe
Murithi, Tim 13
  see also Chapter 13
Museveni, Yoweri 32; 37; 194-195
Mwanasali, Musifiky 10
  see also Chapter 5

N

Namibia 23; 29
Ndinga-Muvumba, Angela 12
  see also Chapter 10

NEPAD 27; 29–32; 80; 93; 126; 141; 237;
244; 255; 268; 277
see also APRM
and democratic governance 20
as core of *Report of the Commission for
Africa* 82–84
AU/NEPAD frameworks for
post-conflict peacebuilding and
reconstruction 13; 243–44; 252–56
credibility 32
Democracy and Governance programme
30–31
establishment of 75; 83; 267
Heads of State and Government
Implementation Committee (HSGIC) 252
Implementation Committee 252
relationship with Commission on Africa 76
Secretariat 31; 253
sectoral priorities 30; 83
Subcommittee on Peace and Security 252
Nigeria 4; 26; 64
APRM missions visits 30
civilian police deployed in Darfur 160
debt 172
Doha trade round, involvement in 34
forces deployed in Darfur 157
Muslim population in 266
oil production 27
peacekeepers in Sierra Leone in 1999 24
peacekeeping operations, support for 251
role in spearheading NEPAD 30
transition in 26
UN anti-apartheid conference in 1977 26
non-governmental organisations (NGOs)
11; 37; 46; 115–16; 123–25; 142; 144; 158–59
Ntaryamira, Cyprien 150
Nyerere, Pres Julius
deconstructing Washington Consensus
167–80

O
Obasanjo, Olusegun 32
Official Development Assistance (ODA)
34; 59; 80; 178; 193; 198; 291
On the Frontline 197
Organisation for Economic Cooperation
and Development (OECD) 34
Organisation for Security and Cooperation in
Europe (OSCE) 119

Organisation of African Unity (OAU)
2; 10; 45; 92; 118; 126; 140–41; 147; 266
and AU's decision to deploy mission to
Darfur 156
Charter of the (*see also* UN Charter) 90
military weakness 24
summit in Zimbabwe, 1997 63
transformation into AU 157
Organisation of American States (OAS) 66–67
Organisation of Petroleum Exporting
Countries (OPEC) 26; 168–69
organised crime
extent of, in Africa 211–13
international response to growth in 208–11
international, security threat 207–20
money laundering 216–18
state capacity-building 218–19
UNODC organised crime index by
region 212

P
Palermo Convention 207–8; 211; 214–17
Article 30 215–17; 219
implementation of 214–18
Pax Africana 9
peacebuilding
recommendation of the High-level
Panel report 78
Peacebuilding Commission
proposed by the High-level Panel
report 78–79
Pan African Parliament (PAP) 31
Plan of Action for HIV/AIDS, Malaria
and Tuberculosis 194
Portugal 134
post-conflict reconstruction 3; 8; 11; 13;
29; 40; 81; 101–5; 107; 237; 243; 280
Memorandum of Understanding 256
symbiosis in 245–46
Post-conflict Reconstruction Unit 255
President's Emergency Plan for AIDS Relief
(PEPFAR) 197–98
protect
responsibility to, AU and UN
perspectives 92–94

R
Radio-Television Libre de Mille Collines
(RTLM) 155

Regional Economic Communities (RECs) 237-39; 253; 255

regional organisations
cooperation proposed by the High-level Panel report 79
UN Security Council relationship with 66-67

'responsibility to protect' 3-6; 10; 28; 40-41; 52; 62; 89-110; 111; 114; 185; 250; 276; 281

Roth, Kenneth 133

Russia 6; 19; 25; 134; 137; 139; 151; 174; 180; 198-99; 237; 251

Rwanda 22-23; 29-30; 61; 67; 270-71
Arusha Agreement of 1993 24; 148-52
Broad-Based Transitional Government (BBTG) 152
genocide in 1994 6; 8; 11; 25; 40; 89; 92; 127; 132-33; 140; 142; 147-61; 173; 244; 248; 277-78
peace operations 250
Radio-Television Libre de Mille Collines 155

Rwandese Patriotic Front (RPF) 148

S
Sachs, Jeffrey 20; 33; 54; 75; 80-81; 178; 199
SaferAfrica 255
Salim, Ahmed Salim 2; 22; 45
Scanlon, Helen 11
see also Chapter 7 and Conclusion
security sector reform (SSR) 256
security threats 207-20
Sese Seko, Mobutu 33; 194
Sierra Leone 4; 26
conflict in 22; 53
cooperation between ECOWAS and UN 23
ECOMOG interventions in 100
natural resources plundering in 213
Nigerian peacekeepers in, 1999 24
post-conflict peacebuilding 60
post-conflict reconstruction 247; 254
refugee camps in 244
Special Court for 254
Truth and Reconciliation Commission 254
UN operations in 24; 29; 41; 66-67
UN peacekeeping in 24; 277
Somalia 4; 10; 22-23; 29; 39; 61; 67; 76; 148; 151; 154; 247; 266-67
South Africa
the UN and human rights 227-39

South African National Defence Force (SANDF)
HIV/AIDS in 186
Southern African Development Community (SADC) 8; 23; 46; 237-38; 253
sovereignty as responsibility 28; 90-91; 122-23; 232; 277
humanitarian intervention and peacebuilding 27-29
state-capacity building 218-19
state failure
international challenge of 111-28
state sovereignty 231-32
Stiglitz, Joseph 178
structural adjustment 173; 209
from economic development to 167-74
Structural Adjustment Programme/ policies (SAPs) 32; 170-75; 200; 209-10
Sudan 4; 67; 125; 127
African troops deployed in 95-96
American support for autocratic government in 39
AU Mission in 149; 278
conflict in Darfur region 67; 76; 95; 142; 148; 158; 161; 244; 277-78
humanitarian catastrophe in 250
Humanitarian Ceasefire Agreement signed 149
Human Rights Council, exclusion from 138
member of Commission of Human Rights 135-36
Operation Lifeline Sudan 124
People's Liberation Army 160
post-conflict reconstruction 247
terrorist threat in 266
UN Human Rights Commission 40; 65
UN Mission in 155; 160
UN operations in 24; 96; 98; 250
Sudan Liberation Army/Movement (SLA/M) 149
Sudanese People's Liberation Movement (SPLM) 148
Sudan People's Liberation Army (SPLA) 160
sustainable development 32-34
Swaziland 3; 25; 32; 82; 184; 217
Syria 262

T

Tanzania 4; 167
 anti-terrorism legislation 39; 263
 health expenditure 196
 terrorist attack on US embassy, August
  1998 50; 265-266
Taylor, Charles 39
terrorism
 and counter-terrorism 261-72
Threats, Challenges and Change 2; 7; 20;
 45; 57; 75-76; 136; 213; 264; 276-77
trade 32-34
Tutu, Archbishop Desmond 27; 142

U

Uganda 4; 153; 266
 adoption of Guiding Principles 119
 APRM missions visits 30
 health expenditure 196
 HIV/AIDS prevalence in 194-95
 HIV infection rate in 183
 human rights commissions established in 142
UN
 aligning HIV/AIDS and security 182-202
 Department of Peacekeeping
  Operations (DPKO) 67
 perspective on 'responsibility to protect'
  92-94
 role in Africa 4
 South Africa, the UN and human rights
  227-39
 war on terror, role of 271-72
UN Assistance Mission for Rwanda
 (UNAMIR) 148-56; 159
UN Charter 28; 51; 63; 99-100; 103;
 107; 132; 250; 262; 267; 269
 Article 27 63
 Article 33 247
 Article 51 250
 Article 65 104
 Article 97 72
 Articles 100-101 68
 Chapter VI 151
 Chapter VII 64; 93-94; 98; 151; 154; 271
 Chapter VIII 66; 269-70
 of 1945 247; 264
UN Children's Fund (UNICEF) 158
UN Commission on Human Rights 116
 reform of 65-66

UN Commission on Human Security 13
UN Conference on Trade and
 Development (UNCTAD) 33-34; 57
UN Convention against Corruption 219
UN Convention against Transnational
 Organised Crime 207; 220
 see also Palermo Convention
UN Department of Peacekeeping
 Operations (DPKO) 22; 67; 152; 155; 189
 Best Practice Unit 147
UN Development Programme (UNDP) 103
UN General Assembly
 reform of 65-66
UN High Commissioner for Refugees
 (UNHCR) 114; 119; 158
UN High-level Panel
 Millennium Declaration and 20-21; 80
UN High-level Panel Report
 an insider's perspective 45-55
 recommendations on collective security
  213-14
UN Human Rights Council 279
 Africa and the 139-42
 establishment 11; 131
 support for a 137-39
UN Industrial Development Organisation
 (UNIDO) 57
United States 1; 39; 57; 63; 70; 77; 134; 137;
 139; 161; 174; 199; 233; 237; 251; 268; 271
 9/11 47; 261; 263-67
 embassies bombings 50; 265
Universal Declaration of Human Rights,
 1948 134-35; 140; 229-30
UN Mission in Sudan (UNMIS) 155
UN Office of the High Commissioner for
 Human Rights (OHCHR) 117
UN Office on Drugs and Crime (UNODC)
 212; 215
 organised crime index by region 212
UN Peacebuilding
 in Africa 21-24
UN Peacebuilding Commision 3; 5; 8; 13; 29;
 40-41; 53; 71; 78; 81; 101-107; 243-44;
 247-48; 256-57; 276-77; 280
 birth and function of 248-52
 Outcome Document, adoption of 58-59; 71; 248
 Post-conflict Reconstruction Mandate 244;
  247-52

proposal for 60-62
structure and membership 251-52
UN Reform Process
Africa's stake in 276-77
key issues in 5-8
rise and fall 19-41
proposed by the High-level Panel report
78-79
UN Reform Reports
critiquing 174-80
UN Secretariat
Chief Operating Officer (COO) 72
reform of 67-69
UN Security Council 3
enlargement of 62-65
humanitarian intervention 27-29
peacebuilding 27-29
reform 25-27
relationship with regional organisations
66-67
Resolution 872 148; 150
Resolution 912 154
Resolution 929 154
Resolution 1590 155; 160
Resolution 1591 158

V
Volker, Paul 72

W
war on terror
Africa 265-69
regional vs international intervention
269-71
Washington Consensus
deconstructing 167-80
Weapons of Mass Destruction (WMDs)
49; 77; 228; 262; 272
World Bank 1; 33; 41; 60; 103; 167; 169;
171-72; 178; 209; 219; 237; 249; 257; 279
World Health Organisation (WHO) 37; 188
World Trade Organisation (WTO) 1; 33; 41;
80; 177; 180; 236

Z
Zimbabwe 26; 65
see also Mugabe, Robert
combating HIV/AIDS 194
health expenditure 196
HIV infection rate in 183
human rights abuses 135; 138; 142
Zimbabwean Human Rights Commission 142